A Missing Link In History

In times such as these, young people need every source possible to navigate through the difficulties of today's communities. *A Missing Link In History* provides an introductory look at a better way of life. The history, contributions, and successes of African Americans in the game of golf are clearly, accurately, and deftly presented in a manner to educate, inspire, and motivate readers.

—J.W. Smith PhD,
Retired Executive Director of
Chicago Public Schools Sports

Incredible work in chronicling the significant evolutionary history of African Americans in golf. These powerful words tell the story of our unsung heroes, and are a focus of study for people of all races. *A Missing Link In History* takes over the reins in paying tribute to African Americans in golf.

—The Honorable Mayor Omar Neal
Former Mayor of Tuskegee, Alabama

A Missing Link In History provides a concise and comprehensive introduction to African American golf history. The biographical information and time line are gateways to a more selective study. A wonderful celebration of a significant point in American history.

—Earnie Ellison Jr., Managing Partner
of Ellison Consulting Group

After years of conscientious effort, Ramona Harriet's *A Missing Link In History* is a welcome addition to the annals of golf. With perseverance and a passionate commitment to compile and corroborate the evidence, she has broadened our understanding of the contributions of African Americans to the game of golf.

—Dr. Calvin Sinnette,
Author of *Forbidden Fairways*

A MISSING LINK IN HISTORY

THE JOURNEY OF AFRICAN AMERICANS IN GOLF

(Left to right) **Althea Gibson and Ann Gregory.** Circa 1963.
Credit: Alexandria Black History Resource Center, Moss H. Kendrix Collection

A Missing Link In History

The Journey of African Americans in Golf

Ramona Harriet

Concluding Comments by Jim Dent

Publisher's Cataloging-in-Publication Data
Harriet, Ramona
    A missing link in history: the journey of African Americans in
golf / Ramona Harriet.
        p. cm.
    Includes bibliographical references.
    ISBN-13: 978-1463622510
    1. African-American golfers—History. 2. Discrimination in
    sports—United States—History. 3. Golf—United States—
    History. 4. Golf—Social aspects—United States—History.
    I. Title.
        GV981.M377
        796.352—dc22

Revised Second Edition. Printed in the United States of America.

Front cover male photograph: Solomon Hughes Sr., professional golfer.
Circa 1940s. Credit: Joyce Hughes and Shirley Hughes.

Back cover photograph (top; also on page 174): Wilberforce University
Golf Class. Circa 1934. Credit: Wilberforce University (Wilberforce, Ohio)
Archives and Special Collection, Rembert E. Stokes Learning Resource
Center

Back cover photograph (bottom; also on page 10): Ormond Golf Course
Caddies Circa 1903. Credit: Ormond Beach Historical Society (Ormond
Beach, Florida)

Cover design: Adam Evans

www.AfricanAmericanGolfHistory.com

For my beautiful daughter, Cherissa Rai.

In memory of my dear friends
Charlie Sifford and Pete Brown.
Thank you for your spirit, wisdom, and
strength of character. In your honor, I
proudly tell the story and cherish the legacy.

Dr. Charles Sifford (*left*) and Charles Lightfoot in Scotland, England, where Dr. Sifford received (in 2006) an honorary Doctor of Laws degree from the University of St. Andrews.
Courtesy Charles Lightfoot

CONTENTS

How to Manage Your Way Through This Book

I was inspired to write *A Missing Link In History: The Journey of African Americans in Golf* after numerous visitors, at my African American golf history traveling exhibition, requested hands-on information about African American golf history.

Parents wanted to share this historical information with their children and grandchildren, teachers wanted to introduce African American golf history to students and colleagues, and others were curious or just wanted to know more. From those requests this book evolved—a huge task, but one of commitment, passion, and joy.

A Missing Link In History is divided into seven chapters:

Chapter I discusses black caddies, the first African American professional golfer–John Shippen Jr., and the first recipient of a United States Patent for a wooden golf tee invention–George Franklin Grant.

Chapter II focuses on African American golf course designers and builders.

Chapter III focuses on prejudices, injustices, defeats, and victories described through court cases, confrontations, and historical accomplishments.

Chapter IV discusses amateur golfers, professional golfers, industry professionals, and golf professionals. This chapter also includes two comparison graphs. Graph one compares the total number of African American LPGA Tour and PGA Tour members to non-African American LPGA Tour and PGA Tour members. Graph two compares the total number of African American LPGA T&CP Members and PGA Members to non-African American LPGA T&CP Members and PGA Members.

Chapter V provides a resource of detailed information about past and current developments of golf facilities, inventions, businesses, publications, organizations, and events.

Chapter VI includes a time line that chronicles African American golf history from 1879 to 2015.

Chapter VII is packed with more than 250 quiz statements. Test your knowledge of African American golf history. Take "Missing Link IQ" as a pretest, and then take it again after you read *A Missing Link In History*.

Finally, this extraordinary journey is celebrated through exclusive concluding comments by legendary professional golfer Jim Dent.

As you navigate through these remarkable life changing experiences, you will find Tee Box spaces with entries of brief facts. To help you find information, there are chapter previews, and also two indexes—an index to chapters one to five, and a general index.

Informative, realistic, and helpful—*A Missing Link In History* gives relevance and respect to the history of African Americans in Golf.

African American golfer demonstrating golf swing at Old Dominion Golf Tournament in Hampton, Virginia. Left of golfer is legendary professional golfer Gary Player. Circa 1960s. Courtesy Burl Bowens

Tee Box

In 1961, the inaugural Old Dominion Golf Tournament was held. For about the first 10 years, Old Dominion Golf Tournaments included amateur and professional divisions; sometime in the 1970s, the event became a competition for amateur players only. Founded more than half a century ago by Old Dominion Golf Club of Hampton Roads, Virginia, the 50th anniversary of Old Dominion Golf Tournament was celebrated in 2011.

where are the accolades?

Introduction

*A legacy of tribulations and triumphs
but where are the accolades?*

As recently as the late fifties and early sixties, I remember segregated schools, theaters, diners, hospitals, and "Colored" signs for water fountains, sinks, and public restrooms.

I remember coming home one night and seeing a Ku Klux Klan cross burning in our front yard.

I remember standing on our front porch seeing hooded white robes and burning crosses at Ku Klux Klan rallies less than a mile away. I remember...!

Engulfed by flames of bigotry, I did not know that a similar injustice occurred at a golf course less than two miles away from our family home.

The word "colored" tells its own story. This designated sink "for Colored People Only" was installed in the locomotive repair area at Seaboard Railroad Company in the Old Midtown neighborhood of Portsmouth, Virginia. Circa 1940s. Courtesy African American Historical Society of Portsmouth Inc. and Mae Breckenridge-Haywood

Bide-A-Wee Golf Club, a private "whites only" facility, was leased property on public land owned by the City of Portsmouth, Virginia—my hometown—rooted in racism.

An October 4, 1992 article in *The Virginian Pilot* titled, *Goodbye to Bide-A-Wee*, plainly told the Bide-A-Wee story— "one of pain and frustration...."—a story too common to African American golf history.

During my childhood, my passion was history and sports. I enjoyed going to basketball games with my father and playing baseball in the backyard with my friends. On rare occasions, I drove through a white neighborhood and passed Elizabeth Manor Country Club. I knew it was a golf course, and I also knew that it was for "whites only".

In school I wasn't taught about Dr. George Grant, an African American who received the first U.S. Patent for a wooden golf tee. I was never introduced to the game of golf or African American golf history. I knew that the sport existed, but I never saw anyone play golf.

That changed in the 1970s when I joined an African American golf club in Tacoma, Washington. I began to enjoy spending hours hitting balls in a field at Fort Lewis U.S. Air Force Base. I looked forward to golf outing bus rides—where I listened to "old timers" talk about their experiences being turned away from golf courses because of the color of their skin. However, I never thought that my experiences then— would later affect my social and professional life.

Playing golf and reading non-fiction golf books became my favorite pastimes. I studied under the great PGA Member Bill "Coach" Strausbaugh and LPGA Member Phyllis Meekins. Golf was my passion. I played the game whenever and wherever I could.

My most memorable golfing experiences were in the early 1990s during a two-year educational work assignment in London, England. I rode buses and trains to courses. People I met at golf facilities, on and off the courses, were cordial. And with never encountering any acts of racism on London's challenging links, playing golf in one of the United Kingdom's largest metropolitan area—was very pleasurable.

Unfortunately, I cannot express the same for my golfing experiences when I returned home to the United States. Caucasian golfers telling the starter that they did not want to be paired with my playing partner and me because they did not want to play with coloreds; or arriving at a course that I had reserved a tee time days before and confirmed prior to arrival, but not playing because a pro says "your tee time is not in the book"—That is what I sometimes encountered at courses in my home country, the USA.

Even though those unforgettable experiences made me bitter, I did not lose my passion for the game. I wanted to be a part of it and yearned to learn more about the African American's past and present role in golf; hence, soon I embarked on a career in golf.

Later led by remarkable experiences and curiosities, combined with encouragement from *Forbidden Fairways* author Calvin H. Sinnette and first female USGA president Judy Bell, I produced a traveling exhibition—*Epochs of Courage: African Americans in Golf*. A week before the inaugural opening in Washington, D.C., I received a call from a representative of an established and well-known golf organization. The caller expressed concern that this exhibition might cause a disturbance and requested that, "certain controversial images and text not be displayed". I cordially acknowledged the call.

In September 1999, the *Epochs of Courage* exhibition opened as planned with no changes and without controversy. Still, that such a call was made showed me that we were not yet at peace with painful parts of our history.

In 2001, I traveled to my hometown—excited to do hands-on research of Bide-A-Wee Golf Club; however, I quickly discovered this to be a challenging task. When I attempted to interview persons about the desegregation of Bide-A-Wee Golf Club, one longtime member told me, "Don't come around here digging up old bad stuff. Yeah, I was there. I know exactly what happened. But I'm not gonna tell you."

The longer I researched this extraordinary history, the clearer it became that African American golf history is like the civil rights history of the United States—rife with suppression and rejection. Maggie Hathaway, Joseph Rice, Charlie Sifford, George Simkins, and many others who worked tirelessly to break the color barriers in the sport of golf had countless Jim Crow experiences. Such racist actions created color lines of economical, physical, and social separations. And now in this new millennium, many of those same separations—generated by elements such as hostility, fear, and ignorance—still exist.

I return to the question posed in the beginning of this introduction, *"where are the accolades?"*.

Although the history of African Americans in golf spans over 115 years, only a few museums display even a small collection of African American golf memorabilia and only a handful of African Americans have been honored by major golf organizations.

There were 150 World Golf Hall of Fame inductees, as of the 2015 induction ceremony; however, only one out of the 150 was African American—Charlie Sifford inducted in November 2004. The PGA Distinguished Service Award was presented to William "Bill" Dickey in 1999 and William Powell in 2009. The PGA of America granted, in November 2009, posthumous membership to Theodore "Ted" Rhodes, John Shippen Jr., and William "Bill" Spiller, and honorary membership to Joseph Louis Barrow Sr. (better known as Joe Louis). Posthumously inducted into The PGA of America Hall of Fame were Jimmy DeVoe and William Powell in February 2013, and Charlie Sifford in November 2015. And in May 2014, World Golf Hall of Fame & Museum opened a permanent exhibition—*"Honoring the Legacy: A Tribute to African-Americans in Golf"*.

I ponder. Are these benevolent gestures grounds for optimism? To put things in perspective, collectively— African Americans in golf have not received their rightful place in history. Therefore, I hope that after you read *A Missing Link In History*, you will applaud and acknowledge the historical contributions within, and help give this rich history the accolades it so well deserves.   —*Ramona Harriet*

African American Golf History

More than golf

African American Golf History is American History!

Epochs of Courage:
African Americans in Golf
Traveling Exhibition

Historical Statement

Through continuous struggles that
African Americans and their supporters
have experienced throughout
the 20th century.

Through confrontation with formidable
barriers to full participation
in the sport of golf.

Through bygone years
of bitter contention.

Legends of golf, both living and
posthumous, are recognized for their
contributions to promoting diversity and
greater equality in the world of golf.

—*Calvin H. Sinnette*

Legends of golf: (*front row, left to right*) James Black (*1st*), James Walker Jr. (*2nd*), Rafe Botts (*4th*), George Johnson (*5th*), and William Wright (*back row, left*); with The Honorable Omar Neal, then Mayor of Tuskegee, Alabama (*front row, center*) and John Inman, then General Manager, Kellogg Hotel and Conference Center at Tuskegee University (*back row, right*) Circa 2011

*I am what time, circumstance, history,
have made of me, certainly, but I am
also, much more than that.*

James Baldwin

Chapter I
First On the Tee

Preview

A group of boy and girl caddies at Ormond Golf Club (Ormond Beach, Florida). Circa 1903. Courtesy Ormond Beach Historical Society

In the period between 1880 and 1900, the Ormond Beach, Florida African American community, located in the vicinity of Tomoka Road and White Street, was called Liberia. A group from the country of Liberia settled there after the Civil War. This picture shows one of the families in the area. In the background is housing that was typical for that community. Another nearby community was called Sudan. Many of the children in the caddie photo (*top of page*) lived in the Ormond Beach Liberia and Sudan communities. (Sudan is the largest country on the African continent. Liberia, in 1821, became the first independent country established in Africa by Freed American slaves.)

First On The Tee

*The colour of the skin is no way connected with
the strength of mind or intellectual powers.*
—Benjamin Banneker

Slaves were the labor force of the United States in the
1700s. Even after lawmakers adopted the Thirteenth and
Fourteenth Amendments to the United States Constitution
in the 1860s, civil liberties and equal protection for blacks
were not lawfully enforced. The color of the labor force did
not change, and this injustice was as real in the sport of golf,
as it was anywhere else.

In the late 1700s, golf
emerged on the United
States as a sport for white
Americans. In the early
1900s, golf continued to be
as segregated as schools,
public transportation,
neighborhoods, theaters, and
churches. Known as a
gentlemen's sport, white men were considered the only ones
who had the finesse to play golf or work in the golf industry.

> In the early 1900s, golf
> continued to be as
> segregated as schools,
> public transportation,
> neighborhoods, theaters,
> and churches.

In spite of these prejudices, African Americans began to
carve a place in golf history. Even though from this vantage
point, African Americans did not receive credit for many of

their accomplishments and were not given equal opportunities at public and private golf courses—African Americans became great caddies, golf course architects, and inventors of golf equipment; and, many caddies became great professional golfers.

This was an epic birth that would later not only impact golf around the world, but also impact the civil rights of African Americans and American history.

◆ ◆ ◆

1

Caddies–First Generation of Black Golf

Stories passed down through generations, described how slaves were used as caddies and golf course laborers—toiling fairways and greens for little or no pay. For decades the vast responsibilities of a caddie were considered demeaning tasks, and caddying was generally classified as a position of servitude.

Caddies cleaned golf shoes, clubs, and balls, assisted players with club selection and reading greens, estimated yardage, searched for players' golf balls, sometimes carried two or more golf bags per round, and maintained golf courses.

Many private country clubs had a caddie staff that was 100% African American. Scorned as a job of humiliation, generally white men were considered too good to caddie. This racial imbalance is an example of how society generally deemed the two races—Whites superior—Blacks inferior.

Caddies were primarily not identified by their names—but by assigned numbers. The caddies' supervisor, known as caddie master, assigned work in numerical order or upon player request.

Example: Caddie number 41 is next in line for assigned work; however, the next player requests a specific caddie—

caddie number 45. The caddie master honors the special request; hence, caddie number 41 must remain in line for another player.

In 1927 at Highland Park Golf Course in Birmingham, Alabama, a white caddie master shot and killed a Negro caddie. According to a June 4, 1927 article on page 2 in *The Birmingham News* titled *Caddy Slain At Municipal Links*:

Caddie master W.H. Derrick accused 24-year-old Eugene Harris of going out to caddie when it was not his turn. Derrick confronted Harris on the first hole and ordered him to give the golf bag to the caddie who he was accused of jumping ahead of.

> In 1927, at Highland Park Golf Course in Birmingham, Alabama, a white caddie master shot and killed a Negro caddie.

Harris denied that he caddied out of turn because his player David Stevens had personally asked him to caddie. Investigative reports indicated that Stevens confirmed that—he did ask Harris to caddie for him.

Caddie master Derrick shot and killed caddie Eugene Harris. Derrick claimed that the one shot he fired was in self-defense—because he felt threatened by the way Harris took a golf club out of the golf bag.

The single bullet entered Harris's neck below the larynx. Harris died within minutes.

It was an hour or more before the coroner arrived. During that wait, Eugene Harris's body remained laying in the first tee box area.

As a result of an investigation by Coroner Russum, and police motor scouts Norrell and Allen, it was reported that Derrick acted hastily and he should be charged for unjustifiable homicide.

Derrick was arrested and denied bail.

(*Documentation of legal actions that occurred after Derrick's arrest was not found under this research.*)

◆ ◆ ◆

Ulysses "Ice Cream" Freeman

In 1944, ten-year-old Ulysses Freeman started running-balls (retrieving balls from a practice area) for Chandler Harper at Glensheallah Golf Course in Portsmouth, Virginia. Freeman watched PGA Tour Member Chandler Harper practice and teach. On weed and gravel fields, Freeman practiced some of Harper's techniques and taught himself the game. Soon after Freeman's 14th birthday, he began to caddie for Harper. About three years later, Freeman was a scratch golfer.

In 1952 Freeman was drafted into the United States Army. In the 1960s while stationed in Europe, an officer saw Freeman hitting golf balls in a field on base and asked him to join a Combat Army (CA) golf team. Freeman accepted the offer.

Ulysses "Ice Cream" Freeman, caddied for PGA Tour Member Chandler Harper

The first time Freeman competed with the CA golf team, he shot the lowest score of the field. Because of his outstanding playing skills, Freeman qualified for a higher-level CA golf team, and later became that team's "A" player. He was the only African American on both CA teams.

During his military career, Freeman won five enlisted men post tournaments including two championship titles at Fort Benning United States Army Post.

After serving 27 years as a paratrooper in the U.S. Army, First Sergeant Ulysses Freeman retired from the military but not from golf. In

1997, Freeman won the Virginia Hampton Roads Golf Association first annual tournament at Chesapeake Golf Course in Chesapeake, Virginia.

Through 2005 Freeman worked with junior golf organizations in South Hampton Roads, Virginia. He also served as assistant golf coach at I.C. Norcom High School, a historically black school in Portsmouth, Virginia.

Freeman encouraged young blacks to do great and positive things—on and off the golf course. He often shared his thoughts regarding young blacks having equal opportunities as a professional tour caddie:

> I think a lot of people would be amazed at the number of black youth who, if given the chance, would become great tour caddies.
>
> Caddying has become very sophisticated and high-tech. Too many people think that young black men can't handle that and don't deserve it.
>
> I don't think there will ever again, be a majority of black caddies on tour or at the Masters. I believe that opportunities were damaged by old myths that all black caddies gambled and got drunk while traveling on tour. Rumors like that hurt everyone.

Even though Freeman was an outstanding caddie and golfer, he chose not to pursue a career in golf.

> Being on tour involves too much traveling, pain, and pressure. I prefer being at home enjoying cookouts and church. I stay busy with my grandchildren and working in the community. I love working with children. Also, I have three hole-in-ones to boast about with my buddies.
> *(Ulysses Freeman interviewed by the author, May 2006)*

Caddying in Pinehurst, North Carolina

African American adult males were not the only ones exposed to caddying. Boys and girls even at the young age of six caddied before, during, and after school, and also on weekends.

In 1925, Mary Gertrude Tufts (daughter of James Tufts, founder of Pinehurst) chaired a committee that arranged Pinehurst school bus transportation for caddies under the age of 16. The bus picked up the children from Pinehurst Country Club, took them to school, picked them up from school, and returned them to the country club. Before this transportation arrangement, many children who worked at Pinehurst Country Club did not attend school.

It was not unusual for a caddie master to interrupt children's school time and request that they go to the golf course to caddie. If a caddie master needed caddies, he would often ask the school principal to send boys to the country club.

Bennie Thomas remembered leaving school early to caddie. When he was six years old (in 1931), Thomas started caddying at Pinehurst Country Club. He caddied for 12 years. Thomas enjoyed talking about his caddie experiences:

> I was eight when I started leaving school to caddie. But I was caddying before then. I started caddying when I was six. I was too small to carry a full bag of golf clubs so the caddie master let me caddie for elderly people who had only a few clubs in their bags. A couple of years later, I could handle two full bags—one on each shoulder.
>
> Most of my friends worked at the golf course. The first dollar that I made was at Pinehurst Country Club. I carried a bag for 18 holes and was paid one dollar. Sometimes I made extra money shagging balls and was paid fifty cents per bag. I used my caddie money to help support my family—five sisters and three brothers. It was about putting food on the table and taking care of family. It was about survival.

The only toy that I ever had was a golf club. All of my friends played golf. We all used the same club. Whoever had a golf club, shared it with everyone. I can't remember playing with my friends when there was no more than one golf club among all of us. When a club would wear down so badly that we could not play with it anymore, we just found another one.

In all the years that I caddied at Pinehurst Country Club, whites were not allowed to caddie and blacks were not allowed in the clubhouse. We did not go up there unless they (the white staff) sent for us. We, the black caddies, sort of knew our place. That's just the way it was. But now Pinehurst Country Club has more white caddies than black caddies. Time brings on changes.

Born in 1925 in Aberdeen, North Carolina, Thomas stopped caddying at Pinehurst Country Club in 1943. That same year, he relocated to Long Island, New York. Thomas continued to play golf but he never caddied again. *(Bennie Thomas interviewed by the author, April 2006)*

♦ ♦ ♦

Many black caddies in the Pinehurst area purchased land to build homes in a segregated community located about three miles from Pinehurst. That property, owned by Demus Taylor, was known as the "colored settlement".

In the early 1900s, Taylor purchased the undeveloped land from the Tuft family. He called his land "Old Settlement"; the community was later renamed "Taylortown" in Demus Taylor's honor. According to 1920s deed records, Demus and his son Robert sold lots for as low as seventy-five dollars.

> Many black caddies in the Pinehurst area purchased land to build homes in a segregated community .... known as the "colored settlement".

In addition to being a wealthy property owner, six feet and four inches tall Demus worked as a tree cutter. During the early 1900s, it was exceptional for an African American to earn a status of wealth such as Demus Taylor acquired.

Told by Richard Tufts:
Demus came into the office to borrow $100 from Mr. Albert Tufts (grandson of James Tufts, founder of Pinehurst). Mr. Albert Tufts was puzzled as to why Demus wanted to borrow money when he truly didn't need it. Demus always paid off the payments with interest promptly. Mr. Tufts finally learned that his reason for borrowing the money was to uphold his prestige among his friends as being the only Negro privileged to borrow money from Mr. Tufts. Demus always sent a young Negro to make an appointment with Mr. Tufts before going to see him. *(From the Tufts Archives Collection. Pinehurst, North Carolina)*

Born into slavery, Demus was a descendant of the Western African Ebu tribe and the grandson of an African slave brought to the New World. Demus's slave master was not sure what year Demus was born, but according to his estimation, Demus died at approximately 105 years old in 1934. *(Pinehurst Archives)*

♦ ♦ ♦

Willie McRae, Robert "Hardrock" Robinson, and Fletcher Gaines were among the many Pinehurst Country Club caddies who lived in Taylortown. McRae started caddying when he was ten years old:

One day in 1943, I was sitting in school and a white man came in and told the teacher that he needed boys to caddie at the country club. I was among the group that was told to go and get on a bus that was parked outside.

The bus took us to Pinehurst Country Club. The caddie master was short on caddies so he came to the school to fill his caddie slots. From then on I, along with other classmates, were often taken out of school to caddie.

No matter what time the bus picked us up from school, that was the end of our school day. School was over by the time we finished caddying.

I got paid $1.25 a bag and about $1.00 to $1.75 for a tip. I caddied six days a week, but not on Sundays. The bosses at the golf course knew that our parents wanted us to go to church on Sundays.

Back then, caddies were not allowed to play any of the golf courses so we sneaked on the courses and played. Most of the time the greenkeeper caught us and told us to leave, but as soon as he was out of sight we went back on the course and played. Finally in the 1960s, caddies were allowed to play.

I love what I do. I get to meet a lot of people. Playing golf and caddying has always been a part of my family. I don't think I'd want to do anything else.

Willie's father Thaddeus McRae was a caddie; Thaddeus taught Willie how to caddie and play golf. Willie taught his son Paul how to play golf, and he taught his grandson Derrick how to caddie.

Both Paul and Derrick work at Pinehurst Resort and Country Club. Derrick McRae is a caddie. Paul McRae, a PGA Class A Member, is the first African American golf professional hired at Pinehurst Training Academy.

Willie McRae sometimes tells his age in golf terms— when he was 73 he said he was one over par. At age 82, the year 2015 marked Willie McRae's 72nd year at Pinehurst Resort and Country Club. McRae still caddies but he drives a golf cart instead of walking.

Just like in his childhood days, Willie McRae does not caddie on Sundays. Now a preacher and singer, McRae goes to church and visits nursing homes. *(Willie McRae interviewed by the author, August 2006)*

♦ ♦ ♦

Robert "Hardrock" Robinson was born January 1, 1914. He caddied at Pinehurst Country Club for many notables including Ben Hogan and golf course architect Donald Ross. Hardrock often talked about the soaring increase of green fees and caddie wages:

> I remember when the green fee for Pinehurst No. 2 was about $25. It's more than $125 now. Today it's all about money. I remember when I made 50¢ for carrying two bags. Imagine what I'd have made if I had caddied for Tiger Woods when he first won a Masters. I would have made more money in that one tournament than I have ever made caddying, and I'm almost 90 years old!

In 2001, Hardrock was inducted into the *Epochs of Courage: African Americans in Golf Wall of Fame*. Robert "Hardrock" Robinson, at age 88, died March 8, 2002. *(Robert Robinson interviewed by the author, April 2001)*

Robert "Hardrock" Robinson
Renowned Pinehurst
Country Club caddie

♦ ♦ ♦

Fletcher Gaines caddied for more than 40 years. He caddied for tour professionals Curtis Strange and Gene Sarazen. Fletcher was also known for his excellent golf game. He won the Pinehurst Caddie Tournament four consecutive times. Fletcher's grandfather Ed Gaines, who was born into slavery, caddied for more than four decades.

The first Pinehurst Caddie Tournament was held in the 1930s. This event gave Pinehurst black caddies an opportunity to exhibit their playing abilities, because caddies were not only noted for their keen caddying skills— they were also well known for their playing abilities.

Jessie Jones has played in more than 50 caddie tournaments and has caddied in Pinehurst for more than 45 years:

> The caddie tournament gave black caddies a time to come together and play on a nice golf course, compete, and have lots of fun. It was a big outing for blacks. Good down-home cooking was often set up on the sixth hole and the 18th hole.
>
> Each golf course had its own caddie tournament but caddies from other courses were invited to play. It was an all-black event because back then, there were only black caddies in Pinehurst. Starting in the 1990s, whites began to enter the tournament.
>
> Today, Pinehurst caddies are about 90 percent white. I think it is about the money. I also think that many blacks do not want to caddie because they relate caddying to slavery days.
>
> When you have caddied as long as I have, you have lived through the changes that the caddie profession has gone through. Caddying is a business now and the tour caddie probably spends just as much time with his golfer than he spends with his family.
>
> I love what I do. I meet great people. I would not change jobs.

I have caddied for more than 50 years—24 at Mid Pines Golf Club and 26 and counting at Pinehurst Country Club. I started caddying when I was 12 years old. My friends, who were four to five years older than me, talked about how good the money was—so I decided to try it. My first day caddying I made $1.50 for nine holes and $2.75 for 18 holes. I counted that money all the way home. Back then I got paid five to six dollars for carrying two bags. Now a caddie gets more than $50 for two bags and about a $50 to $60 tip for 18 holes.

Back then there was no fancy driving range with machinery to pick up golf balls. Caddies did all of that. I could make 50¢ to one dollar a bag shagging balls. When I shagged balls all day, I would walk away with at least pay for 12 or 13 bags. Sometimes we shagged balls while golfers were practicing. Imagine being in a field picking up golf balls while someone is hitting golf balls in your direction. There were many times when caddies were struck and injured by golf balls.

I taught myself how to play golf using tin cans and tree roots. Most of us were self-taught. Then there were some who were taught by other caddies, and lots of guys picked up playing tips watching professional golfers practice. Black caddies are the greatest caddies of all times. *(Jessie Jones interviewed by the author, August 2006)*

Caddying at Augusta National Golf Club

In an era when Blacks were protesting for equal rights and job opportunities across the United States, the caddie shack at Augusta National Golf Club was as segregated as a church service on Sunday morning. And, it was that way for almost half a century.

From 1934 to 1982 Augusta National Golf Club, home of the Masters Tournament, had an all black caddie staff, and the club's mandatory policy required that—all players use an Augusta National Golf Club caddie for the Masters

Tournament. Hence, the Masters Tournament was the only professional major golf event that had an all black caddie field.

The Masters was an opportunity for black caddies to show-off their great caddying abilities, and also to earn a good payday. If his player won, that caddie received approximately ten percent of his player's prize money. Most caddies received good tips, even if their player did not place in the top-10.

Often there were not enough Augusta National Golf Club caddies available for Masters week. To fill the vacant slots, the caddie master assigned walk-on caddies.

Walk-on caddies came to Augusta National Golf Club once a year—to caddie for the Masters Tournament. They were known to work for the players who the club's regular caddies chose not to caddie for—players who were neither favored to win nor finish in the top-10. These potential assignments did not deter walk-ons from wanting to caddie at the Masters. Some drove all night, hitchhiked, and even quit or skipped their jobs—for that one-week opportunity for a big payday.

Walk-on caddie Walter "Cricket" Pritchett, then an Atlanta, Georgia bus driver, got that opportunity when he was assigned to caddie for Charles Coody at the 1971 Masters Tournament. Concerned about being seen on television by his co-workers and supervisors, Pritchett tried to cover his face by draping a towel from his hat. Pritchett's risks resulted in his favor; Coody won. Coody's prize money was $25000, which made a great payday for Pritchett.

Opportunities for blacks to caddie at the Masters took a spiral downfall in 1983; the Masters Tournament was no longer a mandatory all black caddie field. In November 1982, Augusta National Golf Club chairman Hord Hardin announced a policy change—from the 1983 Masters Tournament onward, players were not mandated to use an Augusta National Golf Club caddie.

Hardin's announcement did not reflect the same vision that Augusta National Golf Club cofounder Clifford Roberts had reportedly stated in earlier years, "As long as I'm alive, all the golfers will be white and all the caddies will be black." Roberts died in 1977.

This abrupt policy change, effective at the 47th Masters Tournament in April 1983, was the beginning of a dramatic decline of the black caddie at the Masters Tournament. This new policy also influenced the reduction of blacks on the caddie staff at Augusta National Golf Club.

The new caddie policy was introduced within the same year of reported occurrences at the 1982 Masters Tournament:

> During the third round of the 1982 Masters Tournament, play was stopped because of rain. Later, the third round was suspended; play was scheduled to continue on the following day and caddies were dismissed for the day. Sometime between when the caddies were dismissed and the next morning, the starting times were changed.
>
> Caddies returned the next day prepared to caddie at the original starting times—not the rescheduled times. Hence, many caddies did not arrive in time to perform their duties such as getting their players golf bag, accompanying their player to practice, and even starting the round with their player. Many players were outraged.
>
> The 1982 Masters Tournament had a full caddie field of 76 black caddies. The following year (1983) at the Masters Tournament there were 82 caddies, including 12 black caddies from Augusta National Golf Club. Among the twelve black caddies were Willie "Pete" Peterson who caddied for Jack Nicklaus, and Carl Jackson who caddied for Ben Crenshaw.
>
> After this caddie policy change, Augusta National Golf Club hired its first white caddie and never again was there a full field or majority of black caddies at a Masters Tournament.

The PGA Tour reflected the same caddie color wheel—a diminished hue of black caddies. However, there were a few

PGA Tour players who had long-term black caddies. For more than 15 years Freddie Burns caddied for Hal Sutton, Herman Mitchell caddied for Lee Trevino, and Alfred Dyer caddied for Gary Player.

After Masters week, Augusta National Golf Club's full-time caddies return to the caddie house for work. The racial composition of the caddie staff has changed since 1983, but a few of the old-timers are still there.

William Brown Jr. caddied at Augusta National Golf Club for more than 35 years. He recalled the historical occasion when his brother Henry Brown caddied for Lee Elder:

Henry, my brother, caddied for Lee Elder's first Masters Tournament appearance. After meeting Lee Elder, Henry told Lee that he could beat him playing golf—and most of us caddies felt that he could. Henry was a talented cross-handed golfer.

Smitty Childs started caddying at Augusta National Golf Club in 1939:

I'm the oldest caddie out here. I don't have to carry a bag. They allow me to drive a cart when I caddie. I may be over 80, but I could teach these young caddie boys a few things about caddying. You can't learn how to be a good caddie by reading a book and taking tests—you've got to get out there and learn every nook and cranny on that golf course. That's how I learned. In 1972 when we had to start using a yardage book, that really hurt black caddies. Many could not interpret it, and there were some who could not read. Many great caddies lost their jobs.

(William Brown Jr. and Smitty Childs interviewed by the author, April 2007.)

Many of the Augusta National Golf Club black caddies, including the old-timers, pursued caddie jobs at other private golf clubs and on the PGA Tour. Then, there were others who became discouraged from rejection, and never caddied again.

Carl Jackson, renowned Masters Tournament caddie

Carl Jackson

He caddied in 53 Masters Tournaments, 1961 to 1999 and 2001 to 2014. Jackson did not caddie in 2000 because of health problems. Jackson is a colon cancer survivor.

In April 2014 Carl Jackson, age 66, began his 38th and last Masters Tournament with his friend and professional golfer Ben Crenshaw. Due to health problems Jackson did not caddie at the 2015 Masters Tournament, where Crenshaw announced that 2015 was his last year playing in the Masters. Carl Jackson's brother Justin "Bud" caddied for Crenshaw.

The duo of Carl Jackson and Ben Crenshaw is one of the most popular caddie–professional golfer relationships in Masters Tournament's history. Jackson first caddied for Crenshaw at the 1976 Masters. They were introduced through mutual friends who were confident that Jackson's experience and personality were a good fit for Crenshaw. With Jackson by his side, Crenshaw won the Masters Tournament in 1984 and 1995. Jackson also joined Crenshaw on the PGA Tour for about two years. During that time, Crenshaw won the 1990 Southwestern Bell Colonial.

Carl Jackson was born March 31, 1947 in Augusta, Georgia. He started playing golf when he was seven years old. Using tree branches for flagsticks, he played with friends on a school playground.

"Sometimes a policeman ordered us off the playground, but we always returned to play on our makeshift course. We weren't bothering anybody. We just wanted a place to play golf", Jackson recalled.

The second oldest of nine children, Jackson started working at a young age to help support his mother and siblings. When Jackson was 11 years old, he chose not to work in the cotton fields like many of the boys in his neighborhood; he chose to work close to home at Augusta Country Club, which bordered his neighborhood.

Jackson, also known as "Skillet Jackson", aspired to become a professional golfer or baseball player:

Back then, all public golf courses in Augusta did not allow blacks to play. I had nowhere to practice or play.

When I was 14, I joined a junior baseball league. About two years later I had my best game ever—I struck out 15 batters in one game. Before pitching the last inning of that game, I asked the outfielders to sit down on the baseball field for the entire inning. They thought I was crazy but they all sat down. I struck out every batter in that inning.

Everybody was amazed. My teammates joked that "Skillet cleaned the plate", and from then on I was known as Skillet Jackson. I was a good baseball player but not good enough to go big time."

Jackson caddied six days a week. He was paid 75¢ to $1.25 per hour for shagging balls, and three to five dollars for caddying 18 holes. Two years later, he started caddying at Augusta National Golf Club. The following year (1961), fourteen-year-old Carl Jackson made his debut at the Masters Tournament; he caddied for Billy Burke.

During Carl Jackson's first year at Augusta National Golf Club, he began caddying for Jackson Stephens, who was a member and later served as chairman of Augusta National Golf Club from 1991 to 1998. In addition to caddying for Stephens, Carl began working for Stephens and continued to work for him for more than 40 years.

"Jack Stephens and I were inseparable. I traveled with Jack on his private jet to golf courses throughout the country. I was his golf instructor, liaison, confidante, bodyguard, and Man Friday. When Jack died in 2005, I lost an employer and a dear friend", Carl reflected.

In February 2003, Jackson accepted a management position at Alotian Golf Club in Roland, Arkansas, a private golf club owned by the Stephens family. His position is commonly known as caddie master; however, Jackson is quick to tell anyone that he is a manager, not a master.

"Do not call or refer to me as a caddie master. I am no one's master. I have only one Master and he is up above."

Jackson has hired Augusta National Golf Club black caddies as seasonal caddies at Alotian Golf Club and, he has provided room and board to caddies and their wives.

"There is a strong bond among the Augusta National Golf Club black caddies", Jackson boasts without hesitation.

Jackson also does not hesitate to express his feelings about the Masters Tournament caddie policy implemented in 1983:

I believe what happened at the 1982 Masters was used to force a change that players had wanted for a long time.

Sometime in the afternoon, the first round of play was suspended because of rain. There was no adequate place for the caddies to rest. Caddies were told to go home and come back tomorrow at their regular starting times. I was not aware of any other instructions given to the caddies from the caddie master or tournament officials. Because I was assistant caddie manager, I stayed overnight in a back room in the golf shop where the other caddies were not allowed.

I don't think the caddie master or the tournament officials had a procedure to let the caddies know of any changes. I doubt very seriously if any of the caddies were contacted regarding the changed starting times. So the caddies showed up as they were instructed to do—at their regular starting times. The caddies were not at fault. Because of what happened, many players got rid of good caddies. I was saddened to see that happen.

The black caddie has become an endangered species in major events and on any tour. Even though black caddies show up at tour events, they usually are not selected to caddie, or if selected black caddies are usually the last to be hired. I have seen experienced black caddies rejected for a tour caddie position, but—that same caddie slot was later offered to an inexperienced white caddie. It just seems like some players just don't want a black caddie.

The vision is dim but I still have hope.

(Carl Jackson interviewed by the author, June 2006)

*Through
one century,
a seesaw of changes
occurred.*

❧

*A caddie's job
is no longer
considered a
position of servitude
or a job
dominated
by blacks.*

❧

*It is now a
career profession
dominated
by whites.*

—Anonymous

Preston McClain Jr.
Caddie Master
Temple Hills Country Club

Mike
Troublefield
LPGA Tour Caddie

Reynolds Robinson
Caddie for Cheyenne Woods,
LPGA Tour

Andrew King
Caddied for PGA Tour member
Chandler Harper

Otis "Buck" Moore
Tour caddie

Notable Black Caddies and Caddie Masters/Managers
(Caddie masters/managers denoted by *)

"Big" Henry Avery*–Augusta Country Club

Nathaniel "Ironman" Avery–caddied for Arnold Palmer's four Masters wins (1958, 1960, 1962, and 1964)

Jariah "Bubba" Beard–Augusta National Golf Club— caddied for Fuzzy Zoeller for his 1979 Masters win

Freddie Bennett*–Augusta National Golf Club caddie master for 40 years; retired in 2000

Tommy "Burnt Biscuits" Bennett–Augusta National Golf Club; caddied for Tiger Woods–amateur player at the 1995 Masters

Henry Brown–Augusta National Golf Club; caddied for Lee Elder's debut at the Masters Tournament

William Brown Jr.–Augusta National Golf Club

Billy Budd*–caddie master, Columbia Country Club (Maryland)

Freddie Burns–caddied for Hal Sutton; United States captain's caddie for the 35th Ryder Cup (2004)

Ben Bussey–caddied for Craig Stadler's 1982 Masters win

Smith "Smitty" Childs–Augusta National Golf Club

James "Jim" Clark–Baltusrol Golf Club (retired at age 92)

Alfred "Rabbit" Dyer–caddied for Gary Player for 18 years; first African American to caddie in all four majors

Sam "Killer" Foy–caddied for Hale Irwin for 15 years

George "Fireball" Franklin–Augusta National Golf Club

Ed Gaines–Pinehurst Country Club

Fletcher Gaines–Pinehurst Country Club

Billy Gardenhight Sr.–Biltmore Forest Country Club

Johnny Garret–Augusta National Golf Club

Oscar B. Goings*–Winchester Country Club

Jimmy Green–caddied for Pete Brown

Richard "Jelly" Hansbury–PGA Tour

Neil Harvey–caddied for Lee Trevino

Bennie Hatcher–Augusta National Golf Club

Marion Herrington–caddied for Seve Ballesteros's 1980 Masters win

Earl Hill–Jekyll Island Golf Club

Adolphus "Golf Ball" Hull–tour caddie; caddied for Pete Brown, Calvin Peete, and Raymond Floyd

J.J. Hylton–tour caddie

Carl "Skillet" Jackson*–caddie manager, Alotian Golf Club; caddied for Crenshaw's 1984 and 1995 Masters wins; caddied in 53 Masters

Justin "Bud" Jackson–Augusta National Golf Club

Nathaniel "Smiley" Jenkins–caddied on LPGA Tour

Andrew King–caddied for Chandler Harper

Lonnie Lowe–PGA Tour; caddied for Payne Stewart

Albert Martin*–caddie master Congressional Country Club

Preston McClain Jr.*–first caddie master at Temple Hills Country Club (Texas); retired in 1960; 32 years of service

Leon McClattie–caddied for Tom Watson's 1977 and 1981 Masters wins

Eddie "E.B." McCoy–Augusta National Golf Club; caddied for Gary Player's 1974 and 1978 Masters wins

Willie McRae–Pinehurst Country Club; caddied for U.S. Presidents Ford, Nixon, and Eisenhower

Willie Miller–caddied for Jim Colbert

Herman Mitchell–caddied for Lee Trevino for more than 25 years

Johnny Frank Moore–caddied more than 55 years at Augusta National Golf Club

Jonathan Moore–LPGA Tour caddie for Sadena Parks

Otis "Buck" Moore–caddied for Olin Browne; caddied for Browne's win at the 2011 U.S. Senior Open Championship

Ernest Nipper–caddied for Gary Player's first Masters Tournament win in 1961

Thor "Stovepipe" Norwall–caddied for Gene Sarazan's 1935 Masters win

Jerry "Hobo" Osborn–Senior PGA Tour caddie

Matthew "Shorty Mac" Palmer–Augusta National Golf Club; caddied for Billy Casper's 1970 Masters win

Willie "Cemetery" Frank Perteet–Augusta National Golf Club; caddied for President Dwight Eisenhower

Willie "Pete" Peterson–caddied for Jack Nicklaus for 23 Masters; five Masters wins with Nicklaus (1963, 1965, 1966, 1972, and 1975)

Walter "Crickett" Pritchett–caddied for Charles Coody's 1971 Masters win

Billy Ricks–Augusta National Golf Club

Percy Riley–tour caddie

Reynolds Robinson–LPGA Tour caddie for Cheyenne Woods

Robert "Hardrock" Robinson–Pinehurst Country Club

Leroy Schultz–caddied for Tom Weiskopf and Lanny Wadkins

Orlando Scott–tour caddie

Randy Soul–tour caddie and country club caddie

Tony Smith–Champions Tour caddie for Brad Bryant; caddied for Bryant's win at the 2007 U.S. Senior Open Championship

Willie "Pappy" Stokes–Augusta National Golf Club; five Masters wins: 1938–Henry Picard; 1948–Claude Harmon; 1951 & 1953–Ben Hogan; 1956–Jack Burke Jr.

Cliff Strickland*–caddie and caddie master; Victoria Club, Riverside, California

Del Taylor–caddied for Billy Casper

Tony Terry–tour caddie for Duffy Waldorf

Mike "Country Club" Troublefield–LPGA Tour caddie; began caddying on LPGA Tour in 2000; caddied for M.J. Hur's Safeway Classic win in 2009

Cleveland Wade–Senior PGA Tour caddie

Eddie "Bebe" Wallace–LPGA Tour

Frank "Skinny" Ware–Augusta National Golf Club

Howard "Butch" Wheeler*–caddie master, East Lake Country Club, Atlanta, Georgia

Alonzo "Frog" Wilkins–tour caddie

Charles Frank "Grady" Williams–PGA Tour

John "Eleven" Williams–Augusta National Golf Club

Walter Worthen Sr.–Macon, Georgia

Chuck Wright–Chevy Chase Country Club

Ernest Wright–tour caddie

Caddie Quotes

The following anonymous quotes are from various interviews. The names are withheld by mutual agreement.

Every time I stepped on a golf course, I was out there for a win. It was about survival.

There are tour players who use their family members for caddies. Blood is always thicker than mud.

I call the PGA Tour—*The Friends and Family Tour.*

The way I see it—the PGA Tour has become the *Land of Opportunity for Friends and Family.*

We try not to look at race issues, but they make it hard for us not to.

We are entitled to have the same opportunities as the other caddies.

I survived on blood and guts.

The way I see it, most tour players would rather lose with a white caddie than win with a black caddie.

My first time caddying, the caddie master paid me three dollars for the round. I also got a tip from my golfer—two pieces of peppermint candy.

The unfair treatment that we got—just makes my blood pressure boil.

We were—last to be first, and—first to be last.

The author expresses gratitude to the persons who shared their quotes.

2

John Matthew Shippen Jr.
(December 5, 1879 [Washington, D.C.]–1968). First
American-born professional golfer to enter a U.S. Open
Championship. First African American professional golfer to
win a money prize (1896); granted posthumous PGA
Membership by The PGA of America (2009).

John Shippen Jr.'s early years were spent in the Anacostia
neighborhood in Washington, D.C. His father, a
Presbyterian minister, was a graduate of the Howard School
of Theology (now Howard University, Washington, D.C.).
When John Jr. was about 10 years old, his father received a
mission assignment to pastor a church on the Shinnecock
Indian Reservation in Southampton, New York; thus, the
Shippen family moved from Washington, D.C. to New York.

John Jr. adjusted well to living on the Shinnecock Indian
Reservation. His mother was a homemaker; his father led
the ministry and also taught at the Indian reservation
school. The family was sometimes referred to as Native
Americans; however both parents, John Shippen Sr. and
Eliza Spotswood Shippen were African Americans.

Located close to the Indian reservation was Shinnecock
Hills Golf Club, where John Jr. caddied and learned how to
play golf. It did not take him long to master the game, and
his remarkable talent was quickly noticed by club members
and staff.

In 1896, Shinnecock Hills Golf Club members encouraged
16-year-old Shippen to enter the second U.S. Open
Championship. Club members offered to pay Shippen's
entry fee; Shippen accepted the generous offer. Shippen's
friend Oscar Bunn, a Shinnecock Indian, also registered and
paid an entry fee to the 1896 U.S. Open Championship.

Unfortunately, Shippen's and Bunn's entries caused
contention. Players threatened to withdraw when they
heard about the "colored boy Shippen" and his "Shinnecock
Indian friend" playing in the event. The USGA responded to
the criticisms through an announcement from Theodore
Havemeyer, then USGA president. Havemeyer announced

that both men would be allowed to play. The 36-hole, two-day event opened as scheduled.

At the end of the first round, Shippen posted a 78 on the leaderboard. That score gave him a share of the lead with four other players. On the second day, Shippen was still near the top of the leaderboard after playing the first nine holes. However on the 13th hole, his ball went into a sand bunker; Shippen had a harrowing experience getting his ball out of the bunker, which resulted in an 11 on a par four hole. At the end of the round, Shippen posted an 81.

With a two-day total of 159 John Shippen Jr., the youngest competitor at the second U.S. Open Championship tied for fifth place and won ten dollars. Sixteen-year-old Shippen placed seven strokes behind the winner James Foulis.

After competing in the 1896 U.S. Open, Shippen began to pursue a career in golf. In 1898 at age 19, he became the first to serve as golf professional at Aronimink Golf Club (Newtown Square, Pennsylvania).

> With a two-day total of 159 John Shippen Jr., the youngest competitor at the second U.S. Open Championship tied for fifth place and won ten dollars.

Shippen also competed in the 1899, 1900, 1902, and 1913 U.S. Open Championships. His best finish was in 1902; he again tied for fifth place.

John Jr. had eight siblings—Bessie, Carrie, Clara, Cyrus, Eliza, Henry, Susan, and William. Except for Susan, who died at a very young age, all of John Jr.'s brothers and sisters graduated from college.

His brother Cyrus was the second African American to graduate from Yale College; he graduated in 1899. (Edward Bouchet was the first African American graduate of Yale College; he graduated in 1874. Bouchet received a Doctor of Philosophy degree from Yale Graduate School in 1876; thus, he was the first African American to receive a PhD from an American university.)

CYRUS SPOTTSWOOD SHIPPEN

"Cy"

Born March 29, 1876, at Hillsdale, D. C., but removed to Southampton, Long Island. He happened in New Haven one day in search of a golf ball driven across the Sound in a fit of absent-mindedness. "Ship" dallied awhile at Oberlin. His father, John M. Shippen, is a minister.

John Jr. and his brother Cyrus were golf instructors. In 1924, Cyrus became the golf coach at Dunbar High School in Washington, D.C.; he also taught civics, economics, history, and Latin.

In the early 1930s, John Jr. became the club professional at Shady Rest Golf and Country Club in Scotch Plains, New Jersey. He lived in a clubhouse apartment on the property and worked there for more than 30 years. Shady Rest Golf and Country Club was the first African American-owned country club in the United States.

John Shippen Jr. married two times. Both marriages were to Shinnecock Indian women. Effie Walker, his first wife, died in 1901. Shippen and his second wife Maude Lee had six children.

On May 20, 1968, Shippen died in a New Jersey nursing home. His tombstone reads: John Shippen 1879–1968 The First American Born, African American Golf Professional.

Excerpt from an interview by the author (February 2006) with Hanno Shippen Smith, grandson of John Shippen Jr. (Hanno Shippen Smith died in September 2010):

I want my grandfather to be known throughout the world as the USA's first-born golf professional. It would give me great pleasure for people, who have come after him and achieved even greater things, to recognize him for what he did in 1896, and for what he gave to the game that he lived for. Golf seemed much more to him than anything else in life—even to the detriment of family relationships.

I love the game as well and wish that I could have spent more time with my grandfather when I was growing up, and got the bug for golf like he did. He cared tremendously about getting youth involved in golf.

The John Shippen Foundation provides opportunities to youth. I hope the foundation produces players like my grandfather and Tiger Woods.

While Charlie Sifford and others who followed are great golfers, to my thinking, Tiger will be the best of all times. I wish my grandfather could see Tiger play.

Hanno Shippen Smith, John M. Shippen Jr.'s grandson

I know that Tiger Woods is young and surely has much on his mind, but I am sure that my grandfather would be most grateful if Tiger would mention once in a while that John Shippen Jr. existed and what he did—competed in the 1896 U.S. Open Championship at age 16, led the first round, finished fifth, and was paid ten dollars. By receiving the ten-dollar prize money, my grandfather John Matthew Shippen Jr., an African American, became the first paid American professional golfer.

John Matthew Shippen Jr. is recognized in many record books of today. I hope his name lives as long as the game.

For information about The John Shippen Memorial Golf Foundation and John Shippen Youth Golf Academy visit www.johnshippen.net, or contact chairman Thurman Simmons at 908-322-5486.

3

George Franklin Grant
(September 15, 1846 [Oswego, New York]–August 21, 1910).
First inventor to receive a U.S. Patent for a wooden golf tee;
second African American graduate of Harvard School of
Dental Medicine.

George Grant's parents, Phillis Pitt and Tudor Elandor
Grant, were fugitive slaves. They moved to Oswego, New
York in 1832. Tudor Grant became a successful barber and
well-known abolitionist.

In the May 16, 1838 edition of *Friend of Man* (an
abolitionist newspaper published in Oswego County, New
York), an article titled "Oswego County Society Meeting at
Oswego" referred to Tudor Grant as a "colored gentleman,
once a chattel (slave) although he spoke as though he felt
himself to be a man ...."

That same year (1838), Tudor Grant joined the Oswego
County Anti-Slavery Society's Vigilante Committee (known
for helping fugitive slaves). He also signed an anti-slavery
petition that requested: *Congress not admit any more slave*
states into the Union. Two years later Tudor signed another
petition, which opposed Texas admission into the Union as a
slave state.

Tudor Grant was also involved with the Underground
Railroad, a secret network of people who helped fugitive
slaves escape to free states and to Canada. Oswego, New
York was a major Canadian trade port.

In 1854, Tudor purchased property and built a home at
134 West Bridge Street. He lived there with his second wife
Marie, and four of his seven children from his first
marriage—one son, George, and three daughters, O.C.,
Sophie, and Louisa. (Tudor's first wife died in the early
1850s.)

Oswego County documents show evidence that the
Grant's West Bridge Street residence was an Underground
Railroad site. Oswego's 1855 census records list George
Grant residing at the family's West Bridge Street address.
Based on that 1855 census documentation, George Grant

lived at 134 West Bridge Street while it was an Underground Railroad site. (This historical home later became a part of the Oswego County Historical Society Underground Railroad Tour. In December 2008, the home was destroyed by fire.)

In 1857, Tudor opened a barbershop business in the basement of the Buckout-Jones building located near the city's harbor. Because of the barbershop's harbor location, Tudor's place of business was a suspected passageway for fugitive slaves to escape to Canada.

In 1858, Tudor sold his West Bridge Street property and moved his family to West Seneca Street. Oswego records do not show when George Grant moved out of the family home or when he left Oswego; however, there are unofficial reports that George Grant moved out of the family home in 1861, and left Oswego in 1867.

In 1868, George Grant entered Harvard School of Dental Medicine. He graduated in 1870 and became the school's second African American graduate. Grant ranked number two in his graduating class. Robert Tanner Freeman was the first African American graduate of the Harvard School of Dental Medicine. Freeman graduated in 1869.

In 1871, Dr. Grant was appointed to a position in the department of Mechanical Dentistry; thus, he became the school's first African American faculty member. He served in the department of Mechanical Dentistry for 19 years.

Grant was a founding member and president of the Harvard Odontological Society; and in 1881, he served as president of the Alumni Association.

On December 12, 1899, Dr. Grant was issued the first United States Patent (U.S. Patent Number 638,920) for his invention of a wooden golf tee. Before Dr. Grant's invention, golfers usually teed golf balls on sand mounds. Water and sand were usually situated near each tee box. Golfers would dampen the sand and make small sand mounds to tee up their golf balls.

Even though his invention was a milestone in golf history, Dr. Grant's wooden tees were not commercially marketed; he stored his tees at home and gave many away. And for almost a century, Dr. Grant's U.S. patent invention did not receive its rightful place in history.

The United States Golf Association recognized Dr. William Lowell Sr., a Caucasian, as the first inventor of the golf tee. Lowell received a U.S. Patent (U.S. Patent Number 1,670,267) for his golf tee invention in 1925, more than 25 years after Dr. Grant was awarded a U.S. Patent for his wooden golf tee invention. Due to the efforts of Wornie Reed, an African American university professor, the USGA in 1991 acknowledged Dr. Grant as the first inventor of the wooden golf tee.

Dr. Grant often played golf on meadowlands—ground more suitable for raising farm animals. Even though Dr. Grant was a Harvard School graduate, inventor, and successful dentist, he could not golf at the same country clubs that his white colleagues were welcomed. Dr. George Franklin Grant was denied access because—he was African American.

Dr. George Franklin Grant
1870 Harvard Dental School graduation photograph
Credit Harvard Medical Library

From my life experiences, I have many stories to tell. For as long as you are black, you will always have a story to tell.

William Powell

Chapter II
Building Through the Rough

Preview

African American workers using animals and man-made materials to transplant wiregrass for the construction of Pine Needles Country Club in North Carolina. Circa 1927. Credit: The Tufts Archives

Building Through the Rough

I will not take "but" for an answer.
—Langston Hughes

Man-made tools, horses, wagons, and mules were mainly used to construct golf courses before the invention of tractors or other sophisticated building machinery. For decades, African Americans did not receive recognition for their contributions to golf course construction. For many, there were long and tedious hours of hard labor with insignificant rewards.

African Americans were not allowed to play on the courses that they labored. In 1982, James Barber was hired at Bide-A-Wee Golf Course in Portsmouth, Virginia:

> That was my first job. I was 16 and earned about $2.85 per hour for an eight-hour day. I still have the first dollar that I made. My first day on the job, the supervisor gave me a bucket and a butter knife to prepare the greens for re-seeding. On my knees I pulled out crabgrass, blade-by-blade. It took me more than one hour to do one green.
>
> Blacks were not allowed to play the golf course nor use facilities. We had to use the bathroom in the barn, and we could only purchase food at an outside grill area in back of the pro shop. Back then, to work was the only reason blacks were allowed at Bide-A-Wee Golf Course.

4

Designers and Builders

Joseph Bartholomew Sr.
(August 1, 1881[New Orleans, Louisiana]–October 12, 1971)
Designed and built golf courses in Louisiana.

Joseph M. Bartholomew Sr., renowned golf course architect, was also a philanthropist, investor, and business owner. Bartholomew owned construction and landscaping companies, and also invested in real estate. He was a financial supporter of Dillard University and Xavier University, both historically black universities in New Orleans.

Beginning in the 1920s, Joseph Bartholomew was commissioned to build golf courses in the New Orleans metro area. But even with his wealth, success, and responsibilities of designing and building golf courses— Bartholomew was denied access to play on the public golf courses that he built—because he was African American.

At an early age, Bartholomew began doing odd jobs such as domestic work and caddying. He dropped out of school before entering the ninth grade, and spent most of his time at golf courses working as a caddie and working with grounds crew.

A self-taught golfer, Bartholomew was known as an extraordinary golfer who often scored under par. However, Bartholomew was not only a talented golfer, he was also a skilled landscaper, greenkeeper, and clubmaker.

In the early 1920s, members of the exclusive all-white Metairie Golf Club (located outside New Orleans) queried Bartholomew's exceptional talents in golf course maintenance. Club members offered Bartholomew an all-expense paid trip to the northeast to study golf course architecture; Bartholomew accepted.

Upon completion of his northeast assignment, Bartholomew returned to New Orleans. Metairie Golf Club members requested that Bartholomew have an active role in building an 18-hole golf course for their country club.

Bartholomew accepted, and course construction began in 1922. The 18-hole construction project, which showcased elevated greens and tree-lined fairways, was completed in 1925. Later, Bartholomew became the first golf professional at Metairie Golf Club.

There are conflicting reports regarding what role Bartholomew served for the 18-hole construction project. Was he a laborer or was he lead builder for the golf course construction project? Under research for this publication, Bartholomew is recognized as the lead builder of the Metairie Golf Club first 18-hole golf course construction project.

From the late 1920s through the 1950s, Bartholomew built and was credited for designing City Park Number 1 Golf Course (also known as the East Course), City Park Number 2 Golf Course (also known as the South Course), and Pontchartrain Park Golf Course (all courses located in New Orleans, Louisiana).

In February 1972 (four months after Bartholomew's death), Bartholomew became the first African American inducted into the Greater New Orleans Sports Hall of Fame. In 1979, Pontchartrain Park was renamed Joseph M. Bartholomew Senior Golf Course. This commemoration occurred 23 years after African Americans were granted access to play Pontchartrain Park Golf Course.

Joseph Bartholomew Sr.
Renowned golf course architect
Courtesy Ruth Creech

William Powell
(November 22, 1916 [Butler County, Greenville, Alabama]–December 31, 2009). First African American to design, build, own, and operate a nine-hole golf course.

He started caddying at a very young age, earning 35¢ a bag. Captain of his high school golf team, Powell also played golf in college. He attended Wilberforce University.

In 1942, Powell enlisted in the United States Army. While serving in the military during World War II, he played golf in Europe—experiencing no racial incidences. He returned to the United States in 1946. Unfortunately, Powell's experiences playing golf in the United States were not the same as he encountered in Europe. In his native country, he was denied access to golf courses because he was black. When Powell did have a rare opportunity to play, he was often harassed with racial slurs. As a result of being taunted and turned away, Powell desired to build his own golf course.

After Powell found dairy land property suitable for a golf course, he sought ways to finance his venture. He attempted to apply for a GI loan from local banks, but was told by bankers that no such loans existed. Unable to purchase the property as sole-owner, Powell became an equal partner with two African American physicians. Powell's brother took out a loan on his house to finance William's property investment. In 1946, the land that would later become Clearview Golf Club was purchased.

On October 1, 1946, the Powell family moved to the 130-acre dairy farm. There, they lived in a house that had no indoor plumbing or adequate heating.

Powell worked a full-time job, repaired the family home, and labored to make his dream become a reality. He pulled out all the old farm fence posts, one-by-one, with his bare hands. And, with his own hand-mixed fertilizer, he seeded and fertilized every fairway.

In April 1948, Clearview Golf Club opened with nine holes. During its first year of operation, more than 70 percent of Clearview's clientele were white. Powell now offered his white customers what he had so often been denied by whites—a place to golf. Powell referred to Clearview as "America's Course".

In 1956, Powell bought out his partners and became sole owner of the property. Later he began to expand his course; and in 1978, Clearview Golf Club became an 18-hole golf facility. A family operated course, Powell's daughter Renee served as head golf professional, and his son Larry served as golf course superintendent.

National Aeronautics and Space Administration (NASA) recognized Larry for using a NASA technology, ZeoPro™ nutrients, to change the type of grass on the greens at Clearview. Larry and Clearview's Hole number 15 were featured in the *1998 NASA Annual Publication.*

In 2001, the United States Department of Interior designated Clearview Golf Club as a National Historic Site. That same year, the Clearview Legacy Foundation for Education, Preservation, and Research was established.

William Powell overcame immeasurable obstacles. During a conversation with the author in 2001, Powell was asked if he would do it all over again, he quickly responded:

It was hard, very hard. My lovely, my beautiful wife Marcella supported me—no matter what.

Would I do it again? No! I would not put my family through that—never again!
(William Powell's wife, Marcella, died in 1996. Clearview Golf Club hosts an annual Marcella Powell Memorial Four Lady Scramble.)

William Powell, also known as Mr. P, greeted and talked with customers as he sat by his potbelly wood-burning stove in his pro shop. He often gave customers a glance of history as he talked about his experiences—trials and triumphs—in making Clearview Golf Club a historical landmark.

Powell received numerous honors including the 1999 Unsung Hero Award presented by the Congressional Black

Caucus Spouses, and the 2009 PGA Distinguished Service Award. In 1997 Powell was granted honorary PGA membership from The PGA of America Northern Ohio Section, and in 2013 he was posthumously inducted into The PGA of America Hall of Fame.

After Powell died in 2009, Renee and Larry continued to operate the family business.

A children's book titled—*Twice As Good: The story of William Powell and Clearview, the only golf course designed, built, and owned by an African American*—by Richard Michelson was published in January 2012. *Clearview: America's Course*, William Powell's autobiography by Ellen Susanna Nösner was published in 2000.

(Contact information for Clearview Golf Club, page 184)

William Powell sitting by wood stumps for his potbelly stove that helps keep the pro shop warm.

Zollie Gill and Sam Solomon
Principal builders of the first nine holes at Bull Creek Golf and Country Club in Louisburg, North Carolina.

Zollie Gill and Sam Solomon spent many hours observing and asking questions about golf course construction. Gill and Solomon built the first nine holes at Bull Creek Golf and Country Club that opened in October 1996.

"We didn't know anything about building a golf course, so we went around town and talked to experience people about designing, with a special focus on how to build greens. Building that golf course was hard work, but we did it," Gill told the author during an interview in 2013.

In 1998, the golf course expanded to 18 holes as a 6367 yard par-72 layout; the course closed in 2014. Bull Creek Golf and Country Club was owned and operated by five African American families–Massenburg (Warren Massenburg, principal owner), Strickland, Keith, Brown, and Solomon.

Clifford Sommerville
Owner, designer, builder, and manager of Wedgewood Golf Center in Halifax County, Virginia

For 20 years, Clifford Sommerville worked to transform his 28-acre farmland of corn and soybeans into a nine-hole golf course and learning center. Wedgewood Golf Center opened in 2001. The facility features a nine-hole course, clubhouse with meeting rooms, driving range, and putting green. Sommerville held a ribbon cutting ceremony in 2006. (*Contact information for Wedgewood Golf Center, page 186*)

Wedgewood Golf Center Clubhouse

Prejudice is like a hair across your cheek.
You can't see it, you can't find it with your
fingers, but you keep brushing at it because
the feel of it is irritating.

Marian Anderson

Chapter III
Shifting the Color Line

Preview

State Statute Ruled Nil

The Portsmouth Star. August 29, 1956

The Portsmouth Star
August 29, 1956
Photo Caption
CLAIMS RIGHTS VIOLATED—
These are the three Portsmouth men, shown with
their attorney who say their rights were violated
when they were refused admission to Portsmouth
City Park Golf Course. Judge Walter E. Hoffman
today issued a temporary injunction opening the
course to Negroes. Left to right, Dr. James W.
Holley III, Attorney Mrs. Yolande Chambers,
Linwood C. Bailey and James Gray.

Shifting the Color Line

The problem is the problem of the color line.
—W. E. B. Dubois

In 1896, John Shippen Jr. became the first African American to play in a USGA U.S. Open; that same year a United States Supreme Court ruling, in the case of *Plessy v. Ferguson,* upheld the legalization of segregation.

On June 7, 1892 Homer Ferguson, a 30-year-old shoemaker from Louisiana, purchased a train ticket to travel from New Orleans, Louisiana to Covington, Louisiana. Ferguson, who was biracial (African American and Caucasian), boarded the train and sat in the "Whites Only" section. A train employee informed Ferguson that he had to move to the "coloreds only" coach because he (Ferguson) was sitting in a "whites only" section. Ferguson refused to move to the "coloreds only" coach. Homer Ferguson was arrested.

In the case of *Plessy v. Ferguson*, Homer Ferguson challenged the constitutionality of segregated railroad coaches. The courts referred to the equal protection clause of the U.S. Constitution 14th Amendment, and concluded that separate railroad coaches provided equal services. A United States Supreme Court ruling upheld the lower courts ruling; thus, the *Separate But Equal* clause was upheld.

The 1896 U.S. Supreme Court ruling in the case of *Plessy v. Ferguson* provided a constitutional basis for segregation. The "separate but equal" standard became the foundation of many lawsuits filed by African Americans seeking unrestricted access to public golf courses.

The following sections are focused on: acts and symbols of racism; landmark accomplishments; and federal, state, and local rulings.

◆ ◆ ◆

5
Resent and Rebuff

Fort Worth, Texas

Desegregation policies in the 1940s were very quiet and not really advertised to the public, according to Shirley Apley, Senior Librarian, Fort Worth Public Library. "Usually someone from the City of Fort Worth told the black ministers, who would then tell their congregations."

The city owned and operated four golf courses—Meadowbrook, Rockwood, Worth Hills, and Z. Boaz; all were segregated "whites only" facilities. During the 1940s black golfers set up their golf course at Greenway Park, a city park for blacks. "There were no greens, no fairways, no fancy stuff, just a couple of coffee cups and a stick with a rag on it for a flag. The makeshift course at Greenway was the hand-me-down of hand-me-downs," members of the Fort Worth Negro Golf Association and the Golden Tee Golf Club recalled. *(Angel Beck, Fort Worth Star-Telegram)*

On November 16, 1950, the City Manager received a letter from the Fort Worth Negro Golf Association:

> We the members of the Fort Worth Negro Golf Association, in view of the dissension in the Tyler case of

Park v. People, do not plan any court action because of the promises of the Park Department and Recreation Department to give our association the honor of defending the parks of Fort Worth by providing adequate golf facilities for the year of 1951. However, we are, by no means, using this federal ruling as a "big stick" in contending for what we have asked for, for 13 or more years.

Consequently, we are withholding any action until such time as we may hear from the facilities named herein. —Lawrence B. Sanders, Secretary (Courtesy Fort Worth Public Library Archives)

The City Council held a special closed session and later announced that Negroes were granted access to play one city golf course—one day a year. That designated day was June 19th, known as Juneteenth, Black Liberation Day in Texas.

In 1954, the City of Fort Worth opened Harmon Field Golf Course, a segregated golf course for blacks only. The course was opened for about four years—June 13, 1954 to April 1, 1958. Compared to Fort Worth's whites only courses, Harmon Field Golf Course was underserved.

In June 1955, eight members of the Fort Worth Negro Golf Association attempted to pay green fees at Z. Boaz Golf Course. "They refused to take it. We threatened to bring grass-eating mules and goats to the course if we couldn't play," James Clemons, a member of Fort Worth Negro Golf Association, reported.

Subsequently on August 1, 1955, *Henry Fleming, et al. v. Honorable F. E. Garrison, Mayor City of Fort Worth, Tarrant County, Texas, et al.* lawsuit was filed—*seeking the use and enjoyment of certain designated City-owned and operated recreation facilities.* This class action suit was *for the benefit of the plaintiffs and all other Negro persons situated within the City of Fort Worth, Tarrant County, Texas.*

Plaintiffs were Henry Fleming, M. Whitaker, James Clemons, Henry Martin, Willie Thompson, J. W. Parker,

Thomas Russell, and Eldon Harris. On August 11, the defendants filed a motion to dismiss the suit; motion was denied.

On November 9, 1955, U.S. District Court Judge Estes ruled that all Fort Worth city golf courses desegregate. The next day, Jesse Mitchell became the first African American to officially tee off at a Fort Worth integrated city golf course. Mitchell, along with James Clemons, Vernon Jenkins, and J. Parker, played Rockwood Golf Course.

Federal law granted blacks unrestricted access to all Fort Worth city-owned golf courses; however, what was law was not always enforced. Access sometimes depended on who was behind the counter collecting green fees.

The course is full today. There are no tee times available. False excuses were often used to deny blacks access to city courses.

Orville Person often played Worth Hills Golf Course during its closing hours:

> Sometimes it was so dark I had to use a flashlight. Back then in 1959, I did not know of any courses that we (blacks) had playing privileges on a regular basis.
>
> One evening at Worth Hills Golf Course, I was chipping and putting with Willie Earl Griggs and Thomas Williams. Son Taylor, then head pro, drove up. He didn't say anything and neither did we. He just got out of his golf cart and went into the pro shop. We just kept on chipping and putting.
>
> A few minutes later Son came out and walked over to us.
>
> "You want to play out here?" Son asked.
>
> "I didn't know if we could," I responded.
>
> "You fellows can play out here anytime you want to," Son said.
>
> The next day I paid my green fees and played Worth Hills Golf Course; and from then on, I played there on a regular basis. There were no questions about playing there or getting tee times. I felt welcomed.

Central Valley Golf Club, Orange County, New York
(*Delaney et al. v. Central Valley Golf Club Inc.*)
On October 5, 1940, Hubert Delaney (then New York City Tax Commissioner), Roy Wilkins (then editor of *Crisis Magazine,* official publication of the NAACP), and Edward Morrow attempted to pay green fees at Central Valley Golf Club. Their money was not accepted.

Delaney, Wilkins, and Morrow filed a lawsuit alleging that they were denied the privilege of using the golf course, *...a place of public accommodations...that had...two signs on the highways leading to the golf course, and two on the grounds of the defendant, purporting to indicate that the course was open to the public.*

On May 27, 1941 action on this issue went to trial without a jury in the Supreme Court, New York County. The following is an excerpt from—*Delaney et al. v. Central Valley Golf Club Inc.* court report records:

Delaney testified "though not a member of the club or the guest of any member, he had on a number of occasions prior to October 1940 been permitted to play on the course in question on payment of a fee...." The defendant responded, "Those previous visits there was, whether designedly or inadvertently, a relaxation of the enforcement of the rules. Such relaxation...would not, in and of itself, be sufficient to give to this golf course the character of a place "of public accommodations...."

As to the highway signs, no evidence was introduced showing they had been erected by the defendant; and the evidence seemed to indicate that they had been erected by a group of businessmen in the neighboring town...the fact that the signs on the defendant's grounds near the entrances, qualified the word "public" with the words "under club rules" seems to deprive these signs of whatever probative force as to the "public" character of the course they might otherwise have.

Action by Hubert T. Delaney, and others against the Central Valley Golf Club Inc., involving the alleged denial to the plaintiffs, on the ground of their color, of the privilege of suing the golf course maintained by the defendant. Judgment for the defendant.

The plaintiffs appealed the decision. The appeal was argued in Appellate Court on June 15, 1942. Again, the State Supreme Court decision stood; the Appellate Court ruled in favor of Central Valley Golf Club Inc. Judge Desmond and Judge Finch dissented the decision. The judgment was affirmed for the defendants on July 29, 1942.

Richmond Open – 1948

Ted Rhodes placed 21st and Bill Spiller placed 34th at the 1948 Los Angeles Open. During that same week Madison Gunter placed in the top 60 at another PGA event. According to the PGA's *top 60 Rule*, any player who finished in the top 60 of a PGA event automatically qualified to play in the next scheduled PGA event; therefore Rhodes's, Spiller's, and Gunter's placements qualified them to enter the next scheduled PGA event, the Richmond Open.

Gunter, Rhodes, and Spiller paid their entry fees for the 1948 Richmond Open. However, after they had completed a practice round, an event official informed them that they would not be allowed to play in the event because—they were not members of The PGA of America. The PGA *members' rule* took precedence over the *top 60 Rule;* and the PGA's Caucasian-only clause restricted PGA membership to Caucasians only. Their entry fees were refunded.

As a result of being "denied to compete" at the 1948 Richmond Open Gunter, Rhodes, and Spiller filed a lawsuit against The PGA of America and Richmond Open tournament committee; however, the case was never heard in court. The lawsuit was dropped after the PGA pledged to cease discrimination against black golfers competing at PGA events.

Unfortunately, this verbal agreement was not made in earnest. The PGA's pledge to end discrimination against blacks was not made a part of the PGA tournament entry guidelines, and the Caucasian-only clause was not removed from the PGA Bylaws; hence, discrimination continued.

Subsequent to the 1948 Richmond Open incident with Gunter, Rhodes, and Spiller, the PGA enacted an *Invitation-Only* policy—only professional golfers who received invitations were allowed to play in PGA events. Under the PGA *Invitation-Only* policy, blacks rarely competed in PGA events because—blacks rarely received PGA invitations.

San Diego Open – 1952
Eural Clark, Bill Spiller, and Joe Louis (world heavyweight boxing champion) received sponsor invitations to the 1952 San Diego Open—a PGA sponsored event.

Louis entered the event as an amateur golfer (amateurs did not play the qualifying rounds). Professional golfers Clark and Spiller played the qualifying rounds. The cut was 154. Clark missed the cut by two strokes; Spiller shot a 152 and made the cut. But even after qualifying, Spiller was not allowed to continue to compete in the event. Louis's entry was also denied. Louis and Spiller were not allowed to compete because they were African American.

The PGA's rejection to Spiller and Louis drew media attention. The PGA partially reversed its decision—a sponsor's exemption was granted to Louis but not to Spiller. Louis played in the event and shot a 158.

Tee Box
During a qualifying round at the 1952 Phoenix Open, Eural Clark, Joe Louis, Ted Rhodes, and Charlie Sifford found human feces in the cup on the first green. They waited more than 30 minutes for the cup to be replaced.

Greater Greensboro Open 1961 – Charlie Sifford

The day before the opening round of the 1961 Greater Greensboro Open, Charlie Sifford received telephone calls—warning him that his life would be in danger if he played in the event; Sifford did not withdraw from the event. During play, Sifford was taunted with abusive and verbal threats. In one instance, he found his golf ball covered with beer cans. Event officials and security sometimes walked with Sifford; however, their presence did not stop the racial harassment. On the final leaderboad, Sifford tied for fourth.

Augusta National Golf Club, Augusta, Georgia – 1976
(Avery et. al v. Augusta National Golf Club et. al)

In October 1976 three black males were shot while fishing at Rae's Creek, a popular fishing spot that flows in front of the number 12 green at Augusta National Golf Club. Justin Jackson, age 19, was shot in the right leg; Charles Avery, age 19, was shot in the chest; and Robert Avery, age 12, was shot in the upper right arm and right thigh. Charlie Young, a white male who worked as a guard for Augusta National Golf Club, shot the three young men.

Young never denied that he shot Justin, Charles, and Robert; however, there were conflicting reports on how it happened. One report stated that Young loaded magnum buckshots with the intention to fire warning shots over the boys' heads; but the gun accidentally discharged and the three boys were shot. Another report cited that Young fired at the young men before he ordered them off the course.

The Avery family filed a lawsuit—*denying any malicious and mischievous intent*; and claiming that *the attack made upon the plaintiff and his young black companions was based primarily, or at least part in, upon their race.* The case never went to trial; there was a small out-of-court settlement and Young was not terminated from his job at Augusta National Golf Club. Justin's brother Carl Jackson and the Avery boys' uncle Nathaniel Avery were Augusta National Golf Club caddies at that time.

Separate And Not Equal

St. Louis, Missouri 1923: Public golf courses opened for the "exclusive use and enjoyment of colored persons" on Mondays only, 6:00 AM to 12:00 noon.

Douglass Golf Course (Indianapolis, Indiana) **1928**: Six-hole municipal golf course opened to serve the African American community. Tomato cans were used for flagstick holes. Douglass Golf Course was named in honor of black abolitionist Frederick Douglass.

Norfolk, Virginia 1949: Negroes granted exclusive use of Memorial Park Golf Course on the second weekend (Friday, Saturday, and Sunday) of each month, and Wednesdays and Fridays of the other weeks.

Rogers Park Golf Course (Tampa, Florida) **1952**: Nine-hole golf course built at Rogers Park, then a city-owned segregated park for "blacks only". Volunteers, including local caddies and Willie Black (the club's first head golf professional), were credited for building the course. Most of the work, including tree removal, was done by hand.

Huntsville, Alabama 1956: City Council resolution: Unlawful for blacks and whites to play basketball, baseball, pool, billiards, cards, checkers, dice, dominoes, football, softball, track, or golf together. Blacks permitted—one day a week—to use municipal golf course.

Birmingham, Alabama 1914: Races must be distinctly separated and must be 25 feet apart from one another in any room, hall, theatre, picture house, auditorium, yard, crowd, ballpark, or any other outdoor place.
Birmingham, Alabama 1962: To avoid complying with a federal court order to desegregate all public golf courses, parks, swimming pools, and playgrounds, the city government closed those facilities.

Lincoln Memorial Golf Course (Washington, D.C.) opened in 1924 as a "colored only" golf course. Prior to the opening of this public golf course, blacks were only allowed to play East Potomac Park Golf Course after 3:00 PM on Tuesdays, and West Potomac Golf Course after 12:00 noon on Wednesdays.

An article in The *Washington Post* (December 14, 1938) announced the upcoming construction of a golf course in the Anacostia neighborhood. That site, the present day Langston Golf Course, replaced Lincoln Memorial Golf Course.

Langston Golf Course, built by the United States federal government, opened on June 11, 1939 as a racially segregated, for blacks only, nine-hole golf course. Clyde Martin was the first head golf professional. Inadequate course conditions included poor greens and open sewage flowing close to some of the fairways. Langston Golf Course expanded to 18 holes in 1955. In that same year, Washington, D.C. golf courses were desegregated.

John Mercer Langston
Credit: *From the Virginia Plantation to the National Capitol.* 1894.
John Mercer Langston

Langston Golf Course was named in honor of John Mercer Langston—who was the first African American lawyer in the state of Ohio; served as dean, vice president, and acting president of Howard University Law School; and was the first president of Virginia Normal and Collegiate Institute (now Virginia State University). John Mercer Langston was the great-uncle of renowned poet James Mercer Langston Hughes, known as Langston Hughes.

In 1888, Langston became the first African American elected to the U.S. Congress from the Commonwealth of Virginia. However, election results were contested and it was 18 months after the election before Langston was declared winner; hence, Langston only served six months (September 23, 1890–March 3, 1891) of a 24-month congressional term. After Langston's term in office, it was more than 100 years before an African American represented Virginia in the U.S. Congress. Robert "Bobby" Scott was elected to the U.S. Congress House of Representatives in 1992.

7

Actions Against Injustice

Miami, Florida (*Rice v. H.H. Arnold*)

Miami Springs Golf Course, a municipal property, allowed blacks to play on Mondays only. That one day ruling was later revoked; thus, blacks had no access to Miami's municipal golf course.

Joseph Rice, an ex-caddie, wanted blacks to have access to play Miami's city golf course any day of the week. In the spring of 1949, Rice organized a committee of blacks who were interested in seeking unrestricted access to Miami's municipal course. On Monday, April 12, 1949 Joseph Rice, attorneys John Johnson and Grattan Graves, and four other men went to Miami Springs Golf Course. Their purpose was to challenge Miami Springs Golf Course "whites only" policy.

When Rice and his playing partners attempted to pay green fees, they were told that they could not play. Rice insisted on speaking to Arnold, the course superintendent. Rice informed Arnold that there were two lawyers among them, and if they were not allowed to play—*they just might have to sue.* Arnold told Rice that the law stated—no access to blacks. When the men refused to leave, Arnold telephoned the Miami City Attorney. After talking to the City Attorney, Arnold told the seven men that they could buy tickets and play. "What we was going to do was build a golf course for you guys."

Rice responded, "I don't want you to build a golf course for us; build a golf course for the city. Let everybody play."

After paying, the seven men—with one golf bag among them—proceeded to the starter shack. However, the starter did not allow them to play because of a rule violation—each player did not have a golf bag with clubs; therefore, they could not play. They left the course.

Rice and several friends returned to Miami Springs Golf Course the next day.

> "I don't want you to build a golf course for us; build a golf course for the city. Let everybody play."
> —Joseph Rice

Equipped with individual bags of golf clubs, Rice and his friends were allowed to play. Subsequently, blacks were allowed to play everyday that week at Miami Springs Golf Course. But at the end of that week, the Mondays-only policy was reinstated.

An April 20, 1949 story in the *Miami News* reported that Arnold was considering cutting the Negroes' one day to a half-day if they failed to turn out sufficiently to make up for the club's loss revenue. This too was not acceptable to Rice.

On April 27, 1949, attorneys Graves and Johnson filed *Rice v. Arnold*, petitioning the Dade County Circuit Court to *allow Joseph Rice to play during all hours in which the said course is open to the public*. With Judge Charles Carroll presiding, the city argued that integration of the golf course would stop many whites from playing the course, which would cause a drop in revenue. A few weeks later, Judge Carroll ruled in favor of the City of Miami.

Joseph Rice and his lawyers filed their case to the Florida State Supreme Court. The higher court ruled—there were not enough blacks playing golf at Miami Springs Golf Course to give blacks more time than the one day a week; and, the one-day was equal because there were more than six times as many whites playing than blacks. The Florida State Supreme Court ruling affirmed the previous court's ruling.

On March 24, 1950, Florida Supreme Court Justice Roy Chapman's ruling decision included the following:

> It appears that if the Negroes are permitted the use of the course with the white golfers, then the white golfers will not patronize the course. The green fees paid by the Negro golfers are insufficient to support and maintain the course.... It does not appear by the record that one-day allotment of the facilities of the course to the Negroes discriminated against the Negro race—If an increased demand on the part of the Negro golfers is made to appear, then more than one day each week will be allotted.

On October 16, 1950, U.S. Supreme Court Justices remanded the case to the Florida Supreme Court. Ordering the court to reconsider its ruling, the U.S. Supreme Court Justices referred to two educational U.S. Supreme Court decisions:

(1) a reversed Texas decision that justified barring a black man from the University of Texas Law School; and
(2) a reversed state court decision that allowed the University of Oklahoma to confine black students to designated areas in classroom, libraries, and cafeterias.

In August 1951, the Florida State Supreme Court upheld its decision. Referring to the Texas and Oklahoma cases, Associate Justice Hugh Taylor cited that *education differs fundamentally from golf*.

In March 1952, a final ruling by the U.S. Supreme Court upheld the Florida State Supreme Court's ruling on *Rice v. Arnold*.

In 1957, approximately eight years from the initial filing of *Rice v. Arnold*, Attorney Graves moved forward with another lawsuit to end the Mondays-only rule. This time Graves was successful, and the Mondays-only rule was removed from Miami's municipal golf course policy.

Joseph Rice was born in Milan, Georgia on April 26, 1921. He was seven years old when he started caddying. Rice wanted to learn how to play golf but he did not have money to buy golf clubs or golf balls. Determined to learn the game, Rice used a bent bicycle handlebar for a golf club and tin milk cans for golf balls.

About two years later the country club's resident pro, where Rice caddied, gave Rice one golf club and a few golf balls. Rice and his brothers were allowed to play on the golf course in the afternoons.

Joseph Rice was a United States Army veteran. After serving in the military he moved to Miami, Florida. He relocated to Stamford, Connecticut in 1957. Rice died in March 2010. *(Joseph Rice interviewed by the author in 2001.)*

The Greensboro Six (*Simkins et al. v. Greensboro***)**
In December 1955 Phillip Cooke, Elijah Herring, Samuel Murray, George Simkins Jr., Joseph Studivent, and Leon Wolfe (all later known as "The Greensboro Six") played a round of golf at Gillespie Park Golf Course in Greensboro, North Carolina. That evening at their homes, they were arrested for trespassing on Gillespie Park Golf Course.

Excerpts from George Simkins's personal papers that outline the actions taken from 1949 to 1954—before the arrest of "The Greensboro Six" in December 1955:

In 1949, Waldo Faulkner and a group from the Greensboro Men's Club went before the City Council to seek the rights of Negroes to play on Gillespie Park Golf Course or to get the council to build a golf course for Negroes. After several sessions, the council decided to build a nine-hole golf course for Negroes on city property next to a sewage disposal plant.

The city leased Gillespie Park Golf Course for one dollar to a newly formed white corporation; the city constructed and leased a Negro course to a Negro club.

On April 7, 1949, the city leased the facilities to the Gillespie Park Golf Corporation for $1000 for one year and later the Council requested the Greensboro School District to lease that portion owned by the district and upon execution of it, the city would grant its lease.

About one year later the city authorized a four year lease with the corporation at $1000 per year except that rental for the first year would be one dollar since nine additional holes had been made available and the operations would be very expensive for the first year. For the next two years the rent was waived.

Commencing with 1953, the lease was extended for five years at one dollar per year, with the provision that the group makes the necessary repairs.

In 1954, a committee from the Greensboro Men's Club investigated the Gillespie Park Golf Corporation. During talks, several City Councilmen agreed that Gillespie Park

Golf Course and Nocho Park Golf Course should be opened to all golfers, however, those Council members refused to take any public action on the matter.

Excerpts from personal papers of George Simkins Jr. that describe the occurrences from their arrest to their reprieve:

On December 7, 1955 six Negroes, later to be known as "The Greensboro Six", went to Gillespie Park Golf Course in Greensboro, North Carolina. They went into the clubhouse and began to sign the book for play. The golf course pro informed the six men that the course was private property and they had to belong to the club to play. The men placed seventy-five cents each on the table for green fees, and proceeded to the first tee box to play.

The golf pro followed them around the course cursing and telling them to get off the property. While playing the fourth or fifth hole, two deputy sheriffs arrived. They refused to arrest the group because as far as they were concerned the men were not breaking a law. The group could only be arrested upon procurement of a warrant. They finished playing nine holes and left the property.

That same night they were all arrested at their individual homes. George Simkins's father paid bail. The six Negroes were tried in Municipal Court in early January. They were found guilty of "simple trespass". The North Carolina law on *"simple trespass"* stated: "Whenever a person has any reason to believe that he has a right to be there, he cannot be found guilty of trespassing."

The six men were fined fifteen dollars each—plus court costs. The entire group appealed to the Superior Court and the case came to trial on December 5, 1956.

At jury trial, the men were convicted and sentenced to 30 days in jail. An appeal was noted to the North Carolina State Supreme Court. Their 30-day sentence was acted upon with a reprieve from (then) Governor Luther Hodges.

The six defendants plus four other Negroes, L.E. Reynolds Sr., William Holmes, James Hagins, and Arthur Lee Jr. took out an injunction in Federal District Court—preventing the city from segregating any Negro on any public property in the City of Greensboro (October 1956, *Simkins et al.v. Greensboro*). In March 1957, the court ruled in favor of Simkins; an appeal was filed to the Circuit Court of Appeals.

In June 1957, the North Carolina State Supreme Court threw out the convictions on the trespassing charges. Circuit Court of Appeals ordered the city to cease operating a segregated facility. Within weeks after the Circuit Court of Appeals ruling, Gillespie Park Golf Course clubhouse was severely damaged by fire.

In December 1957, The Greensboro Six was indicted on the initial trespassing charges; they received a guilty verdict from the Municipal Court. They appealed to the county's Superior Court; again they were found guilty. They then appealed to the State Supreme Court; their prior convictions were not overturned. In June 1960, the United States Supreme Court dismissed The Greensboro Six's conviction appeal. In December 1962, Gillespie Park Golf Course desegregated. George Simkins was the first African American to officially tee off.

Tee Box

Credited for spearheading lawsuits to integrate golf courses in the Piedmont Triad of North Carolina, Dr. George Simkins also led lawsuits for the desegregation of public schools and health care. In 1970, Dr. Simkins led a lawsuit to desegregate Greensboro City schools; and in 1963, the landmark U.S. Supreme Court ruling on *Simkins v. Moses H. Cone Memorial Hospital* led to the desegregation of health care. Dr. Simkins was a 1948 graduate of Meharry Dental College. In 2001, Dr. Simkins was inducted into the *Epochs of Courage: African Americans in Golf Wall of Fame*.

(Leeper et al. v. Charlotte Park and Recreation Commission et. al.)

On August 31, 1927 Osmond Barringer offered his land, the Bonnie Brae property, to the City of Charlotte, North Carolina. On February 21, 1929, the City of Charlotte accepted Barringer's offer. Three months later (May 22, 1929), Barringer and his wife deeded and conveyed the designated land as a gift to the City of Charlotte.

Barringer's offer came with specific usage guidelines: *Said lands are to be used by the City of Charlotte through its Park and Recreation Commission for white people's parks and playgrounds, parkways and municipal golf courses only...and requiring that the lands revert to the grantors if such restrictions are not carried out.*

In December 1951, a group of black men attempted to play Bonnie Brae Golf Course. They were not allowed to play the course; hence, they presented to the Parks and Recreation Commission a petition—alleging that their civil rights were violated, and requesting that *"such discrimination cease"*.

The Commission made no policy changes. Subsequently, the petitioners filed, in the Superior Court of Mecklenburg County, a lawsuit seeking access to Bonnie Brae Golf Course.

The petitioners were Charles W. Leeper, I. P. Farrar, Sadler S. Gladden, Robert H. Greene, James Heath, Henry M. Isley, Russell McLaughlin, Anthony M. Walker, Harold Walker, L. A. Warner, Edward J. Weddington, James J. Weddington, Willie Lee Weddington, G. M. Wilkins, Roy S. Wynn, and Rudolph M. Wyche. The attorneys for the petitioners were Robert Carter, Thurgood Marshall, Spottswood W. Robinson III, and T. H. Wyche.

The original plaintiff was the Charlotte Park and Recreation Commission, a Municipal Corporation. The original defendants were listed as Osmond L. Barringer, Abbott Realty Company, a Corporation, and the City of Charlotte.

Upon an appeal, the case went before the Supreme Court of North Carolina—that ruling ordered the City of Charlotte to *either close the park or purchase the land from Barringer.*

In 1957, more than 30 years after the City of Charlotte first accepted the donated land from Barringer, the City of Charlotte returned ownership of the land to Barringer, which now allowed the City of Charlotte to obtain ownership of the Bonnie Brae property.

The City of Charlotte purchased the land from Barringer; thereby, owning the land with no restrictions. In January 1957, African Americans were granted unrestricted access to play Bonnie Brae Golf Course. James Otis Williams was the first African American to officially tee off at the course. A sign on the first tee honors Williams.

In later years, Bonnie Brae Golf Course was renamed Revolution Park Golf Course. In 2011, Revolution Park Golf Course was renamed Dr. Charles L. Sifford Golf Course at Revolution Park, in honor of the first African American PGA golfer Dr. Charles L. Sifford.

(Source: Special Collections, Atkins Library, University of North Carolina, Grier, Joseph Papers. Chapel Hill, North Carolina)

Tee Box

Property...opened to anyone of any race... a stipulation of deeded property gifted on November 7, 1924 by philanthropists Horace and Mary Rackham to the City of Detroit, Michigan. The property included an 18-hole golf course and a clubhouse. In 1925, Rackham Golf Course opened to the public.

Houston, Texas (*Beal et al. v. Holcombe*)
In 1950 Dr. A. W. Beal, Dr. H. Lyman, Dr. W. Minor, J.H. Jamison, and Milton Pruitt (plaintiffs) filed a federal lawsuit seeking access to municipal golf courses in Houston, Texas. Filed against Mayor Oscar Holcombe and the City Council of Houston, the court ruled in favor of the defendants. The plaintiffs filed an appeal; in 1952, the appellate judge ruled in favor of the plaintiffs.

The city appealed the decision to the United States Supreme Court; however, the United States Supreme Court refused to bring the case of *Beal v. Holcombe* up for consideration, and ordered the lower courts to rule on the case. Houston's city officials dropped the appeal and granted African Americans unrestricted access to Houston's municipal golf courses.

Tyrrell Park Municipal Golf Course, Beaumont, Texas (*Fayson, et al. v. Beard, Mayor of Beaumont, et al.*)
In June 1955 *Fayson, et al. v. Beard, Mayor of Beaumont, et al.* was filed in District Court. Plaintiffs Booker T. Fayson, Joseph P. Griffin, William Narcisse, Thomas Parker, Johnnie Ware, and Earl White sought access to play Tyrrell Park Municipal Golf Course. In September 1955, a decision by federal Judge Lamar Cecil granted blacks unrestricted use of Tyrell Park Municipal Golf Course.

Tee Box

In 1947, Hermann Park Golf Course (Houston, Texas) desegregated.

In 1951, Lions Municipal Golf Course (Austin, Texas) desegregated. Lions Municipal Golf Course is also known as "Old Muni".

Louisville, Kentucky

Dr. Pruitt Sweeney Sr. filed a lawsuit in 1947 against the City of Louisville, Kentucky for the desegregation of city golf courses. In 1951, a federal judge ruled that the City of Louisville must allow African Americans to play on all city golf courses or provide separate city golf courses for African Americans. In January 1952, Louisville city golf courses opened all services to African Americans.

Atlanta, Georgia (*Holmes et al. v. Atlanta*)

In 1951 *Holmes et al. v. Atlanta* lawsuit, seeking desegregation of public golf courses and parks in Atlanta, Georgia, was originally filed in United States District Court. The plaintiffs Charles Bell, Alfred Holmes, Hamilton M. Holmes Sr., and Oliver Wendell Holmes filed the lawsuit after they were denied access to play Bobby Jones Golf Course, one of Atlanta, Georgia's public golf courses. Charles Bell, Alfred Holmes, Hamilton M. Holmes Sr., and Oliver Wendell Holmes were denied access to play golf because of their race.

Three years later, a 1954 ruling against the plaintiffs cited that the 1954 *Brown v. Board of Education of Topeka, Kansas* decision applied only to schools; therefore, "separate but equal" golf courses were legal. Hence, segregation was maintained on Atlanta's public golf courses. The Georgia Court of Appeals allowed the City of Atlanta to apply a "different races on different days" policy to one municipal golf course. A district court ruling by Judge Boyd Sloan cited that blacks could play a designated course every Monday and Tuesday. This 1954 ruling was referred to as the first court-ordered desegregation ruling in Atlanta, Georgia.

The plaintiffs continued their fight and the case went before the Court of Appeals; the United States District Court ruling was upheld. With the assistance of then Attorney Thurgood Marshall and the NAACP, the plaintiffs took their case to the United States Supreme Court. On November 7, 1955, the United States Supreme Court overruled the Court of Appeals ruling—the United States District Court was directed to reverse its decision and rule in favor of the plaintiffs. The following month on Christmas Eve, Alfred "Tup" Holmes, Oliver Holmes, and Charles Bell teed off at North Fulton Golf Course in Atlanta. In 1983, more than 25 years after the desegregation of Atlanta's public golf courses, Adams Park Golf Course was renamed Alfred (Tup) Holmes Memorial Golf Course.

Portsmouth, Virginia (*Green, Owens, Johnson, and Cooper v. The City of Portsmouth, Virginia*)
In 1951 James Green, Hugo Owens, Harvey Johnson Jr., and Floyd Cooper filed a lawsuit in Federal District Court seeking access for Negroes to play City Park Golf Course and Glensheallah Golf Course. Upon a court ruling—*the city must provide golfing facilities for Negroes.* The city allowed Negroes to use City Park Golf Course on Fridays only; whites were excluded from the facility on Fridays.

Portsmouth, Virginia (*Holley, Bailey and Gray v. The City of Portsmouth*)
In August 1956 plaintiffs James Holley III, Linwood Bailey, and James Gray filed a lawsuit in Federal District Court seeking unrestricted access for Negroes to play City Park Golf Course. Negroes were only allowed to use the facility on Fridays. The suit was filed under the equal protection clause of the 14th Amendment to the United States Constitution.

According to an August 3, 1956 article in *The Portsmouth Star*, the plaintiffs sought admission to City Park Golf Course on Sunday, July 15 and Tuesday, July 24. Each time, they were *denied the use of these facilities solely because of their race and color....*

On August 29, 1956, Judge Walter Hoffman of the Federal District Court granted a temporary injunction that gave Negroes unrestricted access to City Park Golf Course. A permanent injunction was granted in 1958.

Gleason Park Golf Course (Gary, Indiana)
In 1932, the City of Gary, Indiana built two segregated parks. South Gleason Park, for "whites-only", was about 310-acres with an 18-hole golf course, swimming pool, and recreation areas. North Gleason Park, for "blacks-only", was about 47 acres with a nine-hole golf course, swimming pool, and playground. North Gleason Park Golf Course was recognized as one of the first "black-only" golf courses built by a municipality in the United States.

The two parks, as well as the black and white communities, were separate but not equal. Harsh segregation rules imposed strict restrictions on blacks. A line of separation, known as Little Calumet Bridge, was a passageway with limited access for blacks. Going to and from work—was the only known reason blacks were allowed to cross Little Calumet Bridge.

Legendary golfer Ann Gregory is credited for spearheading the desegregation of the golf course at South Gleason Park:

> Reports indicate that one day in the early 1960s, Gregory went to the segregated "whites-only" South Gleason Park clubhouse and presented money to pay her green fee. A course employee informed Gregory that she could not play. Gregory's response was, "My tax dollars are taking care of the big course, and there's no way you can bar me from it. Just send the police out to get me."

> Police were not called and Gregory was allowed to play.

> "My tax dollars are taking care of the big course, and there's no way you can bar me from it. Just send the police out to get me."
> —Ann Gregory

News about Gregory's experience spread throughout the black community, and blacks began playing the golf course at South Gleason Park; that was the beginning of golf course desegregation at South Gleason Park.

The PGA of America Caucasian-only Clause

In 1934, a Caucasian-only clause—limiting membership to professional golfers of the Caucasian race—was added to The PGA of America Bylaws.

1934 Caucasian-only Clause: The PGA of America
Section 1 of Article III—Members..."Male professional golfers of the Caucasian race, over the age of eighteen years (18), residing in North or South America, who can qualify under the terms and conditions hereinafter specified, shall be eligible for membership or "H" Apprentice status."

The NAACP and other civil rights organizations protested against the Caucasian-only clause. California Attorney General Stanley Mosk also spoke out against the Caucasian-only clause, and was credited for initiating a fight that forced The PGA of America to abolish its racist amendment.

From 1959 to 1964, Stanley Mosk served as Attorney General of the State of California. During his first year in office as California State Attorney General, he received a letter from professional golfer Charlie Sifford. In the handwritten letter dated 1959, Sifford described how he was banned from joining the PGA Tour or entering regularly in PGA events—because he was African American.

Mosk confronted the PGA about what he considered "illegal to bar a competitor because of his race", and Mosk informed the PGA that he would file a lawsuit if Sifford was not allowed to play at the 1962 PGA Championship hosted by Wilshire Country Club in Los Angeles, California. Mosk informed other state attorney generals about his decision and actions taken regarding the PGA's Caucasian-only clause, and asked for their

> Mosk confronted the PGA about what he considered "illegal to bar a competitor because of his race"....

support. The PGA of America moved the 1962 PGA

Championship out of the state of California to Aronimink
Golf Course in the state of Pennsylvania.

In November 1961, The PGA of America passed a
resolution to remove the Caucasian-only clause. In 1962, the
bylaws were amended to reflect that resolution. *(The PGA of
America was founded in 1916. The PGA Tour operated under
The PGA of America until 1968.)*

The PGA of America (Dewey Brown Sr.)

In 1928, Dewey Brown Sr. became the first African
American member of The PGA of America. However, in 1934
Brown's member status was withdrawn. Reports surfaced
that The PGA of America was unable to discern Brown's
ethnicity because of his fair-skinned complexion. The
uncertainty of Brown being Caucasian led The PGA of
America to withdraw Brown's PGA Member status.

In 1965, three years after The PGA of America enforced
the deletion of the Caucasian-only clause and more than 25
years after Brown's PGA status was revoked, Dewey Brown
Sr. was reinstated as a PGA Member. *(More about Dewey
Brown Sr., page 160)*

Masters Tournament (Invitation-Only Policy)

Prior to 1972, the Masters Tournament *invitation-only*
policy included but was not limited to: the PGA Tour money
list top 25 players, two players invited by a majority vote of
the past champions, foreign players who received automatic
exemptions, and winners of major foreign tournaments that
were held the previous year. This strict policy relied on the
discretion of Augusta National Golf Club Masters
Tournament Committee.

In 1972, the Masters *invitation-only* policy was
amended—*any player who won a PGA Tour event within a
calendar year received an invitation to play in the following
year's Masters.* That amendment was *ex post facto* (the Latin
for "from something done afterward") and not *retroactive*

(related things done before the change); hence, the PGA Tour wins in 1964 and 1970 by Pete Brown, and Charlie Sifford in 1967 and 1969 did not earn Brown or Sifford an invitation to play in a Masters Tournament.

Two years after the Masters *invitation-only* policy was amended, Lee Elder won the 1974 Monsanto Open, which qualified Elder to receive an invitation to play in the 1975 Masters Tournament. Hence, Elder became the first African American to be invited to play in the Masters Tournament.

> PGA Tour wins in 1964 and 1970 by Pete Brown, and Charlie Sifford in 1967 and 1969 did not earn Brown or Sifford an invitation to play in a Masters Tournament.

Shoal Creek Golf and Country Club

Established in 1977 as a segregated private club, Shoal Creek Golf and Country Club (Birmingham, Alabama) accepted its first African American member less than two weeks prior to hosting the 1990 PGA Championship.

According to a June 1990 *Birmingham Post-Herald* article, Hal Thompson, founder of Shoal Creek Golf and Country Club, was quoted as saying, "This is our home, and we pick and choose who we want.... We have the right to associate or not associate with whomever we choose."

Thompson's comments drew controversy to the PGA Championship scheduled for August 9–12, 1990. Several event sponsors cancelled, and civil rights organizations threatened to protest the event.

About nine days before the event, Shoal Creek Golf and Country Club accepted its first African American member, Louis J. Willie Jr. who joined as an honorary member. Subsequently, there were no protests.

Following this controversy, The PGA of America, USGA, and PGA Tour announced that tournaments would not be held at segregated facilities.

Bide-A-Wee Golf Club, Portsmouth, Virginia

The site of Bide-A-Wee Golf Club was on city property that was leased to J. Chandler Harper. A former PGA Tour Member, Harper retired from competitive golf in 1955 and in that same year, Harper opened Bide-A-Wee Golf Club and operated the club as a "for whites only" segregated facility.

In July 1976, the Justice Department filed a lawsuit against Bide-A-Wee Golf Club, Chandler Harper, City Council members, and the City of Portsmouth, Virginia. The lawsuit sought the integration of Bide-A-Wee Golf Club.

In that same year (1976), then City Councilman Archie Elliot Jr. attempted to become a member of Bide-A-Wee Golf Club. Board members informed Elliot that all club applicants must be sponsored by two Bide-A-Wee Class A club members. Elliot's request for a list of the club's Class A membership roster was denied. (The Honorable Archie Elliot Jr. is a Portsmouth, Virginia General District Court retired judge).

In December 1977, a U.S. District Court judge ruled that the operation of Bide-A-Wee Golf Club as a private club was not in violation of the 1964 Civil Rights Act. More than ten years after that U.S. District Court ruling, the Portsmouth, Virginia City Council passed an ordinance *prohibiting the lease or use of city property by anyone that discriminates*.

The Honorable James Holley, first African American mayor of Portsmouth, Virginia, was an outspoken protestor against Chandler Harper's segregated policy at Bide-A-Wee Golf Club. Holley served as mayor from 1984 to 1987 and 1996 to 2010.

On April 8, 1988, Bide-A-Wee Golf Club opened to the public. In July 1992, Harper attempted to renew his lease. The City of Portsmouth denied his offer and Harper's lease expired on September 30, 1992. The City of Portsmouth took over operation and management of Bide-A-Wee Golf Club on October 1, 1992.

More Actions Against Injustice

Little Rock, Arkansas 1955: United States Supreme Court banned segregation on public golf courses.

Wichita, Kansas 1958: City Park Board ruled—any golf tournament that excluded blacks would not be held at municipal golf courses; action spearheaded by Chester Lewis, then Wichita Branch NAACP president.

Charleston, South Carolina 1960: Federal District Court ruling ordered Charleston, South Carolina municipal golf course to desegregate. **1961**–Charleston, South Carolina municipal golf course desegregated.

Macon, Georgia 1961: City Council authorized the integration of Charles L. Bowden Golf Course; thus, Charles L. Bowden Golf Course became the first integrated public facility in the City of Macon, Georgia.

Augusta, Georgia, 1964: Federal lawsuit filed by Attorney John Ruffin Jr. led to the desegregation of Augusta Municipal Golf Course, also known as "The Patch". In May 1964, African Americans were granted access; John Elam, Clois Herndon, Dr. Maurice Thompson, and Raymond Jenkins were the first African Americans to officially tee off at Augusta Municipal Golf Course.

Jackson, Mississippi, 1962: Action before the United States District Court requested an injunction to forbid "state enforced segregation of the races" at public facilities. **1971**–City Council ruled to desegregate public golf courses, parks, auditoriums, and the city zoo; however, the five city swimming pools—four swimming pools for whites and one swimming pool for Negroes—were not ordered to desegregate.

Tee Box

In February 2000 at Dunes Golf Club at Seville (Brooksville, Florida), Gordon Fleming and three other men were playing a practice round for a tournament hosted by the African American Golf Club of Hernando County. While playing, they were verbally and physically attacked by Huston Hill, a white male. Gordon Fleming, founder of the African American Golf Club of Hernando County recalled the incident:

Two white guys on the golf course were saying some really nasty things to us. We told the ranger, but he said there was nothing that he could do.

At the 17th hole, the white guys tried to run over us with their golf cart, but instead they ran over my uncle's foot. When they drove by again I hit one of them, Huston Hill, in the jaw. I hit Hill with my fist and I broke his jaw.

When we finished playing the 18th hole, we saw the parking lot full of police cars. Hill had called the police. But after the police investigated, they didn't arrest me—they arrested Hill. He got out on bond the same day.

The confrontation received a lot of attention. As a matter of fact, the trial was scheduled to be on *Court TV*.

Before the trial, I got a telephone call from the State's Attorney. He asked me if I would agree to a *first time offender intervention* for Hill. I told him that I had no problem agreeing to that, and that I carried no vengeance and no hate. My only stipulation—I wanted Hill to apologize to my friends, family, and Hernando County. Hill was not from Hernando County.

At the preliminary hearing, Hill initially refused to apologize. During the hearing, Hill and his attorney stepped outside the courtroom. When they returned, Hill apologized. The judge asked me if I accepted Hill's apology. I said yes—and, that was the end of it.
(Gordon Fleming interviewed by the author, August 2007.)

8

Pressing On

Joseph "Joe" Louis Barrow Sr.

Known as world heavyweight boxing champion Joe Louis, he became the first African American to play in a PGA sponsored tournament when he accepted a sponsor's exemption to play as an amateur in the 1952 San Diego Open. *(More about Joe Louis, page 101)*

Daryl Batey

In 2012, PGA Member Daryl Batey became the first African American Player Development Manager for The PGA of America. Batey was assigned the Atlanta, Georgia region.

Dewey Brown Sr.

In 1928, Dewey Brown Sr. became the first African American PGA Member. Brown was also the first African American member of Golf Course Superintendents Association of America; he became a GCSAA member in 1958. *(More about Dewey Brown Sr., pages 80, 160)*

E. Pete Brown

In 1964, Pete Brown became the first African American to win a PGA Tour sanctioned event when he won the 1964 Waco Turner Open. *(More about Pete Brown, page 123)*

Pearl Carey

In 2005, Pearl Carey became the first African American and first female to receive the Northern California Golf Association Grand Master Award. In 1977, she became the first female president of Western States Golf Association; she served from 1977 to 1981. Carey was also the second female and second African American to receive the USGA Joe Dey Award.

Darryl Crawford and Derrick Crawford
In the 1980s, Derrick became the first African American tour representative for PING; thus, Derrick was recognized as one of the first African American sales tour representatives for a major golf equipment company. In the 1990s, Derrick's twin brother Darryl became PING's second African American tour representative.

A.D.V. Crosby and R.G. Robinson
In 1930, Crosby and Robinson became the first African Americans to enter a University of Michigan All-Campus Golf Tournament. Crosby won the match; thus Crosby became the first African American to win a University of Michigan All-Campus Golf Tournament.

Ben Davis
In 1966, Ben Davis became the first African American PGA Member of the Michigan PGA Section. In 1968, Davis became head golf professional at Rackham Golf Course (Huntington Woods, Michigan). He is recognized as being the first African American golf professional hired at a public golf course in the state of Michigan. Ben Davis died in April 2013; he was 101 years old.

Jonathan DePina
In 2012 Jonathan DePina became president of The Country Club of New Bedford (Massachusetts); thus, DePina is one of the first African Americans to serve as president of a private desegregated golf facility.

William "Bill" Dickey
Bill Dickey was the first African American to receive the PGA Distinguished Service Award (1999) and USGA Joe Dey Award (2001). *(More about William Dickey, page 225)*

Barbara Douglas

In 1993, Barbara Douglas became the first African American and the first minority female to serve on the USGA Women's Committee. In 2009, Douglas became the first African American woman to chair a USGA committee. Barbara Douglas received the Ben Hogan Award in 2011.

Alton Duhon

In 1982, Alton Duhon became the first African American to win a USGA U.S. Amateur Senior Championship. *(More about Alton Duhon, page 99)*

Harold Dunovant

Recognized as the first African American to graduate from PGA Business School, Harold Dunovant graduated in 1960.

Ron Edwards

In 1996, Ron Edwards became Shoal Creek Golf and Country Club's second African American member.

Lee Elder

In 1975, Lee Elder became the first African American to play in a Masters Tournament. *(More about Elder, page 125)*

Earnie Ellison

In 1997, Earnie Ellison became the first African American hired in a senior management position at The PGA of America. *(More about Earnie Ellison, page 148)*

Althea Gibson

In 1963, Althea Gibson became the first African American to join the LPGA Tour. *(More about Althea Gibson, page 119)*

Ann Gregory
In 1956, Ann Gregory became the first African American to play in a USGA U.S. Women's Amateur Championship. *(More about Ann Gregory, page 100)*

Dedric Holmes
In 1995, Dedric Holmes became the first African American hired to an administrative position at the United States Golf Association. Holmes served as coordinator of junior golf and minority affairs.

Lewis C. Horne Jr.
In December 2006, Lewis Horne Jr. was first elected board chairman to The LPGA Foundation; Horne's second term began January 2011.

Ginger Howard
In 2010, Ginger Howard became the first African American female member of a United States Junior Ryder Cup team. *(More about Ginger Howard, page 117)*

Milton Irvin
In 2004, Milton Irvin became the first African American member of Baltusrol Golf Club (Springfield, New Jersey). Baltusrol Golf Club was established in 1895.

Sheila Johnson
In 2013, Sheila Johnson became the first African American female member of the USGA Executive Committee. In 2007, Johnson became the first African American owner of a golf resort (Innisbrook© Resort) and a PGA Tour championship course (Copperhead Golf Course). *(More about Innisbrook© Resort, page 185)*

George Lewis
The first African American board member of The PGA of America, George Lewis was elected in 1995 and served from 1996 to 1998.

Robert "Pete" McDaniel
In 1993, Pete McDaniel became the first African American hired at *Golf World* magazine. *(More about Pete McDaniel, page 206)*

John Merchant
In 1992, John Merchant became the first African American elected to the USGA Executive Committee; he served from 1992 to 1994. Merchant was also the first African American graduate of the University of Virginia School of Law (1958).

Nevin Phillips
First African American to receive PGA Merchandiser of the Year national honors, PGA Member Nevin Phillips was the 2009 PGA Merchandiser of the Year for Public Facilities.

Renee Powell
In 1967 Renee Powell became the second African American member of the LPGA Tour, and in 1996, she became the first African American female PGA Class A Member. In 2015, Renee Powell received honorary membership to The Royal and Ancient Golf Club of St. Andrews in the United Kingdom. *(More about Renee Powell, page 119)*

William Powell
William Powell is recognized as the first African American to design, build, own, and operate a golf course. *(More about William Powell, page 50)*

Condoleezza Rice
In August 2012, former United States Secretary of State Condoleezza Rice was one of two females to become the first female members of Augusta National Golf Club.

Leroy Richie
In 1995, Leroy Richie became the first African American to serve as general counsel of the USGA.

George Roddy Sr.
In 1926, George Roddy became the first African American member of the University of Iowa golf team. *(More about George Roddy, page 103)*

Carrie Russell
In 1974, Carrie Russell became the first African American LPGA Class A Member. *(More about Carrie Russell, page 158)*

John Shippen Jr.
John Shippen became the first African American to play in a U.S. Open Championship in 1896. *(More about John Shippen Jr., page 36)*

Charles "Charlie" Sifford
In 1964, Charlie Sifford became the first African American to receive a PGA Tour card *(More about Charlie Sifford, page 131)*

Kenneth Sims
First African American president of a PGA Chapter, Sims served the West Central Chapter of North Florida Section.

Mariah Stackhouse
She was the first African American woman selected to the USGA USA Curtis Cup team; Mariah Stackhouse was a member of the 2014 USA Curtis Cup team.

Catana Starks
In 1986 at Tennessee State University, Catana Starks became the first African American woman to coach a NCAA Division I men's golf team. A film titled *From the Rough*, based on the true story of Dr. Starks, was released in 2014.

LaRee Sugg
In 1995, LaRee Sugg became the third African American LPGA Tour member. In 2002, Sugg became the first African American female golf coach at a predominantly white university (University of Richmond). *(More about LaRee Sugg, page 120)*

Ron Townsend
In 1990, Ron Townsend became the first African American member of Augusta National Golf Club.

University of Maryland Eastern Shore
In 2008, the University of Maryland Eastern Shore became the first HBCU to receive accreditation to offer a PGA Professional Golf Management™ Program. The PGA PGM™ Program is an accredited program of The PGA of America.

Andrew Walker
In 2013 Andrew Walker, age 14, became the youngest African American to qualify for a USGA U.S. Junior Amateur. In 1991, Tiger Woods qualified for the USGA U.S. Junior Amateur at the age of 15.

Louis Willie Jr.

In July 1990, Louis Willie Jr. became the first African American member of Shoal Creek Golf and Country Club (Birmingham, Alabama). (*More about Louis Willie Jr. and Shoal Creek Golf and Country Club, page 81*)

Eldrick "Tiger" Woods

In 1997, Tiger Woods became the first person of African American ancestry to win a Masters Tournament. *(More about Tiger Woods, page 136)*

Eve Wright

In 2004, Eve Wright became the first African American Director of Legal Affairs for the LPGA. She later served as Senior Director of Legal Affairs and also Senior Director of Business Affairs.

William "Bill" Wright

The first African American to obtain a USGA handicap, William Wright is also the first to win a national golf title; Wright earned that honor when he won the 34th USGA U.S. Amateur Public Links Championship on July 18, 1959.

Tee Box

From his freshman to senior years (1956–1960), William Wright was a member of Western Washington State College men's golf team (now Western State University). During the first three years, Wright practiced at a public golf course without his teammates. Wright did not participate in team practice because the team practiced at a segregated "whites only" facility, Bellingham Country Club. In his senior year, Wright was allowed to practice with the golf team at Bellingham Country Club.

In a *Winnipeg Free Press* (Winnipeg, Manitoba, Canada) June 28, 1961 article on page 54 titled, *PGA Denies Charges of 'Discrimination': Takes Issue with NAACP*, Charlie Sifford and Richard I. Thomas were cited as Approved Tournament Players.

Included in that article was a June 1961 press release by The PGA of America, which included a response to NAACP charges that The PGA of America conducted what could be viewed as "un-American practices".

And also within that press release, The PGA of America recognized Charlie Sifford as the first Negro to be granted Approved Tournament Player status (March 28, 1960); and Richard I. Thomas, of Baltimore, Maryland, as the second Negro to be granted Approve Tournament Player status (June 19, 1961).

Life has two rules:
Rule number one – Never Quit!
Rule number two – Always
remember rule number one.

Duke Ellington

Chapter IV
Leaderboard

Preview

Mary Burton, known as Golfing Granny of the UGA *(center)*, with *(left)* E. Toler, and *(right)* E. Swanson at the 1955 Greater Cincinnati Open Golf Tournament

Leaderboard

*Never give up, for that is just the place
and time that the tide will turn.*
—Harriet Beecher Stowe

In the 1900s, golf continued to emerge as a game dominated by white Americans. However, African Americans began to nudge their way on the playing and business sides of the golf industry, and United States court rulings forced many golf facilities to change its segregated policies.

The beginning of a complex metamorphosis of African Americans in golf also emerged. From golf and industry professionals to amateur and professional players—African Americans became a driving force for change. These legends, men and women, have one thing in common—they all contributed to making a difference in the world of golf.

9

Amateur Golfers

Mary Burton

Known as the *Golfing Granny of the UGA*, Burton won tournaments competing against women who were half her age. She started playing golf at age 47.

Mary's husband Langston, a UGA amateur competitor, taught her how to play golf. Through all four seasons, the couple practiced and played together. Langston and Mary painted golf balls red, which they used to play golf in the snow during the winter months in Ohio.

In 1960, the UGA Mid-West District recognized Mary Burton as the "most honored golferette". An August 10, 1961 article in *The Ohio Sentinel* referred to Burton's trophies as "too many to count—it required an inventory".

During her 29-year golf career, Burton won more than 150 trophies. At age 76, she won her last trophy at a tournament in Columbus, Ohio.

Mary Burton was born in 1897; however, her tombstone at a cemetery in Youngstown, Ohio cannot prove her birth date. Burton gave strict instructions that her date of birth not be put on her tombstone.

Mary Burton died in 1982. Burton was posthumously inducted into the *Epochs of Courage: African Americans in Golf Wall of Fame* in 2001.

Joe "Roach" Delancey

Winner of the UGA Negro National Open Amateur Championship from 1953 to 1955, Delancey was also known for his caddying and coaching abilities. He caddied on the LPGA Tour, and he was a personal golf coach to boxing legend Sugar Ray Robinson.

Delancey also coached Yvette Hemphill, professional golfer and instructor. During a January 10, 2007 interview with the author, Hemphill recalled times spent with Delancey as her instructor and playing partner for ten years:

He was my mentor. When Joe Roach and I talked about racism and golf he would say, *"The only thing that they, white people, respect is the way you play. If you play well, they remember and respect you. If you play lousy, they forget you right then and there."*

Alton Duhon

In 1982 at age 57, Duhon won the USGA U.S. Senior Amateur Championship; thus, Duhon became the first African American to win a USGA Senior Championship and the second African American to win a USGA Championship. In that same year, Duhon also won the California State Senior Men's Amateur Championship. About six years after Duhon's historic USGA victory, he started playing professional golf.

Tee Box

In 1928, Ralph Dawkins Sr. won the first Florida State Junior Golf Tournament. From 1941 to 1949, Dawkins served as teaching professional at Lincoln Golf and Country Club (Jacksonville, Florida).

In the late 1950s, Edna Cohen became the first African American female to win a USGA U.S. Amateur Public Links City Championship.

Ethel Funches, notable amateur golfer for more than three decades, claimed her first of five UGA national victories in 1959.

Bill Fullard

In 2006, Fullard qualified to play in the ING (International Network of Golf) International Pairs World Final. At the final qualifier, Fullard was paired with Bob Dodds of the Professional Clubmakers' Society. Fullard and Dodds won and qualified to represent the United States at the 2006 ING International Pairs World Final competition at Celtic Manor (Wales, England); they placed fifth. Bill Fullard is President of BF Golf Tournament Services. *(More about BF Golf, page 187)*

Ann Gregory

Remembered as the *Queen of Negro Women Golf*, Ann Gregory was the first African American woman to enter a U.S. Amateur Championship—the USGA-sponsored 1956 U.S. Women's Amateur Open at Meridian Hills Country Club (Indianapolis, Indiana). Gregory's best finish in a USGA Amateur was at the 1971 USGA Senior Women's Amateur; she shot a 237, placed second, and lost by one stroke.

Born July 25, 1912 in Aberdeen, Mississippi, Ann's parents died when she was a teenager. After her parents' death, she lived with an older sister. Later she worked as a live-in maid for a Caucasian family (Mr. and Mrs. Sanders). While living with the Sanders, Ann graduated from high school.

In the 1930s, Ann moved to Gary, Indiana and began to play tennis. In 1937, she won the Gary City Tennis Championship.

In 1939, she married Leroy "Percy" Gregory. Percy was an avid golfer and introduced the game to Ann. The couple enjoyed playing golf together; however, their time on the links was interrupted when Percy was drafted into the United States Navy during World War II. Ann continued to play golf during Percy's absence. When Percy returned home at the end of the war in 1945, Ann had developed into a talented golfer.

According to Ann's daughter JoAnn Gregory-Overstreet, Ann Gregory's career lasted more than 40 years, and included more than 300 victories around the world. Included in those victories are the National UGA Women's Amateur Championship (1950, 1953, and 1957), and the Pepsi Cola International Golf Tournament Championship in Puerto Rico (1963, 1964), Madrid (1967), and Hawaii (1968).

In 1989—the same year that her husband died—Ann Gregory, at age 76, won gold medal at the National Senior Olympics golf competition. Entrants were ages 50 and over.

The following year, Ann Gregory died on February 5, 1990. In 2001, Ann Gregory was posthumously inducted into the *Epochs of Courage: African Americans in Golf Wall of Fame.*

Joseph "Joe" Louis Barrow Sr.

He was internationally known as Joe Louis, the world heavyweight boxing champion—a title that he held for 11 years and 10 months. Louis was also well known as a golf tournament host, amateur golfer, and advocate for African American participation in PGA events. He was founder, sponsor, and host of the Joe Louis Open, a major golf competition on the black golf circuit for amateur and professional golfers.

In 1948, Louis won the Joe Louis Open Amateur Golf Championship. Several years later in 1951, he won the UGA Men's Amateur Championship.

At the 1952 San Diego Open, Louis became the first African American to play in a PGA co-sponsored event. With a sponsor's exemption, he played as an invited amateur. Louis missed the cut (150); he shot a 158.

Louis's status as world heavyweight boxing champion helped bring national attention to the PGA's discriminatory practices against African Americans. Known as the *Ambassador of Black Golf*, Louis was an advocate for breaking barriers that banned African Americans from competing in PGA events and becoming PGA Members.

Louis was born May 14, 1914 in Lafayette, Alabama. He held the heavyweight boxing championship of the world title from 1937 to 1949. Joseph Louis Barrow died, at age 66, on April 12, 1981.

In 1986 Pipe of Peace Golf Course, an 18-hole public course in Riverdale, Illinois outside Chicago, was renamed Joe Louis "The Champ" Golf Course. In 2009, The PGA of America granted Joe Louis posthumous honorary PGA Membership. *(More about the Joe Louis Open, page 230)*

Tee Box

Frank Gaskin won the first and second UGA National Men's Amateur Championships (1928 and 1929).

Marie Thompson won the first and second UGA National Women's Amateur Championships (1930 and 1931).

Julia Siler, known as *The Queen of St. Louis*, won more than 100 tournaments. For 27 consecutive years (1931 to 1957), Siler was club champion at Paramount Golf Club (St. Louis, Missouri).

Robert Moss was the only African American to compete in the 1959 San Diego County Amateur Golf Tournament; Moss won the sixth flight.

Donald F. Littlejohn was the first African American to win the Charlotte City Amateur Golf Championship (1989); Littlejohn won the same event in 1991.

George Roddy Sr.

In 1930 and 1937, George Roddy won the UGA Negro National Open Men's Amateur, and he won the Indiana City Championship in 1963 and 1967.

In 1926, Roddy became the first African American to join the University of Iowa's golf team. Roddy's daughter Mary Roddy Molton recalled her father talking about his golf experiences at the university:

> In 1926, riding a bus and carrying one suitcase and one golf club, my father left Keokuk, Iowa (his hometown) to attend the University of Iowa in Iowa City. One of the first things that he did after arriving at the university was—meet the golf coach. My father asked the golf coach if he could play on the team. The coach said that it was not his decision; it would have to be a unanimous team decision.
>
> The team members decided that my father could join the team if he shot the best score in a round of golf with all team members. And that is exactly what he did—at the end of the round my father was the top scorer. He immediately joined the team. Sometime around his sophomore year, he became team captain.
>
> After graduating in 1931 with a degree in engineering, he tried to get an engineering job but no one would hire him. Back then it was hard for a black man to get hired as an engineer, so he pursued a job in education and was hired as a math teacher at Arkansas State College. Later he taught auto mechanics for North Carolina State A&T Vocational School from 1935 to 1948. And from 1948 to 1988 (40 years), my dad worked at Crispus Attucks High School in Indianapolis, Indiana; he started and coached a golf team, and taught auto mechanics at Crispus Attucks.

George Roddy Sr. died in 1988. A decade later (1999), Roddy was inducted into the Indiana Golf Hall of Fame; thus, George Roddy Sr. became the first African American inductee of the Indiana Golf Hall of Fame.

Walter Speedy

Winner of what is known to be the first African American golf tournament, Walter Speedy captured this victory in 1915. This historical event was held at Marquette Park Golf Course (Chicago, Illinois) and hosted by Alpha Golf Club, an organization that Speedy was instrumental in establishing. He also helped establish The Chicago Women's Golf Club and Pioneer Golf Club.

Speedy was an advocate for African American golfers, particularly in the Chicago metropolitan area. He fought against the City of Chicago's policy that banned African Americans from playing in tournaments hosted and sponsored by whites at public golf courses.

Angela Stewart

She won the 2011 North Carolina Women's Senior Amateur Golf Championship; thus, Stewart became the first African American to win a Carolinas Golf Association event. She posted a 151 (76, 75). Stewart served on the USGA Women's Amateur Public Links Committee and the USGA Regional Affairs Committee. Dr. Angela Stewart is a pediatrician.

More notable African American amateur golfers: Lakareber Abe, Ella Able, Alma Arvin, Cleo Ball, Rhutelia Black, Felicia Brown, Barther Cooper, Thelma Cowans, Chauncey Davis, Rhonda Fowler, Tex Guillory, George Harris, Louise Holland, Yvonne Holland, Alfred "Tup" Holmes, Dorothy Johnson, Carrie Jones, Nancy Mason, Elizabeth McNeal, Jean Miller-Colbert, Lucy Mitchum, Omar Neal, George Nelms, Nellie Randall, Exie Shackleford Ochier, Myrtle Patterson, Julia Pettross, Ike Pickney, Leonard Reed, Mary Riley, Dr. Remus Robinson, Bria Sanders, Sarah Smith, Mariah Stackhouse, Alice Stewart, E. Swanson, Clifford Taylor, Eoline Thornton, E. Toler, Vernice Turner, Andrew Walker, Wiley Williams, Geneva Wilson, and Eloise Wright.

(*Left to right*) Joe Louis, Ann Gregory, Eoline Thornton (*fourth*), third and fifth names unknown

An article in the June 13, 1921 issue of *Chicago Defender* announced the opening of Robert P. Ball's Golf School—Private class instruction held daily at 4829 Champlain Avenue, Chicago, Illinois.

Robert "Pat" Ball, a four-time winner (1927, 1929, 1934, and 1941) of the UGA Negro National Open Championship professional division, and a three-time winner (1927, 1929, and 1934) of the Cook County Open held in Chicago, Illinois. His wife Cleo Ball won the UGA Negro National Open Championship women's division in 1941. In 1932, Robert Ball filed an injunction to play in the USGA National Public Links tournament. Filed in Philadelphia, Pennsylvania in Common Pleas Court, the injunction was granted. Robert Ball was one of the first African American golf professionals to work at a desegregated public golf course; in 1938, he joined the staff at Palos Park Golf Course located outside Chicago, Illinois. Circa 1930s

10

UGA Tour Professionals

John Dendy

In 1931 at age 18, John Dendy claimed his first professional victory; he won the Southern Open. He also won the Southern Open in 1934 and 1936. Dendy was a three-time winner of the UGA Negro National Open (1932, 1936, and 1937). John Dendy was inducted into the Western North Carolina Sports Hall of Fame in 1979.

Solomon Hughes Sr.

Winner of the 1935 Negro National Open Championship, Solomon Hughes Sr. also captured victories at the 1945 Midwest Open, Joe Louis Open, and Des Moines Open. In the 1930s, Hughes was a golf instructor in Alabama; his students, men and women, were African American and Caucasian.

Harry Jackson

In 1925, Harry Jackson won the National Colored Golf Championship. The following year (1926) at the first official Negro National Open Championship, Jackson captured first place and won twenty-five dollars.

Tee Box
Solomon Hughes Sr. and Ted Rhodes submitted applications to compete in the PGA Tour's 1948 St. Paul Open; their applications were denied. Hughes attempted to enter the same event in 1951; that application was also denied.

Theodore "Ted" Rhodes

Known as the first African American touring professional golfer, Ted Rhodes is also credited for being the second African American to play in a USGA U.S. Open Championship; he competed in the 1948 U.S. Open Championship. For the first round, Rhodes posted a one under par (70), and placed three strokes from first place; the final three rounds he shot a 76, 77, and 79 respectively. With a final score of 18 over par, Rhodes tied for 51st. Two years later (1950), Rhodes received a sponsor's invitation to play in the Phoenix Open; he made the cut.

Rhodes was a four-time UGA Negro National Open professional champion—three consecutive wins from 1949 to 1951, and a win in 1957. He also won the St. Louis Public Links Invitational Open in 1953, and the Joe Louis Open in four consecutive years, 1946 to 1949. Rhodes served as personal golf instructor and valet to world heavyweight boxing champion Joe Louis, who also financially supported Rhodes as a sponsor.

Theodore Rhodes was born in Nashville, Tennessee on November 9, 1913. During his preteen years, he began working as a caddie at Richland Country Club and also Belle Meade Country Club. In the 1930s, Rhodes enlisted in the United States Navy; he served during World War II.

Ted Rhodes, at age 55, died July 4, 1969. That same year, Cumberland Golf Course (in Nashville, Tennessee) was renamed Ted Rhodes Golf Course. In 1997, Rhodes was posthumously inducted into the Tennessee Golf Hall of Fame. In 2009, The PGA of America granted Rhodes posthumous PGA Membership.

Noted for his countless efforts in trying to break golf's racial barrier, Theodore "Ted" Rhodes was a victim of misleading expectations—that the PGA would ban all discriminatory policies against African Americans. Ted Rhodes was one of the best players—Caucasian or African American—of his time; however, he was denied the opportunity to join the PGA Tour—because he was African American.

William "Bill" Spiller

He turned professional in 1947. Most of Bill Spiller's competitive play was on the UGA professional tour circuit. He rarely competed in PGA Tour events because of the PGA Caucasian-only clause. Spiller was known for his outspoken opinions of the prejudices in the golf world.

In 1986, Spiller was inducted into the UGA Hall of Fame. In 2009, almost two decades after his death in 1988, The PGA of America granted posthumous PGA Membership to William "Bill" Spiller; and in October 2015, Spiller was posthumously inducted into the Oklahoma Golf Hall of Fame.

William Spiller was born October 25, 1913 in Tishomingo, Oklahoma. He attended Wiley College (Marshall, Texas) and graduated in 1938 with a degree in education.

Howard "Butch" Wheeler

A six-time UGA winner (1933, 1938, 1946, 1947, 1948, and 1958), Howard Wheeler also won the 1931 Atlanta Open, 1933 Southern Open, and 1951 Joe Louis Open. He was inducted into the UGA Hall of Fame in 1963.

A native of Atlanta, Georgia, Howard Wheeler was born on April 8, 1911. He began caddying in his pre-teen years. Later he became caddie master at East Lake Country Club in Atlanta, Georgia. Howard Wheeler died in 1968.

More notable professional golfers: James Adams, Herbie Blue, Eural Clark, Harold Dunovant, Herman Duvall, Billy Gardenhight Sr., Nick Gardner, Madison Gunter, Cliff Harrington, Tommy Harton, Zeke Hartsfield, Clyde Martin, Bobby Mayes, Willie McNeal, Bob Miller, Earl Parham, John Roux, Calvin Searles, Warren Sharrock, Cliff Strickland, Cal Tanner, George "Potato Pie" Wallace, Porter Washington, Vance Watts, Joe Whitfield, and Jimmy Wilborn.

Charter Members of United Professional Golfers Association. This group of 23 notable professional golfers included PGA Tour Members Gordon Chavis *(center row 2nd from left)*, and Lee Elder and Richard Thomas *(top row 7th and 8th from left)*. Also PGA Members Harold Dunovant *(top row 10th from left)* and Bill Bishop *(center row 6th from left)*
Courtesy Russell Taylor Black Golf Collection

Organized in 1966, United Professional Golfers Association objectives were to improve the African American professional golfer's status, and to seek fair and equal opportunities for tournament play, work in the golf industry, and golf professional positions at golf courses.

(Photo on left) John Shippen Jr., first African American professional golfer and first African American to play in a USGA U.S. Open Championship (1896).

(Photo below) Theodore "Ted" Rhodes, second African American to play in a USGA U.S. Open Championship (1948).

John Shippen Jr. holding flag stick with putter in hand at Shady Rest Golf and Country Club in Scotch Plains, New Jersey. John Shippen competed in UGA tournaments in the 1920s and 1930s. Circa 1930s.

Theodore "Ted" Rhodes known for his first class golf swing and classy golf attire. Ted Rhodes competed in UGA tournaments in the 1940s and 1950s.
Photo Courtesy Peggy Rhodes-White

What a bleak situation we have right now.

It is extremely hard and difficult for African Americans to play on any professional golf tour.

It is not because we do not have the abilities—because we do.

When I went on the PGA Tour in 1964, I had $2000 and no sponsors.

I cannot think of any African American tour player who had a sponsor at that time....

And furthermore, PGA Tour tournaments that African Americans could play were few and far between.

The problems remain the same—lack of finances, sponsors, and opportunities.

—*William "Bill" Wright*
Former PGA Tour Member

11

Developmental and Mini Tour Players–Men

*There are African American men and women who are
more than capable of taking on the challenges of a
major tour. We have to find a way to get them there.*
—Robert Clark Sr., PGA Member

Kevin Hall

Four years after turning professional in 2004, Hall captured
his first professional victory on the 2008 NGA Hooters Tour.
He carded a 14 under par (70, 66, 66).

Kevin Hall was born prematurely on September 24, 1982.
He suffered with H-Flu meningitis when he was about two
years old. Through his medical challenges, Hall survived—
but lost his hearing. From kindergarten through high
school, Hall attended Saint Rita School for the Deaf
(Cincinnati, Ohio). He aspired to join a high school golf
team, but Saint Rita School for the Deaf did not have a golf
team.

Kevin's parents Percy and Jackie Hall petitioned the
local school district to allow their son, a Saint Rita School for
the Deaf student, to join a golf team at a district high school.
The petition was granted and Kevin joined Winton Woods
High School's golf team. He lettered every year during his
four years on the team. In 2000, Kevin graduated from Saint
Rita School for the Deaf with valedictorian honors.

Hall attended Ohio State University on a full academic
and athletic scholarship; thus, he became the first African
American to attend Ohio State University on a golf
scholarship and the first African American Ohio State
University golf team member. In Hall's collegiate junior and
senior years, he served as co-captain of the men's golf team.
In 2005, he graduated with a degree in journalism.

Through a sponsor's exemption, 22-year-old Kevin Hall
made his PGA Tour debut at the 2005 U.S. Bank
Championship. Even though he missed the cut by four
strokes, Kevin Hall made PGA Tour history—he became the
first profoundly deaf person to play in a PGA Tour event.

Vincent Johnson

Johnson turned professional in 2008. The following year (2009), Johnson made his PGA Tour debut as the recipient of the inaugural Northern Trust Open Exemption; he shot a 144 (70, 74) and missed the cut by three strokes. The inaugural Northern Trust Open Exemption was named Charlie Sifford Exemption Award in honor of the 40th anniversary of Sifford's 1969 Northern Trust Open victory.

Johnson claimed his first professional victory with a 16 under at the 2010 Long Beach Open (an event of the City of Long Beach, California Golf Festival). He won by two strokes.

Vincent Johnson was the first African American member of Oregon State University men's golf team. For the 2005–2006 season, he served as captain and was named MVP; he was co-captain during his senior year. In 2007, Johnson graduated from Oregon State University with a degree in finance. A classical pianist, Johnson minored in music.

Willie Mack III

Prior to turning professional in 2011 and joining the Florida Professional Golf (FPG) Tour, Flint, Michigan native Willie Mack III won the 100th Michigan Amateur Championship; thus, Willie Mack III became the first African American to win a Michigan Amateur Championship. For the 2011–2012 FPG Tour season, Mack ranked number one on the official money list and he was named Player of the Year.

Timothy "Tim" O'Neal

With a third place finish on the 2013 PGA Tour Latinoamérica season-ending money list, Tim O'Neal earned conditional status for Web.com Tour 2014 season. In 2006, he claimed five top-10 finishes on the Nationwide Tour.

In 2000 and 2004 at the final PGA Tour qualifying stage, O'Neal came very close to earning his PGA Tour playing card. In 2000, he needed to post at least a bogey–bogey at holes 17 and 18 in the final round; he bogeyed number 17 and triple bogeyed number 18. In 2004, O'Neal needed at least a bogey on the final hole. He made a double bogey and missed getting his PGA Tour playing card by one stroke.

Before turning professional in 1997, O'Neal won the 1997 Georgia State Amateur Championship. He played collegiate golf at Jackson State University.

Stephen Reed

He turned professional in 2005, and has played the Gateway Pro Tour, NGA Hooters Tour, Canadian Professional Golf Tour, and Nationwide Tour.

At age 18, Stephen Reed won the 2000 American Junior Golf Association TaylorMade-adidas Texas Junior Classic; he shot even par (71, 73), and won by two strokes. With that AJGA victory, Reed became the first African American to win an AJGA event since Tiger Woods won in 1992.

Reed is a 2004 Texas A&M University graduate. In 2013, he received a MBA degree from The George Washington University.

Harold Varner III

He opened the 2015 Web.com season with a second place finish at Panama Claro Championship. On August 30, 2015 at the WinCo Foods Portland Open, Harold Varner III captured, by a margin of $943, the 25th spot on the Web.com 2015 money list. With that top 25 ranking Varner earned a 2016 PGA Tour card.

Varner was the recipient of the 2014 Northern Trust Open Exemption; he tied for 70th. He joined Web.com Tour in 2014. He had two top-10 finishes, tied for second at Rex Hospital Open and tied for sixth at WNB Golf Classic.

A year prior to turning professional in 2012, Varner became the first African American male to win the North Carolina Amateur Championship; he captured the win in 2011 with a 14 under par by three strokes. And in 2012,

Varner was the first East Carolina University student to receive the Conference USA Golfer of the Year Award. Varner graduated from East Carolina University in 2012.

Andy Walker
Walker ranked 10th on the Gateway Pro Tour's 2006 final money list. In 2012, he was the fourth Northern Trust Open Exemption recipient; Walker shot a 150 and missed the cut by five strokes. In 2009, he joined the coaching staff at South Mountain Community College (Phoenix, Arizona).

A graduate of Pepperdine University, Walker was a member of Pepperdine University men's golf team when Pepperdine won the 1997 NCAA Division I men's golf championship; thus, Andy Walker became the first African American member of a Division I-A NCAA men's championship team.

Jeremiah Wooding
After graduating in 2011 from the University of Las Vegas, Nevada, Wooding turned professional. The following year, he joined Web.com Tour with conditional status. Wooding was the 2013 Northern Trust Open Exemption recipient. He made the cut and placed 42nd; thus, Jeremiah Wooding became the first Northern Trust Open Exemption recipient to make the cut. Jeremiah's brother Joshua Wooding was the 2010 Northern Trust Open Exemption recipient.

More notable developmental / mini tour men players:
Levy Adger, Josh Bain, George Bradford, Joseph Bramlett (*Bramlett on the PGA Tour, page 123*), Vern Burns, Brandon Chapman, Albert Crews, John Fizer, Christian Heavens, Randall Hunt, Maurice Jeffries II, Will Lowery, Marcus Manley, Jay McNair, Anthony Miller, Kevin Odum, Jason Seymour, Montrele Wells, Jim White Sr., Joshua Wooding, Donald Wright, and Scott Yancy III.

Developmental Tour Players–Ladies

Dara Broadus
From 2002 to 2005, Dara Broadus played the Futures Golf Tour. She tied for 10th at the 2003 Georgia Women's Open. During her high school years, Broadus was the only female on The Westminster Schools (Atlanta, Georgia) boy's golf team, and she was a two-time recipient of the Most Valuable Player award. Broadus is a graduate of Furman University.

Nakia Davis
From 1996 to 2000, Nakia Davis played the Futures Golf Tour. She was a four-time Louisiana Girls State Champion, and she was featured as a model golf swing in Microsoft's Link 2001 video computer golf game. Davis is a 1996 Vanderbilt University alumna; she was a member of Vanderbilt University women's golf team. In 2006, Davis received a Juris Doctor degree from Loyola University New Orleans School of Law.

Ginger Howard
At 2015 LPGA Qualifying Tournament Stage III, Ginger Howard earned LPGA Tour Member status (Priority List Category 17) for the 2016 season; thus, Howard became the seventh African American member of the LPGA Tour.

In 2010, Howard became the first African American female United States Junior Ryder Cup team member. She turned professional in June 2011, and began competing on the SunCoast Ladies Series Tour; she posted five wins for that season. Howard joined the Symetra Tour in 2012.

Seventeen-year-old Ginger Howard received a special age exemption to enter Stage I of the 2011 LPGA Tour Qualifying Tournament. Entry age requirement was 18 years or older by January 1 of the following year (2012). Howard's 18th birthday, March 15, 2012, came after the January 1 deadline.

Howard won medallist honors at Stage II of the 2011 and 2014 LPGA Qualifying Tournaments; thus, Howard became the first player to medal twice at Stage II. Ginger's younger sister Robbi Howard caddied for Ginger at the 2014 Stage II Qualifying Tournament. Robbi is also a professional golfer; 2014 was her rookie year on the Symetra Tour.

Jameisha Levister

In 2011, Jameisha Levister joined the LPGA Futures Tour. In 2004, she was named Virginia State Golf Association Women's Golfer of the Year; thus, she became the first African American recipient of a Virginia State Golf Association Player of the Year Award. Levister played collegiate golf at North Carolina Central University; she was the only female player on the men's golf team. Levister was named Most Valuable Player, served as team captain, and was honored as the 2001 CIAA Men's Golf Rookie of the Year.

Zakiya Randall

In 2009 at age 17, Zakiya Randall joined the Duramed FUTURES Tour. Prior to turning professional Randall won, against all men, Golf Channel's 2008 Amateur Tour Final Half Championship Flight. At age 15, Randall became the first African American to win first place medal in a USGA U.S. Women's Open Qualifier. In 2005, she received the Georgia PGA Junior Tour Player of the Year Award.

More LPGA developmental golf tour players:

Debbie Adams (Adams is also a LPGA T&CP), Shasta Averyhardt (*Averyhardt on the LPGA Tour, page 121*), Gabriella Dominguez, Lorette Lyttle, Tierra Manigault, Paula Pearson-Tucker (Pearson-Tucker is also a LPGA T&CP), and Darlene Stowers.

12

LPGA Tour Members *(1963 through 2015)*

Althea Gibson

In 1963, Althea Gibson became the first African American LPGA Tour member. Her first professional golf appearance was at the USGA U.S. Women's Open in 1963. Her best finish on the LPGA Tour was in 1970—Gibson tied for second after a three-way playoff at the Lem Immke Buick Open. Gibson played professional golf through 1978; however, her LPGA Tour member status officially ended in 1971.

Internationally known for her outstanding tennis career, Gibson won the 1957 and 1958 U.S. Open Tennis Championships and the Women's Singles at The Championships, Wimbledon.

Althea Gibson, first African American LPGA Tour member. Played on Tour 1963–1971.

A native of Silver, South Carolina, Althea Gibson was born August 25, 1927. She graduated from Florida A&M University in 1953. Althea Gibson died in September 2003.

Renee Powell

The second African American LPGA Tour member, Renee Powell played the LPGA Tour from 1967 to 1980. She is an honorary LPGA T&CP member and the first African American PGA Member; thus, Powell is recognized as the first African American to hold memberships in both The PGA of America and the LPGA.

Powell has received numerous honors and awards including The PGA of America "First Lady of Golf Award" (2003), and the Rolex For The Love of the Game Award (2007). In 2008, she became the first African American female golfer to receive an honorary Doctor of Laws degree from the University of St. Andrews in Scotland, England. In February 2015, Powell was one of seven female members to become the first female members at the Royal and Ancient Golf Club of St. Andrews; she was granted honorary membership.

Born May 4, 1946 in Canton, Ohio, Renee Powell was introduced to golf at age three. Thirteen years later at age 16, she became the first African American to compete in a United States Girl's Junior Championship. She attended Ohio University and Ohio State University, and joined the women's golf team at both universities.

Renee Powell, second African American LPGA Tour member. Played on Tour 1967–1980.

Powell is co-owner and head golf professional at Clearview Golf Club, a family-owned golf facility that was designed and built by Renee's father William Powell.

LaRee Sugg

The third African American to join the LPGA Tour, LaRee Sugg played on Tour from 1995 to 1997, and from 2000 to 2001.

In 2002, Sugg became the first head women's golf coach at the University of Richmond; thus, Sugg was recognized as the first African American female golf coach at a predominantly white university. In 2005, she was promoted to Assistant Director of Athletics and Senior Woman Administrator.

LaRee Sugg, third African American LPGA Tour member. Played on Tour 1995 –1997, 2000–2001.

LaRee Sugg was born November 11, 1969 in Petersburg, Virginia. When she was six years old, her grandfather introduced her to golf. A 1991 UCLA graduate, Sugg was a member of UCLA women's golf team.

Shasta Averyhardt

In 2011, Shasta Averyhardt became the fourth African American to join the LPGA Tour. She also qualified to play on the LPGA Tour for the 2013 season. For both seasons Averyhardt earned partial exempt playing status through LPGA Q-School.

Averyhardt also played the Symetra Tour in 2011 and 2012. She was recipient of the first Symetra Rising Star Award—the most improved player on the official money list from 2011 to 2012. She placed 152nd with total earnings of $1,646 for the 2011 season. At the end of the 2012 Symetra Tour season, Averyhardt was 38th on the official money list with total earnings of $14,362.

Shasta Averyhardt, fourth African American LPGA Tour member. Played on Tour 2011, 2013.

A former Jackson State University golfer, Averyhardt is a 2008 Jackson State University alumna. In 2009, she turned professional and joined the Duramed FUTURES Tour.

Averyhardt was born January 5, 1986 in Flint, Michigan. She became interested in golf when she was about seven years old.

Sadena Parks

The fifth African American LPGA Tour member, Sadena Parks earned a 2015 LPGA Tour card while playing the Symetra Tour in 2014; thus, Parks became the first African American to receive LPGA Tour Member status through the Symetra Tour.

She turned professional in 2012 and began playing on the Symetra Tour in 2013. For the 2014 Symetra Tour season, Parks posted four top-10 finishes—two first-place, a second-place, and a tie for third. Park's total earnings of $57,597 ranked her fourth on the 2014 Volvik Race for the Card money list; that top 10 ranking earned Sadena Parks a 2015

LPGA Tour card. On the final 2015 LPGA Tour's money list Parks ranked 100th with $69,680; thus, Parks retained her LPGA Tour card for the 2016 Tour season.

Parks was the first African American member of University of Washington women's golf team. She is a 2012 University of Washington alumna.

Born May 4, 1990 in Raleigh, North Carolina, Parks was about 9 years old when her father introduced her to golf.

Sadena Parks, fifth African American LPGA Tour member (2015, 2016,)
Courtesy Scott Miller and the LPGA

Cheyenne Woods

In 2014 at LPGA Qualifying School, Cheyenne Woods earned a 2015 LPGA Tour card. She tied for 11th, posting a five under par (355) on the final leaderboard. She also

earned a 2016 LPGA Tour card. She tied for 13th on the final leaderboard.

Woods joined the Ladies European Tour in 2013; the following year she won the Australian Ladies Masters.

Woods was a member of Wake Forest University women's golf team. After graduating from Wake Forest University in 2012, she turned professional and joined SunCoast Ladies Series Tour.

Cheyenne Woods was born July 25, 1990 in Phoenix, Arizona. She started playing golf at age five. Professional golfer Tiger Woods is Cheyenne's uncle.

Cheyenne Woods, sixth African American LPGA Tour member (2015, 2016,)

13

PGA Tour and Champions Tour Members
(1960 through 2015)

James Black

He turned professional in 1962; three years later (1965) at age 22, James Black joined the PGA Tour. For more than 30 years, he held the record as the youngest African American to join the PGA Tour. Black's record was broken in 1996— that is when 20-year-old Tiger Woods joined the PGA Tour.

Joseph Bramlett

In 2010, Joseph Bramlett entered PGA Qualifying School and earned PGA Tour member conditional status for 2011. Thus, Bramlett became the first African American to pass PGA Q-School since professional golfer Adrian Stills in 1985. Bramlett joined the Web.com Tour in 2012. He attempted to rejoin the PGA Tour in 2012, but missed the top-25 cut by three spots and $4,000. Bramlett is a 2010 graduate of Stanford University.

E. Pete Brown

In 1963, Pete Brown joined the PGA Tour. The following year (1964), Brown became the first African American to win a PGA Tour sanctioned event—he posted a 280 (eight under par) and won the Waco Turner Open. In 1970, Brown won the Andy Williams-San Diego Open Invitational; he posted a 275 (13 under par).

Even though Brown captured two PGA Tour victories, he never received an invitation to play in a Masters Tournament. His PGA Tour wins occurred before 1972, the year the Masters Tournament invitation-only policy changed.

The amended invitation-only policy reflected the following—*any player who won a PGA Tour event within a calendar year received an invitation to play in the following year's Masters Tournament*. This change was not *retroactive* (related things done before the change); thus, neither of Brown's PGA Tour wins qualified him for an invitation to play in a Masters Tournament.

Early Brown was born February 2, 1935 in Port Gibson, Mississippi. He turned professional in 1954. During his professional golf career, Brown suffered with non-paralytic polio and had difficulty walking. Yet in spite of distinct medical challenges, he became an exceptional golfer with remarkable achievements. Pete Brown died May 1, 2015.

More Pete Brown Highlights
• Three-time winner of the North and South Tournament
• Won 1961 Michigan Open
• Winner of the UGA National Negro Open Championship (1962 and 1963)
• Head golf professional for more than 20 years at Madden Golf Course (Dayton, Ohio)

James Lacey "Jim" Dent
Former PGA Tour and Champions Tour member, Jim Dent turned professional in 1966 and joined the PGA Tour in 1970. He is a three-time consecutive winner (1976–1978) of the Florida PGA Championship. In 1989, he joined the Senior PGA Tour. Dent was inducted into the Georgia Golf Hall of Fame in 1994. As of 2015, Jim Dent ranked 22nd on the Champions Tour all-time official wins of 10 or more events; Dent had 12 Champions Tour career victories.

James Lacey Dent was born May 9, 1939 in Augusta, Georgia. He caddied at Augusta National Golf Club and Augusta Country Club. He graduated from Laney High School (Augusta, Georgia).

More Jim Dent Highlights
• Tied second–1972 Walt Disney World Open Invitational
• Won 1983 Michelob-Chattanooga Golf Club Classic
• Won 1989–MONY Syracuse Senior Classic, and Newport Cup; ranked 12th on Senior PGA Tour's 1989 money list

• Won 1990–Vantage At The Dominion, MONY Syracuse Senior Classic, Kroeger Senior Classic, and Crestar Classic
• Won 1992 Newport Cup
• Won 1994 Bruno's Memorial Classic
• Won 1995 Bell South Senior Classic at Opryland
• Won 1996 Bank of Boston Senior Classic
• Won 1997 and 1998 The Home Depot Invitational

Robert Lee Elder

He is the first African American to receive an invitation to play in a Masters Tournament. At the 1974 Monsanto Open in a playoff against Peter Oosterhuis, Lee Elder sank a winning 18-foot putt on the fourth hole; that victory qualified Elder to receive his first invitation to a Masters. Hence, this was Augusta National Golf Club's first time inviting an African American to compete at a Masters.

In his first Masters Tournament appearance, Elder posted a 152 (74, 78), and missed the cut, 148, by four strokes. The following year (1976), he did not qualify to receive an invitation to play in the Masters Tournament; however, Elder played in the Masters every year from 1977 to 1981. His best finish—tied for 17th in 1979.

Born July 14, 1934 in Dallas, Texas, Lee Elder began caddying at an early age. He was nine years old when his parents died; his father was killed while serving in World War II and his mother died within a year of his father's death. After his parents' deaths, Elder earned money caddying to help take care of his seven siblings.

At about age 12, Elder moved to Los Angeles to live with his sister. There he attended high school, but later dropped out of school to pursue his dream—a career in golf. Elder worked at golf courses in various jobs including caddying, and working in pro shops and locker rooms.

In 1959, Elder turned professional. That same year, he was drafted into the United States Army. While in the military, he continued to play golf and won two post golf championships at Fort Lewis Military Base.

After Elder's military career he joined the UGA circuit and won numerous UGA tournaments, including 18 of 22 UGA events that were held in 1967. That same year (1967), Lee Elder received his PGA card.

In 1971, Elder became the first African American to compete in a multiracial golfing event in South Africa. Then PGA Tour member Gary Player invited Elder to play in the South African PGA Championship. Because of South Africa's apartheid policy, some civil rights leaders voiced their opposition to Elder participating in an event held in Johannesburg, South Africa.

Elder accepted Gary Player's invitation contingent upon the South African government agreeing to certain conditions. Two of the conditions were—Elder and his family would not be subject to travel restraints throughout the country; and the Elder family would not be subject to the country's segregated policies, such as restrictive seating at events. The South African government agreed to Elder's terms, and also granted Elder permission to raise money for a deprived seminary school for black South African children. In 1972, the U.S. State Department recognized Elder for his goodwill mission to Africa.

In 1979, Elder became the first African American to be selected to a United States Ryder Cup team. The 1979 event was held at The Greenbrier in White Sulphur Springs, West Virginia. In his first match, Elder and U.S. teammate Andy Bean played Nick Faldo and Pete Oosterhuis; Elder and Bean won. (Five years before this Ryder Cup, Elder won against Pete Oosterhuis in a playoff at the 1974 Monsanto Open.) In the Ryder Cup singles competition, Elder played against Nick Faldo; Faldo won. The final score for the 1979 Ryder Cup was 17 to 11—in favor of the United States.

Elder joined the Senior PGA Tour in 1984. The following year he played in 23 events, placed in the top 25 in all events, and had 21 top-10 finishes. With that record, Elder ranked second on the Senior PGA Tour's 1985 money list.

Elder posted four PGA Tour wins and eight Senior PGA Tour wins during his professional career.

More Lee Elder Highlights
- Won 1971 Nigerian Open
- Tied for 11th, 1974 PGA Championship
- Won 1976 Houston Open
- Won 1978 Greater Milwaukee Open (defeated Lee Trevino on the eighth playoff hole)
- Won 1978 American Express Westchester Classic
- Tied for 11th, 1979 U.S. Open Championship
- Tied for 36th, 1979 British Open
- Tied for third, 1981 Atlanta Classic
- Three top-10 finishes, 1983
- Placed second, 1984 United Virginia Bank Seniors
- One top-10 finish on PGA Tour in 1984, tied for ninth at the Bob Hope Classic
- Won in 1984–Suntree Classic, Hilton Head Seniors Invitational, and Jamaica Open
- Tied for second, 1984 du Maurier Champions
- Tied for second, 1984 Quadel Senior Classic
- Eight top-10 finishes in 1984, included a tie for third at General Foods PGA Seniors' Championship
- Won in 1985–Denver Post Champion of Golf, Merrill Lynch/Golf Digest Pro–Am, Digital Seniors Classic, and Citizens Union Senior Golf Classic
- Placed second, 1985 Senior Players Reunion Pro–Am and 1985 Greenbrier American Express Championship
- Tied for second, 1985 Senior Tournament Players Championship
- Eighteen top-10 finishes in 1986, included a win at Merrill Lynch/Golf Digest Commemorative
- Fourteen top-10 finishes in 1987
- Six top-10 finishes in 1988, included a win at Gus Machado Classic
- Two top-10 finishes in 1989
- Tied for fourth, 1993 Better Homes and Gardens Real Estate Challenge
- Golf Writers of America Association Annual Award for service and dedication (2000)

(Source: Lee Elder Chronological, courtesy Lee and Sharon Elder)

George Johnson

In 1964 he turned professional and four years later, in 1968, George Johnson earned his PGA Tour card. During the ten years that Johnson played the PGA Tour, he won the 1971 Azalea Open; thus, Johnson became the fourth African American to win a PGA Tour event. Johnson also played the Senior PGA Tour for three years. In 1997, Johnson became the first African American head golf professional in the state of Kentucky; he was hired at Bobby Nichols Golf Course in Waverly Park (Louisville, Kentucky). He was a lifetime PGA Member. George Johnson died in April 2014.

Walter Morgan

In 1991, Walter Morgan joined the Senior PGA Tour. He won three Tour events—1995 GTE NW Classic, 1996 FHP Health Care Classic, and 1996 Ameritech Senior Open. In 1995, he was selected the Senior PGA Tour Comeback Player of the Year. A Vietnam veteran, Walter Morgan served 20 years in the United States Army.

More Walter Morgan Highlights

• One top-10 finish in 1992
• Four top-10 finishes in 1993
• Four top-10 finishes in 1995
• Ten top-10 finishes in 1996
• Eleven top-10 finishes in 1997, including third place at the Pittsburgh Senior Classic
• Five top-10 finishes in 1998, including third place at Saint Luke's Classic
• One top-10 finish in 1999
• Three top-10 finishes in 2000
• Two top-10 finishes in 2001, tied for second at TD Waterhouse Championship and tied for sixth at SBC Senior Classic.
• Two top-10 finishes in 2002, tied for second at AT&T Canada Senior Open Championship and tied for seventh at 3M Championship

Charles "Charlie" Owens

He was drafted into the United States Army during the Korean War. In 1952 at Fort Bragg, North Carolina, Charlie Owens suffered disabling knee and ankle injuries during a parachute exercise.

A self-taught golfer known for his cross-handed grip, Owens turned professional in 1967. He joined the PGA Tour in 1970 and the Senior PGA Tour in 1981. His professional victories include the 1971 Kemper-Asheville Open, 1974 Florida Open Golf Championship, 1986 Treasure Coast Classic, and 1986 Del E. Webb Senior Tour Roundup. Due to his disability, Owens was sometimes allowed to use a golf cart while competing in events.

Owens is credited for being the first on the PGA Tour to putt with an extended shaft (belly) putter—a 50-inch putter that weighed more than three pounds. He was the brainchild behind the development of the Matzie "Slim Jim Putter"—a 46-inch long putter that featured a heavy brass head. In 1985, Matzie Golf Company began manufacturing and marketing the "Slim Jim Putter".

In 1987, Owens received the Ben Hogan Award from Golf Writers Association of America. He was inducted into the Polk County Sports Hall of Fame in 2000.

Charlie Owens was born February 22, 1930 in Winter Haven, Florida. He played high school football and earned a football scholarship to Florida A&M University.

Calvin Peete Sr.

He qualified for the PGA Tour in 1975 and joined the Senior PGA Tour in 1993. From 1979 to 1998, Calvin Peete won 12 PGA Tour events. Peete held the record for the most PGA Tour wins by an African American or person of African American ancestry until 1999—that is when Tiger Woods won his 13th PGA Tour event at the 1999 National Car Rental Golf Classic/Disney. Peete received the PGA Tour's driving accuracy title for 10 consecutive years (1981–1990); his drive was 80.9 percent accurate.

In 1980, Calvin Peete became the second African American to receive an invitation to play in a Masters Tournament; he shot one under par and tied for 19th. Peete also played in the Masters Tournament from 1981 to 1987. His best finish at a Masters Tournament was in 1986; he tied for 11th.

Peete retired from professional golf in 2001. In the fall of that same year, he and his wife Pepper started a golf team at Edward Waters College in Jacksonville, Florida; thus, Calvin and Pepper Peete became the first known African American husband and wife couple to coach collegiate golf.

A native of Detroit, Michigan, Peete was born July 18, 1943. At age 12, he fell from a tree and broke his left elbow. Surgery was performed; however, Peete could not fully extend his left elbow. Hence, his left arm was permanently bent. Later in Peete's adult life, he suffered with Tourette Syndrome—a neurological disorder that causes involuntary vocalizations and movement of muscles.

Calvin Peete was selected to the 1985 United States Ryder Cup team. However, he lacked one qualification—a high school diploma. U.S. Ryder Cup Team members were required to have a high school diploma or equivalent. To fulfill that requirement, Peete earned his GED (General Educational Development) certificate.

Despite extraordinary challenges, Calvin Peete was an exceptional golfer. Calvin Peete, at age 71, died April 29, 2015.

More Calvin Peete Sr. Highlights
• Won Greater Milwaukee Open in 1979; Anheuser-Busch Golf Classic, B.C. Open, Pensacola Open, and Greater Milwaukee Open in 1982; Georgia-Pacific Atlanta Golf Classic and Anheuser-Busch Golf Classic in 1983; Texas Open in 1984; Phoenix Open in 1985; Tournament Players Championship in 1985; MONY Tournament of Champions in 1986; USF&G Classic in 1986
• Tied for third, 1981 Phoenix Open and Atlanta Classic
• Tied for third, 1982 PGA Championship

- Tied for second, 1983 Bing Crosby National Pro–Am
- Tied for second, 1983 Buick Open
- Tied for fourth, 1983 U.S. Open Championship
- Ben Hogan Award, 1983
- Vardon Trophy, 1984
- Byron Nelson Award, 1984
- Placed fourth, 1984 PGA Championship
- Tied for second, 1986 Phoenix Open
- Placed fourth, 1995 Bell Atlantic Classic
- Four top-10 finishes on Senior PGA Tour in 1996
- Tied for third, 1997 Liberty Mutual Legends of Golf

Charles "Charlie" Sifford

The first African American to earn a PGA Players card, Charlie Sifford is also the first African American inductee into the World Golf Hall of Fame. In 2004 he was inducted under the Lifetime Achievement category, and as of the World Golf Hall of Fame's 2015 induction ceremony, Sifford remained the only African American inductee.

In 1948, Sifford turned professional at age 26. During his professional career he claimed 21 victories. Sifford played the United Golfers Association circuit and won the Negro National Open championship title six times (1952–1956 and 1960). He also served as personal assistant and golf instructor to jazz musician Billy Eckstine.

On March 28, 1960 Charlie Sifford, at age 38, became the first African American to receive PGA Approved Tournament Player status. Even though the PGA granted Sifford ATP status, he was still prohibited from becoming a PGA Member because of the Caucasian-only clause.

In 1962, the Caucasian-only clause was deleted from The PGA of America Bylaws. The abolishment of this racist clause opened doors for African Americans to compete in PGA Tour events; however, it did not open the door for Sifford to play in the Masters. Sifford played professional golf for almost half a century, but he never received an invitation to play in a Masters Tournament.

In 1962, Sifford competed in the Canadian Open, an event that the Masters Tournament Committee recognized as a major foreign tournament; thereby, making it possible for a Canadian Open winner to earn an invitation to play in the Masters under the *invitation-only policy.*

In his autobiography *Just Let Me Play: The Story of Charlie Sifford The First Black PGA Golfer,* Sifford wrote about the Masters Tournament *invitation-only* policy notification of change that was posted for the players at the 1962 Canadian Open, and how this amended policy would affect him, if he won the 1962 Canadian Open:

> After completion of the first round Charlie Sifford posted a 67 for second place, which put him in contention to win the 1962 Canadian Open. If Sifford won (according to the Masters *invitation-only policy*), he would earn an invitation to play in the 1963 Masters Tournament.
>
> However, sometime between the end of the first round and the beginning of the second round, a telephone message was posted in the clubhouse at the Canadian Open. This message announced an immediate change to the Masters Tournament *invitation-only policy*—a 1962 Canadian Open win would not qualify for an automatic invitation to play in the 1963 Masters Tournament.
>
> It seemed peculiar that a Masters *invitation-only policy* change was announced during the time that Sifford was in contention to win the 1962 Canadian Open. Because of this abrupt Masters Tournament policy change, if Sifford won, he would not be eligible to receive an automatic invitation to play in the Masters.
>
> On the final leaderboard, Sifford placed second. He shot a 280, two strokes from the top of the leaderboard.

In 1964, Charlie Sifford was awarded full PGA membership. Three years later, he captured his first PGA Tour win—the 1967 Greater Hartford Open; and in 1969, Sifford won another PGA Tour event—the Los Angeles Open.

In 1975, Sifford joined the Senior PGA Tour. That same year, he won the Senior PGA Championship. As a result of that victory, Sifford was designated to play in a one-day, 36-hole match play against the winner of that year's British Senior Championship, Kel Nagle.

The PGA arranged the competition between Sifford and Nagle and selected, as the host site, Bide-A-Wee Golf Club—a segregated golf facility in Portsmouth, Virginia. Because Bide-A-Wee Golf Club was an all-white member only club, Sifford had to receive permission to play. The Bide-A-Wee board of directors granted Sifford a one-time playing privilege for that event only; thus, Sifford became the first African American to officially play at Bide-A-Wee Golf Club. Nagle won the match.

In 1985, Sifford ranked in the top 28 on the Champions Tour money list. That ranking gave him exempt status; thus, in 1986, sixty-four year-old Charlie Sifford became the oldest player to receive a Champions Tour exemption.

In 2006, Sifford received an honorary Doctor of Laws degree from University of St. Andrews (Scotland, England); thus, Sifford became the first African American golfer to receive this honor. In 2009 Northern Trust Open established an annual Northern Trust Open Exemption in support of diversity in golf. The inaugural exemption was in honor of Charlie Sifford and coincided with Sifford's 40th anniversary of his 1969 Los Angeles Open win. In 2014, Dr. Charles Sifford received the Presidential Medal of Freedom award from President Barack Obama.

Born June 2, 1922 in Charlotte, North Carolina, Sifford started caddying when he was about 10 years old. On May 3, 2011 in Sifford's city of birth—Revolution Park Golf Course was renamed *The Dr. Charles L. Sifford Golf Course at Revolution Park*. This municipal course was formerly named Bonnie Brae Golf Course, a "whites-only" course from the 1920s through the 1950s.

Charlie Sifford died February 3, 2015. He was posthumously inducted into the PGA of America Hall of Fame in November 2015.

More Charlie Sifford Highlights
• Played in 422 PGA Tour events and made the cut in 399
• Won 1957 Long Beach Open, a PGA co-sponsored event
• First African American to play in a PGA sponsored event in the South—Greater Greensboro Open in 1961
• Won 1963 Puerto Rico Open
• Inducted into Northern Ohio Sports Hall of Fame and North Carolina Sportswriters Hall of Fame
• Won 1980 Suntree Senior PGA Tour Classic
• Received 2007 Old Tom Morris Award from Golf Course Superintendents Association of America (GCSAA)
• Honorary Doctor of Laws degree, Lincoln University (2007)
• Named 2008 Ambassador of Golf by Northern Ohio Golf Charities

Jimmy Lee "Jim" Thorpe
In 1972, Jim Thorpe began playing professional golf. Four years later (1976), Thorpe joined the PGA Tour. He captured three PGA Tour victories.

In 1999, Thorpe joined the Senior PGA Tour. As of 2014, Thorpe has posted 13 Champions Tour career victories, which include the Charles Schwab Cup Championship in 2003, 2006, and 2007.

As of 2014, Thorpe was one of four African Americans who have received an invitation to play in a Masters Tournament. Thorpe made the cut at the Masters for three consecutive years, 1985 to 1987. Thorpe's best finish was in 1985; he tied for 18th. He missed the cut in 1982 and 1984, and withdrew in 1988.

Born February 1, 1949, Jim Thorpe was raised with 11 siblings; he was the ninth child. His father Elbert Thorpe Sr. was a green superintendent at Roxboro Country Club in Roxboro, North Carolina. The Thorpe family lived on the country club's property.

A talented football player, Thorpe was a high school star running back. He received a football scholarship to Morgan State University (Baltimore, Maryland).

More Jim Thorpe Highlights

• Won three PGA Tour events—Greater Milwaukee Open in 1985 (Posted a 274 and won by three strokes over Jack Nicklaus.); Seiko-Tucson Match Play Championship in 1985 and 1986
• Won 13 Champions Tour events through 2012: Gold Rush Classic, and The Transamerica in 2000; Allianz Championship, and Kroeger Senior Classic in 2001; The Countrywide Tradition in 2002; Long Island Classic and Charles Schwab Cup in 2003; Farmers Charity Classic, and Commerce Bank Long Island Classic in 2004; FedEx Kinko's Classic, and Blue Angels Classic in 2005; and Charles Schwab Cup Championship in 2006 and 2007
• Won the 1982 Canadian PGA Championship
• Tied for second, 1983 Bank of Boston Classic
• Placed fourth, 1983 Memorial Tournament
• Tied for fourth, 1984 U.S. Open Championship
• Tied for seventh, 1986 PGA Championship
• Tied for ninth, 1987 U.S. Open Championship
• Placed second, 1989 Kemper Open
• Placed second, 1990 Phoenix Open
• Won the 1991 Amoco Centel Championship
• Tied for second, 1999 Foremost Insurance Championship
• Tied for second, 1999 Bell Atlantic Classic
• Placed second, 2001 MasterCard Championship
• Placed second, 2001 Senior PGA Championship
• Placed third, 2001 State Farm Senior Classic
• Placed fifth, 2001 AT&T Canada Senior Open Championship
• Tied for second, 2002 Ford Senior Players Championship
• Tied for third, 2002 ACE Group Classic
• Tied for fourth, 2002 Senior PGA Championship
• Tied for fourth, 2002 Farmers Charity Classic
• Placed fourth, 2002 Napa Valley Championship
• Placed second, 2003 Greater Hickory Classic at Rock Barn
• Tied for second, 2003 Ford Senior Players Championship
• Tied for fourth, 2003 Verizon Classic
• Tied for fourth, 2003 Kinko's Classic of Austin

• Tied for fourth, 2004 Kroeger Classic and 2004 Allianz Championship
• Tied for fifth, 2004 Royal Caribbean Golf Classic
• Ranked in the top 10 on the Champions Tour's money list for 2004 and 2006
• Placed second, 2006 Ford Senior Players Championship
• Placed fourth, 2006 Regions Charity Classic
• Tied for fifth, 2008 SAS Championship
• Tied for fourth, 2009 Regions Charity Classic
• Tied for fifth, 2012 Mississippi Gulf Resort Classic
• One hundred Champions Tour career top-10 finishes through 2012

Eldrick "Tiger" Woods

At age two, Tiger Woods made a national public television appearance putting with Bob Hope on the "Mike Douglas Show". At age five, he appeared on ABC's *That's Incredible*. Fifteen years later (1996), at age 20, Tiger Woods joined the PGA Tour and claimed his first PGA Tour win—the Las Vegas Invitational. The following year, Tiger Woods won his first major, the 1997 Masters Tournament; thus, Woods became the first person of African American ancestry to win a Masters Tournament.

From 1996 through November 2015, Woods claimed 79 official PGA Tour wins and 14 professional major golf events. Woods ranked second highest of any player for career PGA Tour and major golf championship wins; Sam Snead had 82 PGA Tour career wins and Jack Nicklaus had 18 career major championships.

Eldrick Tont Woods was born in Cypress, California on December 30, 1975 (Coincidentally, the same year Lee Elder became the first African American to play in a Masters Tournament.) Eldrick's mother, Kultida Woods, is a native of Thailand, and his father Earl Woods was a retired U.S. Army lieutenant colonel. Earl Woods died in May 2006.

Eldrick was nicknamed "Tiger" by his father, who also had given the same nickname to a friend named Vuong

Dang Phong. While serving in the Vietnam War, United States Army soldier Earl Woods met Colonel Dang Phong, a Vietnamese Army soldier.

Tiger attended elementary through high school in Orange County, California; he graduated from Western High School in Anaheim, California. Before turning professional and joining the PGA Tour, he attended Stanford University through a full golf scholarship.

On April 13, 1997, at age 21 years-three months and 14 days, Tiger Woods became the youngest Masters Tournament champion and the first major championship winner of African or Asian heritage. Through 2015, Woods has claimed four Masters Tournament victories—1997, 2001, 2002, and 2005. Due to back surgery, Woods did not compete in the 2014 Masters Tournament.

On June 15, 1997, in his 42nd week as a professional at age 21 years-24 weeks, Woods became the youngest "number one" golfer. Beginning in 1998, Woods held the official world number one player position for 264 consecutive weeks. In September 2004, Woods lost the official world number one ranking to Vijay Singh. In June of the following year (2005), Woods regained number one world ranking.

Through 2013, Woods ranked as the year-end world number one golfer in 1998, 1999, 2000, 2001, 2002, 2003, 2005, 2006, 2007, 2008, 2009, and 2013; and Woods received the Mark H. McCormack Award from 1998 to 2010, and in 2013. (The Mark H. McCormack Award is presented annually to the golfer who has the most weeks ranked as number one during the calendar year.)

In 2001, Woods became the first player to hold all four professional major titles at once—2000 U.S. Open champion, 2000 British Open champion, 2000 PGA Championship winner, and the 2001 Masters Tournament champion.

In 2006 at age 30 Woods captured his 10th major win, the 2006 British Open; thus, Woods became the youngest player to win 10 major golf events. In 2007, Woods was champion of the inaugural FedExCup. He captured the FedExCup title again in 2009.

At the U.S. Open Championship in 2008, Woods won his 14th professional major under remarkable circumstances—he played with an injured left knee. His golf club sometimes became a walking cane to help keep weight off his left knee, and he often grimaced after hitting shots. A few days after the event, Woods announced that he required constructive knee surgery and would miss the remainder of the season.

After an eight-month layoff, Woods returned to the PGA Tour in February 2009. The following month at the Arnold Palmer Invitational he posted his first 2009 win. Making a 15 foot birdie on the 18th hole, Woods won by one stroke.

In 2009, Woods was inducted into Stanford University's Athletic Hall of Fame, and the *Associated Press* named him Athlete of the Decade. *Sports Illustrated* named Woods Sportsman of the Year in 1996 and 2000. In July 2013, Woods received the ESPY Best Male Golfer Award.

Woods has received the same awards multiple times. As of December 2014, he was named the *Associated Press* Male Athlete of the Year (1997, 1999, 2000, and 2006); Player of the Year by the PGA Tour and The PGA of America (1997, 1999–2003, 2005–2007, 2009, and 2013); Golf Writers Association of America's Player of the Year (1997, 1999–2003, 2005–2007, and 2009). He received the Vardon Trophy (1999–2003, 2005, 2007, 2009, and 2013), and ESPY Best Male Athlete Award (1997, 1999, 2000, 2001, and 2008).

In 1998, Woods became the seventh athlete to be selected spokesperson for the *Wheaties* brand. As of 2014, Woods has 14 *Wheaties* box depictions; Michael Jordan is the only athlete who has more than 14 depictions on a *Wheaties* box. Jordan has 18 depictions.

More Tiger Woods Highlights
(Portions of this chronological, courtesy Tiger Woods Foundation)
1978–1989
• Shot 48 for nine holes at Navy Golf Club in Cypress, California (age 3)
• Appeared on the *Today Show* and *Good Morning America* (age 6)

• Made first hole-in-one (age 6)
• Won Optimist International Junior World (ages 8, 9, 12, and 13)
• Had a zero handicap—scratch golfer (age 13)
1990
• Won Insurance Youth Golf Classic National (age 14, youngest ever to win)
• Southern California Player of the Year
1991
• Won U.S. Junior Amateur Championship (age 15, youngest ever to win)
• Won Southern California Junior Championship
• Won PING/Phoenix Junior (AJGA)
• Won Los Angeles City Junior Championship
• AJGA Player of the Year
• *Golf Digest* Player of the Year
• Southern California Player of the Year
1992
• Won Ping Phoenix Junior (AJGA)
• Won U.S. Junior Amateur Championship (only golfer to win twice)
• *Golf Digest* Player of the Year
1993
• Played, as an amateur, in the following PGA Tour events: Nissan Los Angeles Open, Honda Classic, and GTE Byron Nelson Classic
• Won U.S. Junior Amateur Championship (third time)
• *Golf World* Player of the Year
1994
• Won U.S. Amateur Championship (youngest to win; largest come-back)
• Won Pacific Northwest Amateur Championship
• Entered Stanford University on a full scholarship
• Won William Tucker Invitational (first collegiate event)
1995
• Tied for 41st at the Masters Tournament (first professional major); only amateur to make the cut
• Won U.S. Amateur Championship

1996
- Won U.S. Amateur
- Won Disney/Oldsmobile Classic
- Won Las Vegas Invitational
- PGA Tour Rookie of the Year

1997
- Won the Masters Tournament (first professional major championship victory); set Masters Tournament 72-hole record with a total of 270, a 12-stroke victory margin, and also largest 54-hole lead (nine strokes); youngest 36-hole and 54-hole Masters Tournament leader
- Won Mercedes Championship
- Won Asian Honda Classic (Thailand)
- Won GTE Byron Nelson Classic
- Won Motorola Western Open
- Qualified for the United States Ryder Cup Team
- 42nd week as a professional, became the youngest professional to achieve a number one world ranking

1998
- World's top ranked No. 1 player
- Won BellSouth Classic
- Won PGA Grand Slam
- Qualified for United States Presidents Cup Team

1999
- World's top ranked No. 1 player
- Won Buick Invitational
- Won Memorial Tournament
- Won Motorola Western Open
- Won PGA Championship
- Won WGC-NEC Invitational
- Won National Car Rental Golf Classic/Disney
- Won THE TOUR Championship
- Won WGC-American Express Championship

2000
- World's top ranked No. 1 player
- Won Mercedes Championship
- Won AT&T Pebble Beach National Pro–Am
- Won Bay Hill Invitational

- Won Memorial Tournament
- Won U.S. Open Championship
- Won British Open Championship
- Won PGA Championship
- Won WGC-NEC Invitational
- Won Bell Canadian Open
- Won PGA Grand Slam of Golf
- Received Byron Nelson Award and Vardon Trophy

2001
- World's top ranked No. 1 player
- Won Bay Hill Invitational
- Won The PLAYERS Championship
- Won Masters Tournament
- Won Memorial Tournament
- Won WGC-NEC Invitational
- Won PGA Grand Slam of Golf
- Recipient of the Epochs of Courage Award (*Epochs of Courage: African Americans in Golf Traveling Exhibition*)

2002
- World's top ranked No. 1 player
- Won Bay Hill Invitational
- Won Masters Tournament
- Won U.S. Open Championship
- Won Buick Open
- Won WGC-American Express Championship
- Won PGA Grand Slam of Golf

2003
- World's top ranked No. 1 player
- Won Buick Invitational
- Won WGC-Accenture Match Play Championship
- Won Bay Hill Invitational
- Won 100th Western Open
- Won WGC-American Express Championship

2004
- Won WGC-Accenture Match Play Championship
- Won Target World Challenge

2005
- World's top ranked No. 1 player

• Won Buick Invitational
• Won Ford Championship at Doral
• Won Masters Tournament
• Won British Open Championship
• Won WGC-NEC Invitational
• Won WGC-American Express Championship
• Won PGA Grand Slam of Golf
• First player to become a six-time Vardon Trophy recipient

2006
• World's top ranked No. 1 player
• Tied for third at the Masters Tournament
• Won Ford Championship at Doral
• Won British Open Championship
• Won Buick Open
• Won WGC-Bridgestone Invitational
• Won Deutsche Bank Championship
• Won Buick Invitational
• Won PGA Championship (12th major win—ranked second behind Jack Nicklaus with 18 career major wins)
• Won WGC-CA Championship
• Won PGA Grand Slam of Golf
• Won Target Championship

2007
• World's top ranked No. 1 player
• Won Buick Invitational
• WGC-CA Championship
• Tied for second at the Masters Tournament
• Won Wachovia Championship
• Won WGC-Bridgestone Invitational
• Won BMW Championship
• Inducted into the California Hall of Fame
• Became tournament host of the AT&T National, a PGA Tour event
• Won PGA Championship
• Won THE TOUR Championship presented by Coca-Cola
• Winner of the first PGA Tour FedExCup
• Won Target World Challenge
• Tied for second at Deutsche Bank Championship

2008
- World's top ranked No. 1 player
- Won Buick Invitational
- Won WGC-Accenture Match Play Championship
- Won Arnold Palmer Invitational presented by MasterCard
- Tied for second at the Masters Tournament
- Won U.S. Open Championship

2009
- World's top ranked number one player
- PGA Tour Player of the Year
- Won Arnold Palmer Invitational presented by MasterCard
- Won Memorial Tournament
- Won BMW Championship
- Won AT&T National
- Won Buick Open
- Won WGC-Bridgestone Invitational
- Winner of the PGA Tour FedExCup
- Won Australian Masters
- Became the third person in Presidents Cup history to win all five matches at a Presidents Cup
- Named *Associated Press* Athlete of the Decade

2010
- Tied for fourth at the Masters Tournament
- Placed fourth at the U.S. Open Championship

2011
- Tied for fourth at the Masters Tournament and placed third at the Emirates Australian Open
- Scored the winning point for the United States at the Presidents Cup
- Won the Chevron World Challenge

2012
- Won Arnold Palmer Invitational presented by MasterCard, Memorial Tournament presented by Nationwide Insurance, and the AT&T National

2013
- Won Farmers Insurance Open, WGC Bridgestone Invitational, and WGC-Cadillac Championship
- Tied for fourth at Masters Tournament

• Tied for second at U.S. Open Championship
• Placed third in the final PGA Tour FedExCup standings
• Won Arnold Palmer Invitational; this win placed Woods number one in Official World Golf Ranking—this was his first number one world golf ranking since October 2010
• Won THE PLAYERS Championship
• Placed second in the final PGA Tour FedExCup standings
• Has 79 PGA Tour career wins; second behind Sam Snead's 82 PGA Tour career wins
• Named Player of the Year (for the 11th time) by the PGA Tour and The PGA of America

2014
• Played in seven PGA Tour events; withdrew in two events; made five cuts with one top 25 finish

2015
• Tied for 10th at the Wyndham Championship
• Named a vice captain for 2016 U.S. Ryder Cup team

Tiger Woods at a press conference in Norfolk, Virginia
Courtesy Joseph Ricks

More African American PGA Tour Members and Champions Tour Members

(Senior PGA Tour renamed Champions Tour in 2003)

Henry Baraben	Played the PGA Tour; became a PGA Member in 1968
Rafe Botts	Joined PGA Tour in 1961
Cliff Brown	Played the PGA Tour from 1964 to 1969
Howard Brown	Joined PGA Tour in 1969
Lee Carter	Joined PGA Tour in 1980
Gordon Chavis	Joined PGA Tour in 1962
Al Green	Joined PGA Tour in 1973
Al Morton	Joined PGA Tour in 1981
Curtis Sifford	Joined PGA Tour in 1969 (Charlie Sifford's nephew)
Nathaniel Starks	Joined PGA Tour in 1973
Adrian Stills	Joined PGA Tour 1986
Bobby Stroble	Joined PGA Tour in 1976; Senior PGA Tour in 1995
Ron Terry	Joined PGA Tour in 1976
Richard I. Thomas	Joined PGA Tour in 1961 (Second African American to receive PGA APT Status)
Chuck Thorpe	Joined PGA Tour in 1972; played the Champions Tour (Jim Thorpe's brother)
Harold Varner III	Earned (in August 2015) PGA Tour card for the PGA Tour's 2016 season
James Walker Jr.	Joined PGA Tour in 1965
Tom Woodard	Joined PGA Tour in 1981 *(More–page 165)*
William Wright	Joined PGA Tour in 1964 *(More–page 92)*

Figure 1. Combined total percentage of African American active members of the PGA Tour, Champions Tour, and LPGA Tour compared to the combined total percentage of PGA Tour, Champions Tour, and LPGA Tour active members who are not African Americans (other). *(Percentages are estimated and based on the 2015 player rosters.)*

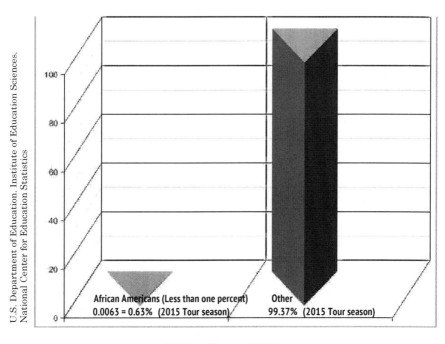

U.S. Department of Education. Institute of Education Sciences, National Center for Education Statistics

LPGA Tour–2015
Approximately 183 active roster members
Two African American LPGA Tour members
Sadena Parks and Cheyenne Woods

PGA Tour and Champions Tour–2015
Approximately 450 combined active roster members
PGA Tour: One person of African American ancestry—Tiger Woods
Champions Tour: One African American—Jim Thorpe

Courtesy Margaret Brown

Why haven't we,
African Americans,
dominated golf
like we dominate
other sports?
My thoughts are....

There are talented African American golfers who are player-ready to join major tours.

There are young African American golfers who have the skills, and yearn to be coached and groomed for future play on a major tour, but....

There are not commensurable opportunities and financial support for the aspiring African American professional tour golfer.

Will African Americans ever dominate a major golf tour?

Will such an extraordinary history making moment ever take place?

Maybe not in my lifetime, but...I believe, it is only a matter of time.

Circa 2012

—*Pete Brown*
First African American to win
a PGA Tour sanctioned event
(Died May 1, 2015)

Earnie Ellison, Managing Partner of
Ellison Consulting Group, consultants
to The PGA of America Golf Industry
Supplier Diversity Initiative. Ellison
served as former Director of Business
and Community Relations of The PGA
Foundation. In 2013, Ellison retired
from The PGA of America.

14

Industry Professionals

Joe Louis Barrow Jr.
In 2000, Joe Barrow became chief executive officer of The First Tee. He has served as president and chief operations officer of Izzo Systems Inc., and executive vice president of World Golf Foundation. Barrow is the son of world heavyweight boxing champion Joe Louis.

Farrell Evans
In 2011, Farrell Evans joined the *ESPN.com* staff as senior golf writer. Prior to working at *ESPN*, Evans was a golf writer for nine years at *Sports Illustrated*. He played collegiate golf at Florida A&M University.

Leon Gilmore
Former executive director of Champions Tour Charles Schwab Cup and western regional division director for The First Tee, Leon Gilmore's experience also includes general manager at Oakland Golf and Associate Director, Outreach for The First Tee. He is a Hampton University alumnus.

Calvin Peete Jr.
In 2010, Peete acquired the position of National Sales Manager for STX Golf. Calvin Peete Jr. is the son of legendary tour player Calvin Peete Sr.

Golf Channel
Anthony Anderson (actor), host for *Golf in America* (premiered in 2009); **Damon Hack**, co-host for *Morning Drive*, and contributing writer for GolfChannel.com (joined staff in 2012); **Iain Page**, reporter and host for *Golf Central* (from about 2004 to 2010); **Ahmad Rashad** (former NFL player), host for *Morning Drive* (2013).

Golf Channel (continued)
Brandi Seymour, production assistant, commentator, and features reporter (from about 2002 to 2009); **Scott Walker**, anchor/reporter for *Golf Central* (joined staff in 2008).

LPGA Headquarters
Ashleigh Anderson, Manager of Programs and Events–The LPGA Foundation and LPGA/USGA Girls Golf Club
Zandria Conyers, Senior Director of Legal Affairs
Brooke Hollins, 2009 Solheim Cup Tournament Coordinator
Shameeka Quallo, Associate Counsel

PGA Tour and Champions Tour
Keith Newton, Champions Tour Director of Tournament Operations; **Aaron Spearman**, PGA Tour Manager ShotLink Producers; **Don Wallace,** PGA Tour Director of Operations of ShotLink

The PGA of America
Daryl Batey, Player Development Regional Manager
Earnie Ellison, Director of Finance for Tournament Operations (1997 to 1999); Director of Business and Community Relations of The PGA Foundation (2000 to 2013); **Wendell Haskins**, Director of Sports and Entertainment Relations; **Julius Mason**, Senior Director of Communications and Media Relations

United States Golf Association (USGA)
Erin Alexander, U.S. Open Ticket Marketing Manager
Michael Herndon, USGA Rules Official
Michael Phillips, GHIN Technical Support Liaison
Carter Rich, Manager, Equipment Standards
Ellen Thomas, Assistant Manager U.S. Open Admissions

15

Golf Professionals

Selected notable men and women golf professionals including United States Golf Teachers Federation Members

Levy Adger

A self-taught golfer, Lee Adger has played and instructed golf for more than 40 years. He served as head golf professional and teaching instructor at Jeremy's Golf Center and Academy (North Ellis County, Texas). In 2010, he joined Country View Country Club (Lancaster, Texas) staff as Director of Golf Instruction. Adger is also an author. (*Levy Adger's publications–pages 202, 205*)

Peter Andraes

In 1990, Peter Andraes conducted a PGA Teaching Summit at Ferris State University; thus, he was recognized as one of the first African Americans to conduct a PGA Teaching Summit. He has served as director of golf at Chiang Mai Lamphun Golf Club in Northern Thailand. A former Asian Senior Tour member, Andraes joined the Asian Senior Tour in 2005. He is internationally known for teaching Golf Qi-Gong (a fusion of yoga, meditation, golf, and martial arts).

Burl Bowens Jr.

For more than 20 years, Bowens was head golf coach at Hampton University; he started the men's golf team in 1984 and women's golf team in 1997. He retired in 2010. Bowens was a charter member of Old Dominion Golf Club. He held a bachelor's and master's degree from Hampton University. Burl Bowens was a United States Army veteran.

Carlos Brown

In 2010 and 2012, *Golf Digest* named Carlos Brown one of the "Top 40 Best Young Teachers under 40 in America". Brown is also noted for teaching golf to the disabled.

John Coleman
In 1997, he received his USGTF certification. In 2000, John Coleman became an instructor for The First Tee of Washington, D.C. Coleman served in the U.S. Army and U.S. Air Force. While stationed in Germany and Vietnam, he taught golf to enlisted personnel and their families.

Richard "Dick" Forest
A well-known teaching professional in the greater Philadelphia, Pennsylvania area, Forest gave lessons at Brownies Driving Range, and he was an assistant golf professional at Freeway Golf Course.

Forest encouraged his students with intriguing phrases such as "if you stick with me, I'll put you on TV"; and for a good wedge shot Forest would often say, "that ball landed like a butterfly with sore feet". (*Tee Off Newsletter*, August 2004.)

In spite of having an arm amputated due to a hunting injury, Dick Forest became an accomplished golfer.

Charles French
A USGTF member, Charles French began teaching golf in the 1990s. His roster of former students includes United States Vice President Joe Biden, and several Congressional members. In the Washington, D.C. metropolitan area, French held golf professional positions for Capital City Golf School at East Potomac Park Golf Course and The First Tee of Washington, D.C.

James "Jimmy" Garvin
A USGTF member, Jimmy Garvin earned his certification in 2000. Garvin's former positions include general manager of Langston Golf Course and president of Golf Course Specialists (concessionaire for National Park golf facilities in the District of Columbia).

Jamila Johnson

The first woman to coach a men's golf team at the University of Maryland Eastern Shore, Jamila Johnson served as men's golf coach from 2009 to 2012. She was also hired, in 2009, as Academic Coordinator for the UMES PGA/PGM™ (Professional Golf Management) Program. Johnson is a graduate of Jackson State University.

Eddie Payton

Head golf coach at Jackson State University for more than 25 years, Eddie Payton has received eight National Minority Coach of the Year Awards and 28 SWAC Coach of the Year Awards.

Under Payton's tutelage as of June 2015, the men's team has won 13 National Minority College Golf Championships and 23 SWAC Championships; and the women's team has won 14 SWAC Championships. A Jackson State University alumnus, Payton graduated in 1973. He is a former NFL player. *(More about Jackson State University page, 176)*

Sam Puryear

For more than a decade, Sam Puryear has coached collegiate golf. In July 2011, Puryear became director of golf operations at Queens University of Charlotte (North Carolina). From 2007 to 2011, he served as head men's golf coach at Michigan State University; that position made Puryear the first African American head golf coach in Division I BCS Conference. In 2008, Michigan State University won the Big Ten Conference title and Puryear received the Big Ten Coach of the Year Award.

Prior to joining Michigan State University staff, he was full-time assistant men's golf coach at Stanford University. He has also served as director of East Lake Junior Golf Academy (Atlanta, Georgia).

A 1992 graduate of Tennessee State University, Puryear has a bachelor's degree in speech and theater.

Julius Richardson
In 2000, Richardson was named USGTF Teaching Professional of the 20th century. That same year, Richardson became the first African American to be listed among the 100 top teachers in *Golf Magazine*. He is author of *Better Golf*. Julius Richardson died in September 2007. (More about *Better Golf*, page 201)

Guster "Gusto" Robinson
In 2000, Guster Robinson became general manager at Maggie Hathaway Golf Course. Active in the African American golf community, he served as Western States Golf Association's eighth president from 1987 to 1993, and 10th president from 1999 to 2002. In 2012, Robinson was elected vice president of WSGA's southern California section.

Conan Sanders
Former head golf professional and director of golf at Augusta Municipal Golf Course, Sanders has also served as head golf professional at The First Tee of Augusta. A golf consultant, Sanders has provided services to Nike, and the Boys and Girls Club of Augusta, Georgia. Conan Sanders is a United States Army veteran.

Raymond "Ray" Savoy
Founder and director of Langston Junior Boys and Girls Golf Club (Washington, D.C.), Ray Savoy has worked with junior golf programs for more than 15 years. He is a certified master USGTF instructor. Savoy has conducted *Hook-A-Kid on Golf* workshops for United States Air Force dependents in the United States and Aviano, Italy.

Savoy's career also includes 30 years of service with the Washington, D.C. Department of Parks and Recreation, and playing professional sports with the Pittsburgh Pirates and Baltimore Broncos.

Vernon Stewart

Stewart was the first golf professional at Nocho Park Golf Course (Greensboro, North Carolina). A 1959 graduate of North Carolina State A&T University, Vernon Stewart earned a degree in sociology.

Russell Taylor

Taylor served as head golf coach of Brebeuf Jesuit Preparatory School boy's team, head golf professional at Douglass Golf Course, and Director of Junior Golf Operations for Indy Parks and Recreation Program (Indianapolis, Indiana). From 1987 to 1991, Taylor worked for Pebble Beach Company; he was one of the first African Americans hired by Pebble Beach Company. Russell Taylor, at age 54, died in June 2007.

Andia Winslow

In 2012, Andia Winslow became teaching professional for The Golf Club at Chelsea Piers (New York City). In April 2006 with a sponsor's exemption, Winslow entered the LPGA Ginn Clubs and Resorts Open; thus, she became the fourth African American to play in a LPGA Tour event. She shot a 166 and missed the cut by 18 strokes. A 2004 Yale University graduate, Winslow was a member of Yale University women's golf team.

More notable African American golf professionals:

Carlton Bolden III, Craig Bowen, Paris Brown, Ralph Dawkins Sr., Charles Foster, Zeke Hartsfield, Yvette Hemphill, Almay Fay Horn, John Linton, Clyde Martin, Catana Starks, and Timothy Thomas.

Tee Box

Maggie Hathaway worked for more than a decade as golf instructor and director at Jack Thompson Golf Course (Los Angeles, California). In 1997, Jack Thompson Golf Course was renamed Maggie Hathaway Golf Course.

An advocate for golf course desegregation, Hathaway often described herself as a militant—working to open doors for others. In the 1950s, she applied for membership at Western Avenue Women's Golf Club (Los Angeles). It took about eight years for her member application to be accepted. Thirty days after becoming a member, Hathaway resigned. "Thank you for accepting me, but I have other countries to conquer."

In 1960, she petitioned Los Angeles County to hire black starters at the county's golf courses; blacks were hired. In 1964, she led a group to picket segregated Fox Hills Country Club; blacks were admitted as members.

Hathaway was also a columnist for the *Los Angeles Sentinel*, a weekly African American newspaper. Her popular column included topics from protesting segregated golf facilities to praising black golfers. Hathaway was the only African American granted a media pass to the 1975 Masters Tournament—the history making moment when Lee Elder became the first African American to compete in a Masters Tournament.

A recipient of many awards, including the distinguished Silver Award at the NAACP 25th Anniversary (1994), Hathaway also helped to honor others. She spearheaded the organization of the NAACP Beverly Hills/Hollywood chapter, and cofounded with entertainer Sammy Davis Jr., the NAACP Image Awards—honoring people of color for outstanding achievements in social justice and the arts. Hathaway was also a talented singer and actress. She often worked as a double for celebrity Lena Horne. Maggie Hathaway died in September 2001.

16

LPGA Teaching & Club Professionals

Wendy Boyd

In 2001, Wendy Boyd turned professional; in that same year she entered the LPGA T&CP program. Five years later in March 2006, Boyd earned LPGA T&CP Class A Member status. As an amateur, Boyd won two Chicago Women's Amateur Championships.

Wendy Boyd

She earned a degree in finance from Loyola University and a degree in accounting from the University of South Florida.

Wendy Boyd died, at age 57, in February 2009.

Oneda Castillo

In 1998, she entered the LPGA T&CP program, and in 2003 Castillo received LPGA Class A Member status. In 2012, Oneda Castillo was named LPGA Southeast Section Teacher of the Year. In 2009, she was selected to the LPGA Golf Clinics for Women instructor's team, an eight-person team that conducted premier celebrity clinics throughout the United States. Castillo became an LPGA national evaluator in 2006, and in 2013 she began serving as a LPGA Global Education Instructor.

Courtesy Oneda Castillo

Oneda Castillo

Castillo serves as director of golf for the Women In Golf Foundation. She owns and operates ONEDAGOLF Systems.

Gladys M. Lee

She entered the LPGA T&CP certification program in 2007, and in June 2012, Gladys Lee received Class A status. She is founder and CEO of Roaring Lambs International Junior Golf Academy based in Dallas/Fort Worth, Texas.

Courtesy Gladys M. Lee

Gladys M. Lee

Lee served as head women's golf coach at Estrella Mountain Community College (Avondale, Arizona), and head boy's and girl's golf coach at Estrella Foothills High School (Goodyear, Arizona). Prior to entering the golf industry, she was production coordinator for Dick Clark Productions, American Bandstand. Lee has received numerous community awards including the Renaissance Cultural Center of Fort Worth Texas "Living Legend Award".

Phyllis Meekins

In 1981, she became a LPGA T&CP Class A Member, and in 2001, Meekins received Life Member status. In 1973, she established the Phyllis G. Meekins Golf Clinic Inc.—a junior golf program based in the Philadelphia, Pennsylvania metropolitan area. She also held clinics at Freeway Golf Course.

Meekins died in February 2005. Her daughter Denise McBride established, in her mother's honor, The Phyllis G. Meekins Scholarship—a need-base scholarship awarded annually to a minority female high school graduating senior.

Carrie Russell

The first African American LPGA Class A Member, Carrie Russell earned Class A status in 1974. Two years later (1976), Russell became the first president of the LPGA

T&CP Northeast Section; she served from 1976 to 1978. Russell was also the first golf coach at Delaware State University; she coached men's golf from 1972 to 1980.

Russell earned a bachelor's degree from Delaware State University, a master's degree from West Chester State University, and LPGA Master Life Professional member status (the highest honor for LPGA T&CP Membership).

In August 2012, Carrie Russell died at age 83.

Jamie Taylor
In 2013, Jamie Taylor received LPGA Class A Member status. Taylor has served as head LPGA Golf Professional at Seneca Golf Course (Broadview Heights, Ohio) and golf professional at Shawnee Hills Golf Course (Bedford, Ohio). She is a 2007 Gannon University alumna.

♦ ♦ ♦

African American LPGA Teaching & Club Professionals
Roster through 2014. List may not be complete.
"A"-Class A   "H"-Honorary   "D"-Deceased

Debbie Adams	Angelique Johnson
Robin Aikens	Gladys Lee (A)
Ashleigh Anderson	Phyllis Meekins (A/D)
Toby Bolton	Paula Pearson-Tucker
Wendy Boyd (A/D)	Renee Powell (H)
Oneda Castillo (A)	Judith Rhodes
Maulana Dotch	Carrie Russell (A/D)
Paula Edmondson (D)	Jamie Taylor (A)

17
PGA Members

Bill Bishop
Head golf professional emeritus at Freeway Golf Course in Sicklerville, New Jersey, Bill Bishop was hired in 1967 as an assistant golf professional at Freeway Golf Course, and the following year he became head golf professional. Bishop received his PGA Class A Member status in 1973.

He turned professional in 1974, and that same year he represented Gulf Oil Company at the Nigerian Open. He has won 84 amateur events and more than 90 professional wins.

A native of Americus, Georgia, Bill Bishop was born in 1926. When he was about twelve years old he started caddying at Americus Country Club, where his grandfather was caddie master. In the 1940s, Bishop's family moved to Philadelphia, Pennsylvania. After graduating from Ben Franklin High School, he served in the U.S. Army from 1945 to 1947.

In 2013, the 42nd Bill Bishop Benefit Golf Classic was held. Bill Bishop Benefit Golf Classic supports the Bill Bishop Junior Golf Foundation, which has served more than 5,000 girls and boys.

Dewey Brown Sr.
He was born September 21, 1898. Three decades later, in September 1928, Dewey Brown Sr. was elected into The PGA of America; and six years later (1934), the same year that the Caucasian-only clause was added to The PGA of America Bylaws, Brown's PGA Member status was withdrawn.

Because of Brown's fair-skin complexion, he could have been mistaken for being Caucasian. Reports indicated that Brown received his PGA Member status because his African American heritage was unknown to The PGA of America.

In September 1965, more than three decades after Brown's PGA membership was withdrawn and three years after the PGA Caucasian-only clause was eliminated from

The PGA of America Bylaws, Dewey Brown Sr. was reinstated as a PGA Member.

Brown started caddying when he was nine years old, and earned 25 cents for 18 holes. At 17, he began pursuing a career in golf. He worked at golf facilities in the New Jersey area including Baltusrol Golf Club and Morris County Golf Club. Brown cut fairways at Madison Golf Club. The crew had one horse that pulled a fairway cutter. The horse wore leather boots to prevent damaging the turf. Cutting the fairways involved sitting on a horse for 8 to 9 hours per day.

Brown also worked as an apprentice at Shawnee Inn and Country Club (Shawnee on Delaware, Pennsylvania) from 1917 to 1918, and from 1925 to 1936. From these experiences and more, Brown crafted his talents and became an accomplished golf club maker and professional golfer.

In 1958, Brown joined Golf Course Superintendents Association of America; thus, Dewey Brown Sr. became the association's first African American member. He was a GCSAA member from 1958 to 1973.

In 1947, Brown purchased Cedar River House and Golf Club; he served as club professional at his nine-hole facility in Indian Lake, New York. In 1972, Brown turned over proprietorship to his son Dewey Jr., who sold the Cedar River House and Golf Club property about four years later.

Dewey Brown had three sons, Roland, Dewey Jr., and Edward. His firstborn Roland later became Major Roland Brown Sr., a Tuskegee Airmen during World War II.

Dewey Brown Sr. selected his grave plot to be in a cemetery adjacent to Cedar River Golf Course. He died December 22, 1973.

Robert Clark Sr.
The first African American PGA Professional in the state of Oregon, Clark entered the PGA program in 1993 and remarkably completed the program in 20 months. In November 1995, Robert Clark Sr. received PGA Class A Member status. He played professional golf for two years.

For his achievements and dedication to the game, Clark has received numerous awards including the Oregon Chapter PGA Junior Golf Leader Award (2000–2003) and Pacific Northwest Section 2005 Junior Leader of the Year Award.

In 2011, Clark was hired as assistant golf coach at Alabama State University. He is a Central State University alumnus.

Ted Countee

He became a PGA Class A Member in 1998. Ted Countee has served as assistant professional at LPGA International, assistant professional and teaching professional at Andrews Air Force Base Golf Course, and head professional for The First Tee of Washington, D.C. and The First Tee of Prince George's County (Maryland). In 2007, Countee was a recipient of the PGA President's Council on Growing the Game national award.

James "Jimmy" DeVoe

He was a professional golfer, instructor, entrepreneur, and *TEE-CUP* columnist. James DeVoe was the first African American to receive PGA Member status after the elimination of the PGA Caucasian-only clause.

In 1962 James DeVoe, at age 74, became a PGA Member; thus, DeVoe was the oldest person elected to The PGA of America. Also recognized as the first African American to compete in the Los Angeles Open, DeVoe earned that title in 1944.

In the 1950s, DeVoe served as assistant golf professional at Fox Hills Country Club (Culver City, California). In the 1930s, entrepreneur DeVoe owned and operated a golf school in Harlem, New York.

James DeVoe died March 19, 1979, less than one week from his 91st birthday (March 24). He was posthumously inducted into The PGA of America Hall of Fame in February 2013.

Maulana Dotch

The first African American female PGA Member in the state of Texas and the second African American female PGA Class A Member, Maulana Dotch became a PGA Member in 2010. Dotch is also a LPGA Teaching and Club Professional.

Dotch turned professional in 2003; that same year, she joined the Futures Golf Tour. A Bethune-Cookman University graduate, Dotch has a degree in accounting.

Harold Dunovant

He is credited for being the first African American graduate of the PGA Business School; Harold Dunovant graduated in 1960.

He received, in 1974, a PGA Class A Member status. He was a member of the Carolinas PGA Section, and in 1999 Dunovant received the Carolinas PGA Section Junior Golf Leader of the Year Award. He was a PGA Life Member.

In 1986, Harold Dunovant founded the National Black Golf Hall of Fame. After Harold's death in 2002, his son Jeff continued his legacy and became the organization's executive director. Harold and Jeff were the first father and son African American PGA Class A Members. (*Read about Harold Dunovant's son, Jeff Dunovant—next.*)

Jeff Dunovant

When he was 12 years old, his father introduced him to golf. About 19 years after his father Harold Dunovant earned his PGA Class A certification—Jeff Dunovant became a PGA Class A Member in 1993.

Dunovant's experience includes program director of the National Minority Golf Foundation, assistant general manager at Stonecreek Golf Club (Phoenix, Arizona), and Assistant Director for The First Tee of East Lake (Atlanta, Georgia). In 2001, Dunovant was named Southwest Section PGA Junior Golf Leader of the Year and he was PGA Georgia Section's 2012 Junior Golf Leader.

Jeff Dunovant earned a Bachelor of Science degree from Fayetteville State University. He was a member of Fayetteville State University's golf team.

Rodney Green
In 2009, he became Director of Golf at Innisbrook©, A Salamander Golf and Spa Resort (Palm Harbor, Florida). This position made Green among the first African American directors of golf at a premium resort. PGA Member Rodney Green has also served as head golf professional and director of instruction at Walt Disney World. In 2009, Green was appointed to the PGA.com Board of Directors.

Quincy Heard
He became a PGA Class A Member in October 2006. Four years later, the Oregon Golf Association named Quincy Heard 2010 Golf Professional of the Year. From 2006 to 2011, he served as executive director of The First Tee of Greater Portland. In 2011, he became CEO at Summit Golf Foundation, a junior golf school in Vancouver, Washington.

During an interview with the author, Heard talked about some of his initial golfing experiences:

> When I was about 13 years old, my uncle and I watched Calvin Peete play golf on television. Eight years later, on my 21st birthday, I played golf for the first time—that was my birthday present to me. I could not believe that something so frustrating could be so much fun. I just had to try it again and again. I became a PGA Member 16 years later.

Steve Hogan
The first African American member of the Nebraska PGA Section, Steve Hogan became a PGA Member in 1997. In 2003, Hogan became the first Nebraska PGA Section

Member to receive a PGA Junior Golf Leader award. He was founder and director of Hogan's Junior Golf Heroes.

An Omaha, Nebraska native, Hogan worked for more than 25 years at the City of Omaha Department of Parks and Recreation. He held several positions including head professional at city-owned Miller Park Golf Course. Steve Hogan died in November 2008. In May 2009, Miller Park Golf Course was renamed Steve Hogan Golf Course.

Renee Powell

She earned her PGA Class A status in 1996; thus, Powell became the first African American female PGA Member. She is head golf professional at Clearview Golf Club, a family-owned facility. *(More about Renee Powell, page 119)*

Tom Woodard

Woodard began working in the Denver metropolitan area golf community in 1987. PGA Member Tom Woodard became general manager and director of golf at Foothills Park and Recreation District in 2006. Other former positions include head professional at Buffalo Run Golf Course, City Park Golf Course, Littleton Golf Club, and South Suburban Golf Course. A supporter of junior golf, Woodard cofounded The First Tee of Denver. In 2013, he was inducted into the Colorado Golf Hall of Fame.

Woodard played the PGA Tour in 1981, 1982, and 1985. He competed in the PGA Championship in 1991 and the U.S. Open Championship in 1989 and 1993.

Woodard was one of the first African Americans to receive the Eisenhower-Evans Caddie Scholarship. In 1978, he graduated with a degree in marketing from the University of Colorado. During Woodard's collegiate year, he served as team captain and he became the first black golfer recognized by the NCAA as an All-American. Woodard was also the first African American to join the University of Colorado's golf team.

African American PGA Members

2014 roster–list may not be complete

Obiekezie Agbasi	Michael Day	Jeffery Jones
David Alexander	Geoffrey Dean	Leonard Jones
Fred Barr	Jim Dent	Michael Jones
Daryl Batey	William Dixon	Richard Jones
Bill Bishop	Maulana Dotch	Arden Kersey
Paul Blockoms	Jeffrey Dunovant	Boris King
Gregory Bond	Robert Lee Elder	Brian King
Chris Brown	John Eubanks	Eric Klevin
Richard Brown III	Horace Evans	Steven Latimer
Melvin Bryant	Justin Ford	William Lewis
Milton Carswell Jr.	Rodney Green	Archer Logan
Eric Clark	Theophilus Gregory	Matthew Marino
Loritz Clark	Charles Hammond	Ira McGraw Jr.
Robert M. Clark Sr.	Burdette Hawkins	Paul McRae
William Clopton Jr.	Christopher Hawkins	Ira Meachem
Earl Cooper	Quincy Heard	John Mercer
Damian A. Cosby	Davie Hendrix	Walter Morgan
Ted Countee	Jessie Hodge Jr.	Kendall Murphy
Ashley Cox	Marlon Holloway	Mark Nance
Kamal Dames	Randall Hunt	David Newsom
Todd Daniel	Franklin Johnson	Ashley Nicks
Alvar David	Michael Johnson	Steven Outlaw
Robert Davis III	Willie Johnson	Nevin Phillips

African American PGA Members
2014 roster (continued)

Andre Pillow	Keith Robertson	Anthony Stepney
Henry Pointer	Timothy Sanders	Willie Toney Jr.
Kenneth Pope	Henry Sandles	James Vie-Carpenter
Orlando Pope	Carl Seldon	Lanier Waters
Renee Powell	Willie Shankle	Kenneth Weaver
Robert Powell	Kenneth Sims	Don Wilburn
Lawrence Price	Otis Smith	Matthew Williams
Howard Pruitt	Todd Smith	Jon Wilson
Henry Ravenell Jr.	Willie Smith	Tom Woodard
William Reid	Henry Spivey	Wyatt Worthington II
Eltoria Renwick	Burley Stamps Jr.	
Malcolm Rhodes	Gregory Stephens	

♦ ♦ ♦

Posthumous PGA Membership
(granted in 2009)
Theodore "Ted" Rhodes
John Shippen Jr.
William "Bill" Spiller

Posthumous PGA Honorary Membership
(granted in 2009)
Joseph Louis Barrow Sr.
(better known as Joe Louis, world heavyweight boxing champion)

PGA Member Kenneth Sims with his trophy awards. Sims served, from 2004 to 2006, as president of the West Central Chapter of the North Florida Section. Courtesy Kenneth Sims

Figure 2. Total combine African American membership of The PGA of America and LPGA Teaching & Club Professionals is less than one percent of the total combined membership of The PGA of America and LPGA T&CP. The numbers are shown graphically below.

U.S. Department of Education. Institute of Education Sciences, National Center for Education Statistics

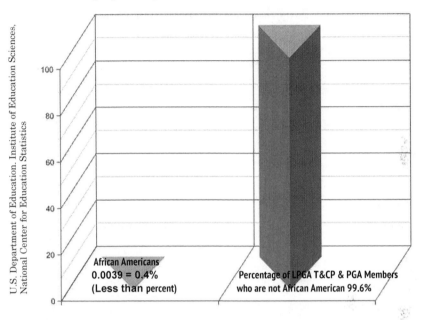

(*Estimated figures based on data from the last quarter of 2014.*) The PGA of America has approximately 27,000 PGA instructors. Among that 27,000, there are approximately 101 African American PGA Class A Members.

The LPGA Teaching & Club Professional division has approximately 1,600 members, which includes approximately 12 African Americans. Three of the 12 African American LPGA T&CP Members are Class A Members.

I got my start by giving myself a start.

Madam C. J. Walker

Chapter V
Black Golf Directory

Preview

Courtesy Dr. William R. Harvey

Golf is not just a game. The benefits
from playing golf are social, athletic,
and competitive experiences. Bonds
are developed on the golf course. A
game that was once not affordable for
many minorities has now become one
of many social vehicles for economical
status for minorities.
    —Dr. William R. Harvey, President
                    Hampton University

Black Golf Directory

Accomplishments have no color.
—Leontyne Price

Chapter five is designed to be an informative guide to finding data in the following categories: black colleges and universities that have golf teams or golf programs; African American-owned/co-owned golf facilities and golf industry businesses; inventors and manufacturers; publications and media that are owned, published, or authored by African Americans; organizations; and events.

Due to large number of listings in certain categories, only a select group is listed. The omission of any listing is not intentional.

Every effort was made to provide dependable data; however, contact information, function, and other descriptive information are subject to change.

Wilberforce University men's and women's golf program indoor session.
Circa 1934. Credit: Wilberforce University (Wilberforce, Ohio) Archives and Special Collection,
Rembert E. Stokes Learning Resource Center

18

Colleges and Universities

Intercollegiate Events

Wilberforce University vs. Ohio Northern University
In 1937 the first golf competition between an all-white university, and a historically black college and university was held. Ohio Northern University men's team played against HBCU Wilberforce University men's team. Wilberforce University is the oldest private historically black college or university in the United States. Two matches were played and Wilberforce University was victorious in both matches.

On April 13, 2002, the two universities' golf teams met for a rematch. In attendance were the only surviving members of the 1937 teams—The Honorable Joseph Mallone of the Ohio Northern University team and William Powell of the Wilberforce University team. Powell, recognized as the first African American to own, design, build, operate, and manage a golf course, was the event's host. This historical rematch was held at Powell's course, the historical Clearview Golf Club in East Canton, Ohio.

**Southern Intercollegiate Association of Colleges
Tuskegee Institute, Tuskegee, Alabama** *(now Tuskegee University)*
In 1938, the first Historically Black Colleges and Universities Southern Intercollegiate Association of Colleges golf tournament was held at Tuskegee Institute. The event took place at Franklin Road Golf Course, a nine-hole golf course owned by Tuskegee Institute. The participating men's teams were Alabama State College, Florida A&M College, Morehouse College, Morris Brown College, and Tuskegee Institute.

The participating women's teams were: Florida A&M College, Fort Valley State College, Morris Brown College, and Tuskegee Institute.

Alabama State University

As of 2015, Alabama State University women's golf team has won four Southwestern Athletic Conference (SWAC) Women's Championships (2011, 2013, 2014, and 2015); and, the Alabama State University men's golf team has won the SWAC Men's Championship four consecutive times, 2012 to 2015. These historic victories were under the tutelage of head coach Dr. Gary Grandison and assistant coach Robert Clark Sr., PGA.

Jackson State University

The first HBCU to compete in both NCAA women's and men's golf, Jackson State University women's team entered a NCAA regional championship in 2001; and, the men's team qualified, in 1996, to play in a NCAA regional post seasonal event at the University of Michigan.

The men's team was also honored for capturing more collegiate wins in the 1995–1996 season than any other Division I university in the United States. Under the tutelage of head coach Eddie Payton, Jackson State University men's and women's golf teams have collectively captured more than 40 championship titles, as of the 2014–2015 golf season.

Jackson State University men's golf started in 1949; women's golf started during the 1990–1991 school year.

Black Colleges & Universities Golf Teams & Programs

2015–2016 school year. This list may not be complete.
Alabama A&M University–Normal, Alabama
Alabama State University–Montgomery, Alabama
Alcorn State University–Lorman, Mississippi
Benedict College–Columbia, South Carolina
Bennett College–Greensboro, North Carolina
Bethune-Cookman University–Daytona Beach, Florida
Bluefield State College–Bluefield, West Virginia
Delaware State University–Dover, Delaware
Edward Waters College–Jacksonville, Florida
Elizabeth City State University–Elizabeth City, North Carolina

Fayetteville State University–Fayetteville, North Carolina
Florida A&M University–Tallahassee, Florida
Grambling University–Grambling, Louisiana
Hampton University–Hampton, Virginia
Jackson State University–Jackson, Mississippi
Johnson C. Smith University–Charlotte, North Carolina
Kentucky State University–Frankfort, Kentucky
LeMoyne-Owen College–Memphis, Tennessee
Lincoln University of Missouri–Jefferson City, Missouri
Livingstone College–Salisbury, North Carolina
Miles College–Fairfield, Alabama
Mississippi Valley State University–Itta Bena, Mississippi
Morehouse College–Atlanta, Georgia
North Carolina Central University–Durham, North
  Carolina
Paine College–Augusta, Georgia
Prairie View A&M University–Prairie View, Texas
Saint Augustine's University–Raleigh, North Carolina *(also golf
  course owner–see listing, page 186)*
Savannah State University–Savannah, Georgia
South Carolina State University–Orangeburg, South Carolina
Southern University and A&M College–Baton Rouge, Louisiana
Spelman College–Atlanta, Georgia
Talladega College–Talladega, Alabama
Tennessee State University–Nashville, Tennessee
Texas Southern University–Houston, Texas
University of Arkansas at Pine Bluff–Pine Bluff, Arkansas
University of Maryland Eastern Shore–Princess Anne,
  Maryland (first HBCU to offer a PGA/PGM™ Program)
Virginia State University–Petersburg, Virginia
Virginia Union University–Richmond, Virginia
West Virginia State University–Institute, West Virginia
Winston-Salem State University–Winston-Salem, North
  Carolina
Xavier University of Louisiana–New Orleans, Louisiana

I am still of the opinion that if all the active clubs in the east got together and pooled their available funds with those of some of our business men, we could secure a golf course similar to the former Rising Sun, which we once owned and operated. I think it could be well supported by our many interested golfers at large. We should all remember that we must sacrifice to be successful in all our undertaking.

—John L. Singleton
New York City

Gazing and Listening
On The Ball Magazine
Winter Edition, 1962

19

Golf Facilities
Selected list of African American-owned golf facilities that no longer exist or are no longer owned/co-owned by African Americans.

Apex Golf Club
Pomona, New Jersey
Owner: Sarah Spencer Washington
Established in the 1940s; Charter membership–$250
Nine hole facility
Apex Golf Club was named after businesses founded and owned by Sarah Washington. Apex News and Hair Company was one of several businesses that Washington owned. Sarah Spencer, also known as Madam Washington, was one of America's first black millionaires. In a June 29, 1948 *Baltimore AFRO-American Newspaper* article by John Jasper, Sarah Spencer Washington was quoted as saying "I founded the business without any financial aid from anybody". Washington died in 1953. Since her death, Apex Golf Club was sold and renamed twice. The second purchase was in 1970; the course was renamed Pomona Golf and Country Club.

Big Walnut Country Club
Gahanna, Ohio (outskirts of Columbus, Ohio)
Founder: Nimrod Booker Allen
Incorporated 1927; ownership listed as Nimrod Allen and Rocky Fork Outing Club
Private club
Closed in the 1960s

Cedar River House and Golf Club
Indian Lake, New York
Owner: Dewey Brown Sr., first African American PGA Member
Nine-hole facility purchased in 1947
In 1972, Brown gave the property to his son Dewey Jr.; four years later Dewey Jr. sold Cedar River House and Golf Club.

Celebrity Golf Club International

Tucker, Georgia
Owner: Julius Erving (former NBA player known as Dr. J)
Semi-private establishment
Formerly named Heritage Golf Club
Erving became sole owner of Heritage Golf Club in 2008; establishment was renamed Celebrity Golf Club International in November 2008. Erving relinquished ownership in 2010.

Jeremy's Golf Center and Academy

North Ellis County, Texas
Owner: Susan Lee-Hargrave
Nine-hole golf course and practice area
Opened in 2003; closed in 2009
Susan Lee-Hargrave is recognized as the first African American female to own and operate a golf course.

Lake Arbor Golf Club

Mitchellville, Maryland
Owner: Hercules Pitts
Eighteen hole golf course
Purchased in June 2005; relinquished in 2009

Lincoln Golf and Country Club

Jacksonville, Florida
Established in 1926; opened in 1927
Founded by Abraham Lincoln Lewis who was also founding partner of Afro-American Industrial & Benefit Association, the first chartered black insurance company in Florida.

Mapledale Country Club

Stow, Massachusetts
Owner: Robert Hawkins
Established in 1926
Nine-hole golf course, tennis courts, and clubhouse
USCGA tournament host site from 1926 to 1928
Hawkins gave up this venture in 1929.

Marlborough Country Club
Upper Marlboro, Maryland
Owner: Hercules Pitts
Eighteen-hole golf course
Purchased in July 2006; relinquished in 2009

Meadowbrook Country Club and Golf Course
Garner, North Carolina
Founded in 1959
Sold to Saint Augustine's University in 2007; renamed Saint Augustine's University Golf Course and Recreational Complex at Meadowbrook *(See listing–page 186)*

Shady Rest Golf and Country Club
Scotch Plains, New Jersey
Purchased in 1921, Shady Rest Golf and Country Club was the first African American-owned and operated country club in the United States. The facility featured horseback riding, croquette, a tennis court, and a nine-hole golf course. Shady Rest Golf and Country Club was a social hub for celebrities such as Count Basie, Duke Ellington, and Sarah Vaughn. In 1938, the Township of Scotch Plains took ownership of the property through a tax lien foreclosure; however, African Americans were allowed to continue to operate the facility. In 1964, the Township of Scotch Plains took over operations and opened the facility to the public; the property was renamed Scotch Hills Country Club.

Shellbanks Golf Course
Hampton, Virginia
Owner: Hampton Normal and Agricultural Institute *(became Hampton Institute in 1930; attained university status in 1984–renamed Hampton University)*
Eighteen-acre property purchased in the late 1920s
Site development began in 1930
In addition to a golf course, the land was also used for agricultural studies. Only faculty had access to play the golf course. Faculty and students developed, maintained, and

Shellbanks Golf Course (continued)
operated the golf course. Hampton Institute later sold the property to the United States Air Force. Hampton University is recognized as the first HBCU to own, develop, manage, and operate a golf course.

Tuskegee Institute Golf Courses (Tuskegee, Alabama)
Recognized as the first HBCU to own a golf course, a five-hole course was developed in 1923 on property that is now the site of Tuskegee University College of Veterinary Medicine. In 1926 under the guidance of athletic director Cleveland Abbott, the school opened a nine-hole course located on Franklin Road. In 1962, Tuskegee Institute developed another nine-hole golf course at Moton Airfield; that course existed until 1971. Tuskegee Institute attained university status (Tuskegee University) in 1985.

More notable golf facilities that no longer exist or are no longer owned by African Americans.

Booker T. Washington Country Club
Buckingham, Pennsylvania
Owner/Founder: John W. Lewis
Purchased in 1924

Bull Creek Golf and Country Club
Louisburg, North Carolina
Owned/operated by five families: Massenburg, Strickland, Keith, Brown, and Solomon. First nine holes (principal builders–Sam Solomon and Zollie Gill) opened in October 1996; expanded to 18 holes in 1998; closed in 2014.

Lincoln Country Club
Atlanta, Georgia
Founded in 1932; built on unused cemetery property.

Mill Cove Golf Course
Jacksonville, Florida
Owners: T.C. & Ruby Newman
Purchased in 2001
Went into foreclosure 2008

Parkridge Country Club
Corona, California   663 acres
Purchased in 1928 by a group of African American businessmen.

Spring Lake Golf Course
Glen Allen, Virginia
Purchased in 1978 by Thomas Kenney

The New Rogell Golf Course, Detroit, Michigan. First African American-owned golf course in the state of Michigan. Purchased in 2007 by Greater Grace Temple; closed in 2013.

Julius Erving, former NBA basketball player known as Dr. J.
Erving was sole-owner, from 2008 to 2010, of Celebrity Golf Club
International in Tucker, Georgia.

♦ ♦ ♦

The following golf facilities were operating in January 2015.

Al's 4-Par 3 Holes
3606 County Road 36
Tuskegee, Alabama 36083
Owner: Alphonso Moore
Family-owned property since the 1800s
Opened in 2003
Seven-hole, par 3 executive golf course

Clearview Golf Club
8410 Lincoln Highway
East Canton, Ohio 44730
Phone: 330-488-0404
www.clearview-gc.com
Designed and built by William Powell
Family owned and operated
Renee Powell, PGA/LPGA Head Golf Professional
Larry Powell, Golf Course Superintendent
In April 1948, Clearview Golf Club opened for play with nine holes. In 1978, the golf course expanded to 18 holes. Clearview Golf Club became a historical landmark in February 2001. *(More about Clearview Golf Club and William Powell, page 50)*

Freeway Golf Course
1858 Sicklerville Road
Sicklerville, New Jersey 08081
Phone: 856-227-1115
www.freewaygolf1967.com
18 holes   Par 72
First African American owned and operated 18-hole golf course in the United States. In 1966, four businessmen—Bob Salsbury (motel owner), James Blocker (bank vice-president), Al Letson (realtor), and Maxwell Stanford (business owner)—initiated a plan to purchase the golf

course property. Together, with 100 men who each pledged $1000 toward buying the property, a purchase offer of $250,000 was made. Their offer was accepted and in 1967 the property was purchased. In June 1968, Freeway Golf Course opened for play. In 1969, shareholders founded The Greater Philadelphia Golf and Country Club. Later transformed into a culturally diversified group of men and women, The Greater Philadelphia Golf and Country Club continues to hold ownership of Freeway Golf Course, and Freeway Golf Course continues to be managed by African Americans.

Grand Marais Golf Club
5802 Lake Drive
Centreville, Illinois 62203
Phone: 618-398-9999
www.grandmaraisgolf.com
Owner: Bob Bonner
Purchased in October 2008
18-hole golf course

Innisbrook©, A Salamander Golf and Spa Resort
36750 US Highway 19 North
Palm Harbor, Florida 34684
Phone: 727-942-2000
www.innisbrookgolfresort.com
Owner: Sheila C. Johnson, Founder & CEO, Salamander©
Hotels and Resorts
Purchased in 2007
Johnson is the first African American sole-owner of a golf resort and PGA Tour championship course (Copperhead Golf Course), one of four championship golf courses at Innisbrook© Resort. A noted entrepreneur, Johnson cofounded BET (Black Entertainment Television), and she is the first African American woman to hold ownership or partnership in three professional sports franchises— WNBA's Washington Mystics, NBA's Washington Wizards, and NHL's Washington Capitals.

Saint Augustine's University Golf Course and Recreational Complex at Meadowbrook (formerly named Meadowbrook Country Club and Golf Course)
8025 Country Club Drive
Garner, North Carolina 27529
Phone: 919-516-5010
Owner: Saint Augustine's University (HBCU)
Purchased in 2007
Opened to the public in 2008
Facility features a nine-hole golf course

Wedgewood Golf Center
2131 Mountain Road
Halifax, Virginia 24558
Phone: 434-476-7715
Owner: Clifford Sommerville; opened in 2001
Nine-hole par 3 golf course, miniature golf course, lighted driving range, and banquet facilities. *(More on page 53)*

Woodridge Golf Club
301 Woodridge Drive
Mineral Wells, West Virginia 26150
Phone: 304-489-1800
www.woodridgegolfclub.com
Owner: Bill Neal (acquired sole-ownership in 2013)
Features an 18-hole golf course and tiered driving range

20

Businesses

A-Game Global Sports
Ed Coleman, Founder and President
Las Vegas, Nevada
www.agameglobal.com
Golf apparel and golf shoes; features "A-Game Brisole" footwear

Advanced Lesson Academy of Golf
Charles Lightfoot, Founder and Director
Brooklyn, New York
www.advancedgolfacademy.com
Private and group training
Business Interactive™ program; parent and junior program; autistic junior program

BF Golf Tournament Services Inc.
Bill Fullard, Founder and President
Hempstead, New York
www.bfgolfservices.com
Tournament, event management, and consulting services

Bogey Boyz®
Al Quarles, Cofounder and Co-President
Philadelphia, Pennsylvania
www.BogeyBoyz.com
Clothing line, Bogey Kidz Mentoring Program®, Investment Group, Travel Agency

CSI Golf
Craig Stingley, Founder
Craig Stingley and Derrick Stingley, Proprietors
West Allis, Wisconsin
www.csigolf.com
Product development and manufacturing
CSI Golf is a division of CS Innovation LLC
(Stingley's inventions–pages 193, 194)

Golf Quests Inc.
Ty DeLavallade, Founder and President
Orlando, Florida
www.mygolfconcierge.net
Luxury golf travel and event management

New Attitude Sports International
Tony Peters, Co-owner and CEO
Suzanne Peters, Co-owner
Stamford, Connecticut
www.New-Attitude.com
Multi-cultural golf lifestyle wear

Nirvana Golf Technologies
Tyrone Wallace, Chairman/President/CEO
Pullman, Michigan
Custom-designed golf clubs
(Nirvana's patents–page 193)

ONEDAGOLF Systems
Oneda Castillo, Owner and Operator
Fayetteville, Georgia
www.onedagolf.com
Coaching system for all player skill levels; club fitting

Scooter's Sports Enterprises Inc.
Wanda Sheffield, Founder and Proprietor
Miami, Florida
Design and distribution of golf accessories
(Sheffield's inventions–page 194)

Sweet Spot Apparel Inc.
Golf apparel and accessories
Anthony Shareef, Founder and CEO

SydMar Golf and Sports Management Inc.
Marie Dunovant, President
Decatur, Georgia

TGA of Gwinnett County (TGA Junior Golf franchise)
Tenesha Davis, Owner/Chapter Director
Duluth, Georgia
www.playtga.com/gwinnettcounty

The Grass Ceiling Inc.
Rose Harper, Chief Executive Officer
Washington, D.C.
www.thegrassceiling.com
Professional and consulting golf services

Tee Box

John Bailey owned and operated the first African American Mizuno dealership in the United States. Bailey's Golf Shop, located outside Richmond, Virginia, was established in 1998 and closed in 2009.

Robert "Pat" Ball owned and operated a golf school in Chicago Illinois; Ball's school opened in June 1921.

James "Jimmy" DeVoe owned and operated a golf school in Harlem, New York in the 1930s. In the 1950s and 1960s, DeVoe's golf business known as "Harmonization" was based in Los Angeles, California.

Ray Mitchell, in the 1950s, owned and operated the Golf School of Harlem in New York City, New York.

Freddie MacLaughlin established Gotham Promotion Association in 1958. In addition to promoting major golf tournaments, MacLaughlin set up sponsorships for black professional golfers who played in major tournaments.

Weldon and Shirley Coleman, proprietors of Pro Golf at Camp Creek, a golf retail store in East Point, Georgia (outskirts of Atlanta, Georgia). Pro Golf at Camp Creek opened in 2005 and closed in 2008. During years of operation, Pro Golf at Camp Creek was the only African American-owned Pro Golf franchise in the United States.
Pro Golf at Camp Creek Logo: Courtesy Shirley Coleman

Five On The Back Side
by Samuel A. Barnes
Sam Barnes Original Fine Art Golf Prints
Samuel A. Barnes, Artist
Augusta, Georgia

(*Left to right*) Craig Stingley and Derrick Stingley.
Craig Stingley is inventor of The Club Scrub System
and BMR2-Putters™. Brothers Craig and Derrick are
the proprietors of CS Innovation LLC.

21

Inventions

BMR²-Putters™
Craig Stingley, Inventor
West Allis, Wisconsin
www.csigolf.com
P.T.T. (Putting, Tempo, Tuning) Technology, Gradu-Weighted Training Ball System
USGA and The R&A compliant for tournament play under the Rules of Golf.

Cajun Wind Sok
Bobby Brown, Inventor
Shreveport, Louisiana
Determines the wind velocity, intensity, and direction

Device for Altering the Angle-between the shaft and the head of a golf club
Assignee: The Nirvana Group LLC
Pullman, Michigan
U.S. Patent Number: 6,431,993
Award date: August 13, 2002
Used in designing the Swagie Putter by The Nirvana Group

Golf Club Hosel Interface
Assignee: The Nirvana Group LLC
Pullman, Michigan
U.S. Patent Number: 6,270,425
Award date: August 7, 2001
Used in designing the FeraLon System II Woods and Irons by The Nirvana Group

Golf Flag
Bobby Brown, Inventor
Shreveport, Louisiana
U.S. Patent Number: D,266,832
Award date: November 9, 1982
U.S. Patent description for Golf Flag–page 199

Golf-Tee Cigar/Cigarette Holders
Golf-Tee Club/s Holders
Wanda Sheffield, Inventor
Miami, Florida
www.scooterssports.com
Holders' sizes—small, medium, large, and double

Hook-Up and Swing™
Bobby Brown, Inventor
Shreveport, Louisiana
Elastic golf swing exercising device

Jiro Putter
Alexander McKinnon, Inventor
Washington, D.C.
U.S. Patent Number: 6,110,057
Award date: August 22, 2000
McKinnon was 78 years old when he received a U.S. Patent
for his Jiro Putter invention.

Putting Training Device
Bobby Brown, Inventor
Shreveport, Louisiana

The Club Cane
Jonathan E. Wilson II, Inventor
United States Patent Number: D600,300 S
Award date: September 15, 2009
www.whole9golf.com
U.S. Patent drawing for The Club Cane—page 198

The Club Scrub System
Craig Stingley, Inventor
www.csigolf.com

The Twister Golf Ball Cleaner
Alfonzo Dowe Sr., Inventor
www.thetwistercleaner.com

Wooden Golf Tee
George Franklin Grant, Inventor
U.S. Patent Number: 638,920
Award date: December 12, 1899
U.S. Patent description for Wooden Golf Tee, pages 196–197
(Read about George Franklin Grant, pages 40–42)

ZipAir Sport Shirt
Jonathan Wilson II (for Whole 9 Golf), Inventor
U.S. Patent Number: US D491,713 S
Award date: June 22, 2004
www.whole9golf.com
Side vented sport shirt with concealed side closure
mechanism

◆ ◆ ◆

*The following is an excerpt from the United States Patent
Office certified copy of George F. Grant of Boston,
Massachusetts. Golf–Tee. Specification forming part of
Letters Patent Number 638,920 December 12, 1899.*

"To all whom it may concern:

Be it known that I, George F. Grant, of Boston, county of Suffolk, State of Massachusetts, have invented an Improvement in Golf-Tees, of which the following description, in connection with the accompanying drawings, is a specification, like letters on the drawings representing like parts.

This invention has for its object the production of a simple, cheap, and effective tee for use in the game of golf, obviating the use of the usual conical mounds of sand or similar material formed by the fingers of the player on which the ball is supported when driving off.

While the tee must firmly, yet lightly, support the ball until hit by the player's club, the tee must be so constructed that it will not in any manner interfere with the swing or "carry through" of the club in making the stroke. These requisites are possessed in full by my invention, and the annoyance and sometimes discomfort attendant upon the formation of a sand tee are obviated thereby.

Figure 1 represents a golf tee embodying one form of my invention shown as inserted in the ground and supporting a bill ready to be struck. Fig. 2 is a side elevation of the base portion of the tee, the head being shown in section; and Fig. 3 is a transverse section on the line xx, Fig. 2.

In accordance with my invention the tee comprises a rigid base portion a and an attached flexible head b, the base being preferably made of wood and tapering to a point at its lower end to be readily inserted in the ground. Near its upper and the base is preferably reduced in diameter, as at a', to leave an annular shoulder a^2, and over the reduced portion is stretched one end of a piece of rubber tubing forming the head b, the tubing being drawn down to the shoulder a^2. I prefer to cement the head to the base around the part a' of the latter, the open upper end of the head presenting an annular seat b', in which the ball B rests as in a cup as shown in Fig. 1.

In practice the base is driven into the ground to substantially the shoulder a^2, the head projecting upward about three-quarters of an inch. When the ball is struck, the head will yield in the direction of travel of the ball, offering no obstruction to its flight, and if the club strikes the head, as will frequently be the case, the yield will not in any way retard or stop the proper swing of the club as it is carried through the stroke.

The tee may be withdrawn after the drive and again used for the next drive, and so on, or the tee may remain permanently in the teeing-ground, as desired or found most convenient.

By the use of the tee, as described the player is sure that his ball is uniformly elevated from the ground at each drive and the uncertainty of a sand tee is overcome, as it is practically impossible to make them of uniform height each time."

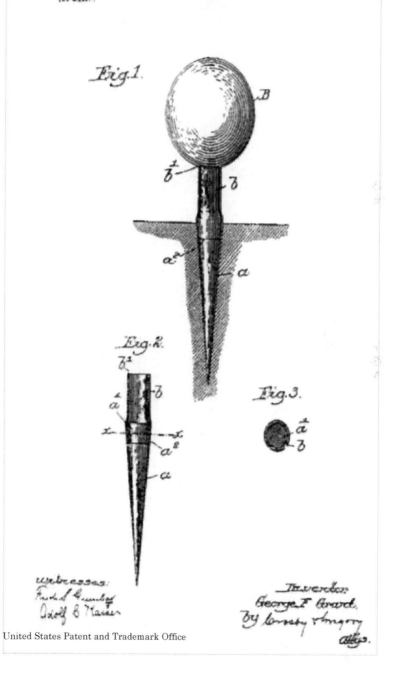

The Club Cane:
Inventor Jonathan Wilson II

US00D600300S

(12) **United States Design Patent**
Wilson, II

(10) **Patent No.:** **US D600,300 S**
(45) **Date of Patent:** ** **Sep. 15, 2009**

(54) **SELF STANDING GOLF CLUB SUPPORT**

(76) Inventor: **Jonathan E. Wilson, II**. 1710 Stefan
Cole La., Apopka, FL (US) 32703

(**) Term: **14 Years**

(21) Appl. No.: **29/294,343**

(22) Filed: **Jan. 8, 2008**

(51) **LOC (9) Cl.** **21-02**
(52) **U.S. Cl.** **D21/796**
(58) **Field of Classification Search** D21/789,
D21/796; 473/282
See application file for complete search history.

(56) **References Cited**

U.S. PATENT DOCUMENTS

D318,090 S * 7/1991 Bahns D21/796
5,149,087 A * 9/1992 Thompson, Jr. 473/286
D360,248 S 7/1995 Wright
D360,451 S 7/1995 Levocz et al.
D400,612 S 11/1998 Rubin
D407,774 S * 4/1999 Weiss D21/796
D458,660 S 6/2002 Stealey

D472,598 S * 4/2003 Lawrence D21/796

* cited by examiner

Primary Examiner—Mitchell I Siegel
(74) *Attorney, Agent, or Firm*—William B. Noll

(57) **CLAIM**

I claim the ornamental design for a self standing golf club support, as shown and described.

DESCRIPTION

FIG. **1** is a front perspective view illustrating the self standing golf club support of this invention;

FIG. **2** is a rear perspective view of the self standing golf club support of FIG. **1**;

FIG. **3** is a partial, enlarged front perspective view of the golf club support bracket shown at a midpoint of FIGS. **1** and **2**;

FIG. **4** is a partial, enlarged rear perspective view of the bracket of FIG. **3**; and,

FIG. **5** is a top view of the bracket of FIGS. **3** and **4**, where the bottom view is a mirror image thereof.

1 Claim, 1 Drawing Sheet

Golf Flag: Inventor Bobby Brown

United States Patent [19]

Brown

[11] Des. 266,832

[45] ** Nov. 9, 1982

[54] GOLF FLAG OR SIMILAR ARTICLE

[76] Inventor: Bobby Brown, 453 Fuller St., Shreveport, La. 71108

[**] Term: 14 Years

[21] Appl. No.: 111,835

[22] Filed: Jan. 14, 1980

[51] Int. Cl. .... D11—05
[52] U.S. Cl. D11/166; D11/170
[58] Field of Search D11/165-170, D11/172-174; 116/173-175

[56] References Cited

U.S. PATENT DOCUMENTS

D. 2,599	3/1867	Rogers	D11/166
2,853,046	9/1958	Meade	D11/166 X
3,016,035	1/1962	Asbury	D11/166 X

Primary Examiner—Louis S. Zarfas

[57] CLAIM

The ornamental design for a golf flag or similar article, substantially as shown and as described.

DESCRIPTION

FIG. 1 is a perspective view of a golf flag or similar article, showing my new design;
FIG. 2 is a sectional view taken along lines 2—2 in FIG. 1;
FIG. 3 is a side elevational view; and
FIG. 4 is a front elevational view thereof.

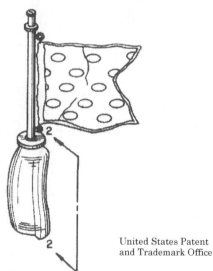

United States Patent and Trademark Office

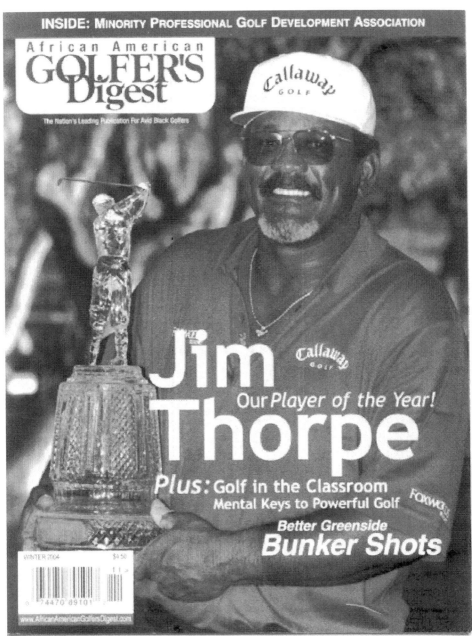

African American Golfer's Digest front cover 2004 issue
Courtesy Debert Cook, Publisher

22

Publications and Media

A Tearful Journey for Freedom: The Life and Time of Maggie Hathaway
Conrad Bullard, Author
ISBN-13: 978-1403311825

African American Golf History Brain Aerobics
Ramona Harriet, Author
ISBN: 978-1463622398

African American Golfer's Digest
Debert Cook, Publisher
www.AfricanAmericanGolfersDigest.com
Nationally distributed print magazine
First edition published March 2003
Subscription based—four issues annually

African American Golfers During the Jim Crow Era
Marvin P. Dawkins and Graham C. Kinloch, Authors
ISBN-10: 0275959406

Anatomy of The Perfect Golf Swing: The Surest Way to Better Golf
Glennon Bazzle, Author
ISBN-13: 978-0966707908

Better Golf: A Skill Building Approach
Julius Richardson, Author
ISBN-13: 978-1886346536

Carl Jackson: Through the Eyes of a Caddy
DVD
Cathy Durant, Director/Executive Producer

Chicago Golf on the Soul Circuit
Aaron Browning, Author
ISBN-13: 978-0615758039

Children's Golf A to Z
Amie J. Greer, Author
ISBN-13: 978-1414032894

Epochs of Courage: African Americans in Golf
Traveling Exhibition (multi-media)
www.AfricanAmericanGolfHistory.com

Forbidden Fairways: African Americans and the Game of Golf
Calvin H. Sinnette, Author
ISBN-13: 978-1574781229

Foundation To Fairways: The Everyman's Guide to Golf Through Fitness and Strategic Performance
Anthony L. Wilkins, Author
ISBN-13: 978-1483504179

From Tee to Green: Seeing God...In the Middle of the Fairway
Marvin R. Wamble, Author
ISBN-13: 978-0595696185

God, You & Golf
Levy Adger, Author

Golf: The Sport of Business
Jandie Smith Turner

Heroines of African American Golf: The Past, the Present, and the Future
M. Mikell Johnson, Author
ISBN-13: 978-1426934193

How I Found My Sweet Spot...and How You Can Find Yours
Robin Aikens, Author
ISBN-13: 978-0976510901

How I Play Golf
By Tiger Woods with the Editors of *Golf Digest*
ISBN-13: 978-0446529310

How to Be Long and Strong
Video
By Jim Dent
www.tourexperience.com

I Come To Play: America's Golf Song
Instrumental and vocal CD
By Selina Johnson

I Hate to Lose: How a little-known handicapped black man beat the best of the best on the PGA Tour. Charlie Owens: His Life and Times
By Charlie Owens and Ed Smith with Robert Bruce Woodcox
ISBN-13: 978-1440106620

Invisible Golfers: African Americans' PGA Tour Quest
J. C. Callaway, Author
ISBN-13: 978-0967604701

Just Let Me Play: The Story of Charlie Sifford The First Black PGA Golfer
By Charlie Sifford with James Gullo
ISBN-13: 978-0945167440
ISBN-10: 094516744X

Let Them Play: The Story of the MGAA
John David, Author
ISBN-13: 978-0977674305

Minority Golf Magazine
Herschel Caldwell and Patricia Caldwell, Founders
Herschel Caldwell, Publisher
First published in 1996

Music, Golf, and Motivation
DVD (Instructional)
By Robin Aikens

Playing In the Dark
John H. Perry, Author
ISBN-13: 978-1448948925

Playing Through: Straight Talk on Hard Work, Big Dreams, and Adventures with Tiger
Earl Woods, Author
ISBN-13: 978-0062702227

Powerful Golf: Lower Your Golf Score By Changing The Way You Think
Audio CD
By Michael J. Russ
ISBN-13: 978-0972023405

Rainbow on the Green
Documentary; an *American Legacy Series* production
Actor Tim Reid created *American Legacy Series*
Byron Hunter and Omar Akil, Producers/Writers
Released March 2008

Skins & Grins: The Plight of the Black American Golfer
Lenwood Robinson Jr., Author
ISBN-13: 978-1886094673

Sports Opportunity and Information Center
(Formerly named Black Golf Information Center)
Charles Dorton, Director
A complimentary service that compiled, printed, and distributed a 12-month schedule of African American golfing events. First publication distributed in 1987; view 1987 schedule–pages 239 to 243; 2010 schedule–pages 245 to 251. Many of the 2010 listed events continue to be held annually.

Start Something: You Can Make a Difference
Earl Woods and Tiger Woods Foundation, Authors
ISBN-13: 978-1416537045

Stories From the Caddyshack
Edward S. Wanambwa, Author
ISBN-13: 978-0977234516

TEE-CUP Magazine
Official publication of Western States Golf Association
First published in 1988

The African American Woman Golfer: Her Legacy
M. Mikell Johnson, Author
ISBN-13: 978-0313349041

The BogeyMan: True Confessions of a Golf Addict
Ilee Coleman, Author
ISBN-13: 9780985361716

The Last Colored Caddy
Documentary Film
Jada Harris, Film Maker
Edward S. Wanambwa, Lead Consultant

The Pendulum Swing: Your Personal Pocket Golf Coach
Levy Lee Adger, Author

The United Golfer
First published in 1936, The United Golfer became the official publication of United Golfers Association in 1938; distribution stopped in the 1940s. The Moss H. Kendrix Organization resurfaced *The United Golfer* in 1959. Kendrix announced: "*The United Golfer* will first appear in the fall of 1959 and will be published subsequently three times a year—spring, summer, and fall." *The United Golfer* is no longer in publication.

Training a Tiger: A Father's Guide to Raising a Winner in Both Golf and Life
Earl Woods, Author; Pete McDaniel, Coauthor
ISBN-13: 978-0061013263

Uneven Fairways
Pete McDaniel and Dan Levinson, Co-writers
Documentary hosted by actor Samuel L. Jackson

Uneven Lies: The Heroic Story of African-Americans in Golf
Pete McDaniel, Author
ISBN-10: 1888531363; ISBN-13: 978-1888531367

Robert "Pete" McDaniel, author and freelance golf writer. McDaniel served as contributing editor and senior writer at *Golf Digest* and *Golf World* magazines. He is a recipient of the Harlem YMCA Black Achiever in Industry Award.

Dr. Calvin Sinnette (center), author of *Forbidden Fairways*, with members of the Knickerbocker Golf Club

Courtesy Patricia E. Williams

Enterprise Ladies Golf Association, *(left to right)* Carolyn Tabor (guest), and members Barbara Collaso, Paulette Savoy, and Patricia E. Williams
Circa 2007

23

Organizations
Selected list of notable active and inactive African American golf organizations.

African-American Golf Foundation
Edward Oden, Founder and Executive Director
Services the Atlanta, Georgia metropolitan area
Founded in 1987
www.aagf.org

African American Golfers Hall of Fame
Malachi Knowles, Founder
Palm Beach Gardens, Florida
Supports Inner City Youth Golfers' Inc.
www.africanamericangolfershalloffame.com
Eleventh celebration and induction ceremony held in May
2015

Alpha Golf Club
Chicago Illinois
Established in 1915
Sponsored what is known as the first black golf tournament

Arlington Divots Golf Club
Arlington, Virginia
Organized in 1948 by Cassell Butler

Black Jewels Ladies Golf Association (BJLGA)
New York, New York
Founded in 2004
Chapters throughout the United States, including Florida,
Washington, D.C., and Chicago, Illinois

Bogey Boyz Golf®
Al Quarles and Lawrence Faison, Co-Presidents
Philadelphia, Pennsylvania
www.bogeyboyz.com
Hosts events including charity golf events and golf retreats

Bunker Club
Pittsburgh, Pennsylvania
Established in 1927

Camp Hart
Dr. Thomas Hart, Founder
Founded in 1947; Washington, D.C.
Junior program included overnight summer camps. Curriculum included golf, swimming, hiking, and other sports; golf was added to the curriculum in 1997.

Capital City Golf Club
Washington, D.C.
Originally named Citizens Golf Club
In 1933, renamed Royal Golf Club

Chicago Women's Golf Club, The
Anna Mae Robinson, Founder and first elected president
Founded in 1937
First women's organization to obtain affiliation to United Golfers Association (1939); and the first African American women's golf club to become a USGA member club (1956).

Citizens Golf Club
Washington, D.C.
Established in 1925
Between 1927 and 1928, Citizens Golf Club was renamed Capital City Golf Club.

Cosmopolitan Golf Club
Los Angeles, California
www.cosmogolfclub.com
Established in 1944; celebrated 70th anniversary in 2014.

Del Val Golf Club
Philadelphia, Pennsylvania
www.delvalgolfclub.org
Established in 1954

Desert Mashie Golf Club Inc.
Phoenix, Arizona
www.desertmashie.org
Organized in 1946
Known as the oldest public golf member club in the state of Arizona, the 67th Annual Desert Mashie Invitational Golf Tournament was held in May 2015. Recognized as one of the first African American golf clubs to become a USGA member club, Desert Mashie Golf Club became a USGA member club in 1950.

Ebony Ladies Golf League
Headquartered in Youngstown, Ohio
www.ebonyladiesgolf.org
Established in 1997
Scholarship program for high school seniors offered through the Ebony Ladies Golf and Youth Foundation.

Enterprise Ladies Golf Association
Mitchellville, Maryland
Patricia E. Williams, Founder
Established in 1999
Home course–Enterprise Golf Course (Mitchellville, Maryland)
Primary objectives: to introduce women to golf, offer competitive amateur golf for women, and provide network opportunities.

Fairview Golf Club
Philadelphia, Pennsylvania
Organized in the late 1920s

Fir State Golf Club
Seattle, Washington
Founded in 1947
Fir State Golf Club was among the first African American golf clubs to become a USGA member club. Fir State Golf Club joined the USGA between 1952 and 1953.

Fore Wood Golf Club
Detroit, Michigan
Gus Barksdale, Contact person
Former member of the Midwest district of United Golfers Association
Offered inner city youth program that focused on staying in school and career choices in golf.

Friends Golf Club Inc.
Camden, South Carolina
In 2004, management of Pickett-Thomas Golf Course was turned over to Friends Golf Club. Due to lack of maintenance, this South Carolina state-owned nine-hole course was in unplayable condition; nevertheless, for several years Friends Golf Club kept the course open for play and held junior golf clinics at the course.

Friends Golf Club member Hampton Wright recalled the early days of Pickett-Thomas Golf Club:

> Before golf courses were integrated in Camden, South Carolina, Pickett-Thomas Golf Course was the only place that we, African Americans, could play. Pickett-Thomas Golf Course was named after Dr. Thomas Pickett, the first African American doctor to practice in Camden. To me, it is a piece of history and should be preserved.

Golden Tee Golf Club
Fort Worth, Texas
Founded in 1982
Hosts the Annual Open Golf Scholarship Tournament; 33rd Annual Open Golf Scholarship Tournament was held in 2015; event benefits a junior golf scholarship fund.

Green's Ladies Golf Club
Lorraine Sawyer, Founder
Founded in 1954, Green's Ladies Golf Club hosts an annual event at Freeway Golf Course, the club's home course; event supports health issues facing African American women.

Gulf City Golfers Association
Mobile, Alabama
www.saag-inc.com/gulfcity
Established in 1960
Gulf City Golfers Association filed, in 1960, a lawsuit seeking access to play Mobile Municipal Park Golf Course in Mobile, Alabama. In 1961, a U.S. District Court ruling was made in favor of Gulf City Golfers Association. (Mobile Municipal Park Golf Course was later renamed Azalea City Golf Club). In 2015, Gulf City Golfers Association celebrated its 55th anniversary. Known for community involvement, this association of men and women has donated more than a quarter million dollars to colleges, students, golf teams, and charities.

Hollywood Golf Institute
Detroit, Michigan
Selina Johnson, Founder and President
Founded in 1983
Hollywood Golf Institute is a national award-winning junior golf program; also emphasizes reading and math.

Inner City Youth Golfers Inc.
Malachi Knowles, Founder
Palm Beach Gardens, Florida
www.icyg.org

Knickerbocker Golf Club
New Haven, Connecticut
Established in 1944
Recognized as one of the oldest African American golf clubs on the east coast.

Langston Junior Boys and Girls Golf Club
Ray Savoy, Founder and Director
Langston Golf Course, Washington, D.C.
www.langstonjunior.org
Offers an annual summer program for ages six through 18.

Langston Ladies Golf Association
Washington, D.C. metropolitan area
www.orgsites.com/md/assoc
Founded by Georgia Leeks
Purpose—to promote, stimulate, and develop a broader interest in the game of golf among women.

Les Birdies Golf Club
Cincinnati, Ohio
www.lesbirdies.com
Established in 1976
Scholarships awarded to deserving young African American females.

Lone Star Golf Association
Houston, Texas
www.lsgahoustongolf.com
Established in 1946
Host of the Annual Charles M. Washington Memorial Golf Classic; 69th anniversary was celebrated in 2015. Annual golf classic supports Lone Star Golf Association's scholarship and junior golf programs.

Madden Women's Association (MWA)
Dayton, Ohio
www.maddenwomensgolf.org
Established in 1983, Madden Women's Association 29th Invitational Golf Tournament was held in 2015. MWA supports junior golf, and also awards college scholarships to female college students and high school seniors.

Mid Island Golf Club
Springfield Gardens, New York
Established in 1961
Hosts the Dr. Fred Richards Annual Memorial Golf Tournament; 52nd Dr. Fred Richards Annual Memorial Golf Tournament was held in 2013; event supports Mid Island Golf Club's youth scholarship program.

Midwest Golf Association
Founded in 1950
www.midwestgolf.net
Supports amateur golf, junior golf, and education

Minority Association for Golfers
Los Angeles, California
Established in the early 1960s; Founder, Maggie Hathaway advocated for jobs and access to golf facilities

Multicultural Golf Association of America (MGAA)
John David, Founder and President
Established in 1991
National junior golf training program

National Black Golf Hall of Fame
Jeff Dunovant, Executive Director
Founded in 1986 by Harold Dunovant
www.nationalblackgolfhalloffame.com

National Minority Golf Foundation (NMGF)
Founded in 1995, National Minority Golf Foundation served as a minority golf resource center and advocate for minority participation in all aspects of golf. Reorganized in the early 2000s, NMGF went under the umbrella of the World Golf Foundation. NMGF ceased operation in 2004.

National Minority Junior Golf Scholarship Association
Renamed, in 2005, The Bill Dickey Scholarship Association
(The Bill Dickey Scholarship Association listing–page 218)

National Negro Golf Association (NNGA)
www.nnga.us
Established in 1965. National Negro Golf Association started as a small group of men coming together for social gatherings. In 1966, NNGA held its first tournament in Pittsburgh, Pennsylvania. Since its inception, NNGA has

National Negro Golf Association (continued)
developed into an association with chapters in cities
throughout the United States. National Negro Golf
Association hosts celebrity tournaments to raise money for
United Negro College Fund.

New Amsterdam Golf Club
New York City, New York
Organized in the early 1930s

**Northern California Minority Junior Golf
Scholarship Association Inc.** (NCMJGSA)
Willie L. Simmons Jr., Founder and President
Sacramento, California
Established in 1990
NCMJGSA provides junior golf training, and awards
collegiate academic scholarships to minority youth.

Oxon Blades Golf Club
Washington, D.C. metropolitan area
Founded in 1959
Founders: Henry Davis, Lowell Scott, Elliott Sickles, Guy
Smith, Marcel Wilson, and James Wright

Par Putters Golf Club
South Bend, Indiana
www.parputters.com
Founded in 1973
Originally named The Michinana Golf Club

Pro Duffers Golf Club, USA
www.produffersusa.org
Established in the late 1950s

Project One Junior Golf Academy
Atlanta, Georgia
Vic Clark, Founder
Established in 1995

Riverside Golf Club
Organized in Washington, D.C.
Established in 1925

Roaring Lambs International Junior Golf Academy
Fort Worth, Texas
Gladys M. Lee, Founder and CEO
Established in 1986
Youth golf and life skills program; provides assistance in career choices, college selections, and obtaining college scholarships. In 2000, Roaring Lambs International Junior Golf Academy was featured on "Making A Difference"—a NBC Nightly News television segment. News anchor Tom Brokaw recognized the organization's success in working with youth.

Royal Golf Club
Washington, D.C.
Established in 1933; formerly named Capital City Golf Club. Royal Golf Club was a major force in the desegregation of public golf courses in Washington, D.C.

St. Nicholas Golf Club
New York City, New York
Organized in 1926

Sisters Across America Inc.
Orlando, Florida
www.sistersacrossamerica.com
Esther Wilson, Founding President; established in 2006
Sisters Across America supports minority women who aspire to become professional golfers.

TEE-Lo Golf Inc.
Orlando, Florida
Robert Biggers, Founder and President
Established in 2006; Youth golf program
www.tee-logolf.org

Teens On the Green LLC
Atlanta, Georgia
Renny Roker, Founder; established in 2000
International junior golf program; offered opportunities to earn college scholarships and interact with different cultures on a global level.

The Bill Dickey Scholarship Association Inc. (BDSA)
Phoenix, Arizona
William "Bill" Dickey, Founder
www.nmjgsa.org
Incorporated in 1984; The Bill Dickey Scholarship Association has awarded more than three million dollars in college scholarships to more than 1000 minority students.

The Darby Foundation
Chris Arceneaux, Founder and CEO
Freeport, New York
www.darbyfoundation.org
Offers a youth enrichment program
Presented the first Brooklyn Golf Show, in partnership with *African American Golfer's Digest*; event held in September 2012 at Medgar Evers College (Brooklyn, New York).

The Lady Drivers Golf Club
Gloria S. Whitley, Founder
Jackson, Mississippi
www.ladydriversgolf.com
Established in 1996, The Lady Drivers Golf Club is recognized as the first African American female golf member club in the state of Mississippi.

The Midnight Golf Program
Detroit, Michigan
Renee Fluker, Founder and Director; established in 2001
www.midnightgolf.org
In addition to an introduction to golf, The Midnight Golf Program focuses on enhancing lifestyles, financial literacy,

community involvement, career exploration, and college preparatory skills. From The Midnight Golf Program's inception through 2014, more than 600 program graduates were admitted to college or university.

Tidewater Youth Golf Association Inc.
Al Hatten, Founder
Established in 1987
Headquartered in Portsmouth, Virginia

United Golfers Association (UGA)
Originally named United States Colored Golfers Association, United Golfers Association was comprised of districts throughout the United States.

Officially established in 1928, United Golfers Association was founded as an all male organization. From 1926 to 1929, UGA tournaments were restricted to "men only". A women's division was added in 1930. In 1939, UGA accepted its first female club, The Chicago Women's Golf Club.

Two years later (1941), Paris Brown was elected vice president of United Golfers Association; thus, Paris Brown became the first female to hold an elective office with UGA. In 1954, Brown was elected UGA's national tournament director. Paris Brown was known as "The First Lady of Golf".

During a time when most golf courses and events operated under an "all white" policy and The PGA of America operated under a restrictive Caucasian-only clause, the United Golfers Association provided opportunities for African American professional and amateur golfers to play competitively. The UGA Tour was fondly referred to as the Chitlin Circuit.

From the 1920s to the 1960s, UGA Tour was the only major golf tour circuit for African American professional and amateur golfers. UGA events were not closed to "Caucasians"; however, very few "Caucasians" played in UGA events. United Golfers Association ceased operation during the 1980s.

United States African American Golf Association
Formerly named African American Golf Association
Renamed, in 2006, United States African American Golf
Association (USAAGA)
USAAGA hosts the Myrtle Beach Winter Golf Invitational.

United States Colored Golfers Association (USCGA)
Organized by Robert Hawkins
Established in 1925
First USCGA meeting was held in Washington, D.C. at the
12th Street YMCA Branch. Between 1928 and 1929, United
States Colored Golfers Association was renamed United
Golfers Association.

Vernoncrest Ladies Golf Club
Los Angeles, California
Mae Crowder, Founder
www.vernoncrestgolfclub.com
Established in 1947
Originally named Vernondale Women's Golf Club

Wake-Robin Golf Club Inc.
Helen Harris, Founder
Washington, D.C. metropolitan area
www.wake-robingolf.org
Founded April 22, 1937
Noted for being the first African American women's golf club
organized in the United States, Wake-Robin Golf Club
celebrated its 78th anniversary in 2015. Wake-Robin Golf
Club was a major force in lobbying the federal government
to desegregate public golf courses (properties funded by
federal taxes) in the District of Columbia. Wake-Robin Golf
Club's presence has heightened the awareness of African
American women golfers, and motivated women of color to
play golf. Among the many community and outreach
involvements, Wake-Robin Golf Club supports junior golf
and African American females who aspire to become LPGA
Tour members.

Western States Golf Association (WSGA)
www.westernstatesgolf.org
Founded in 1954
Incorporated in 1972
Parent organization for organized African American golf clubs located in the western United States.
Created by eight chartered golf clubs:
> Bay Area (San Francisco, California), Cosmopolitan (Los Angeles, California), Desert Mashie (Phoenix, Arizona), Fir State (Seattle, Washington), Leisure Hour (Portland, Oregon), Los Angeles Postal (Los Angeles, California), Paramount (San Diego, California), and Vernoncrest Ladies (Los Angeles, California).

Western States Golf Association's roster includes more than 25 member clubs from the above listed states and also the states of Colorado and Nevada. Among WSGA's many community outreach activities, WSGA awards scholarships to youth golfers and conducts junior golf clinics.

Windy City Golf Club
Chicago, Illinois
Organized in the early 1920s

Women In Golf Foundation Inc.
LaJean Gould, Founder and President
Atlanta, Georgia metropolitan area
www.womeningolffoundation.org
Women in Golf Foundation offers life skills and junior golf programs, and hosts the Women's Collegiate Golf Classic. (*Women's Collegiate Golf Classic listing–page 235*)

Yorkshire Golf Club Inc.
Founded in 1937 by Lewis "Ted" Owens, (who also served as the club's first president); Yorkshire Golf Club is credited for being one of the oldest African American golf clubs in Western Pennsylvania. A member of United Golfers Association, Yorkshire Golf Club hosted the UGA Negro National Open Championship in 1946, 1952, and 1958.

Yorkshire Golf Club Members, Yorkshire, Pennsylvania
Circa 1958

Ray Savoy speaking at the Langston Junior Boys and Girls Golf Club
Second Annual Scholarship Golf Tournament opening ceremony.
Circa 1996. Courtesy Ray Savoy

Willie L. Simmons Jr., Founder and President, Northern California Minority Junior Golf Scholarship Association. NCMJGSA services youth in the Greater Sacramento Metropolitan area and has awarded (as of 2014) more than 75 collegiate academic scholarships to deserving students.

William "Bill" Dickey *(1928–2012)*. Founder, The Bill Dickey Scholarship Association (formerly National Minority Junior Golf Scholarship Association) and a cofounder of National Minority College Golf Championship (now the PGA Minority Collegiate Golf Championship), Bill Dickey was also the first African American to receive the PGA Distinguished Service Award (1999), and the USGA Joe Dey Award (2001).

13th Annual Negro Open Championship
September 1938
Palos Park Golf Course
(outside Chicago, Illinois)

135 players: 34 African American men professionals, 84 African American men amateurs, 16 African American women amateurs, and one white male amateur who plays daily at Palos Park Golf Course and chooses to continue his daily routine by entering the tournament.

First place prize money (professional only): $200

Caddies optional: Should players prefer not to carry their own bags, white caddies are available for one dollar per round.

24

Events
Selected notable active and inactive events.

Advocates Professional Tour
www.advocatesgolf.org
Presented by: The Advocates USA
First event held in 2010
Professional mini-tour featuring top African American professional golfers
The Advocates USA presented, in 2010, the inaugural Adrian Stills Award to professional golfer Vincent Johnson. In addition to receiving the Adrian Stills Award, Johnson received financial support to help cover expenses for PGA Tour Qualifying School. The Advocates USA was established in 2004. This non-profit organization is recognized for its community involvement particularly in education, health, and economic development.

African American Golf Classic of Hernando County
Gordon Fleming, Founder
gflemin3@yahoo.com
Two-day / 36-hole flighted event
Hernando County, Florida
Traditionally held in the month of February
Proceeds benefit a scholarship fund for high school graduates

Barb Young Golf Classic
Lincoln Park, Michigan
Gus Barksdale, Tournament Director
Fore Wood Golf Club hosted and sponsored the Barb Young Golf Classic for more than 20 years.

Bill Bishop Annual Benefit Golf Classic
Freeway Golf Course
Sicklerville, New Jersey
Inaugural event held in 1971
Pro-Am tournament

Bill Bishop Annual Benefit Golf Classic (continued)
Named in honor of Bill Bishop, PGA Member and head golf professional emeritus at Freeway Golf Course. Event benefits the Bill Bishop Junior Golf Foundation. The 43rd Bill Bishop Benefit Golf Classic was held in August 2013. *(Read about Bill Bishop–page 160)*

Black Enterprise Golf & Tennis Challenge
www.blackenterprise.com
Hosted by Black Enterprise, this event is held during Labor Day weekend. The 22nd Black Enterprise Golf & Tennis Challenge was held in 2015.

Capital City Open
Langston Golf Course
Washington, D.C.
Langston Golf Course has hosted the Capital City Open for more than 40 years. Notable African American professional and amateur golfers, including Lee Elder and Joe Louis, have competed in the Capital City Open.

Clyde E. Bailey Jr. and Rapheal M. Prevot Jr.
National Bar Institute Annual Golf Tournament
www.nationalbar.org
Previously named National Bar Institute Golf Tournament; in 2010, renamed in honor of deceased National Bar Institute members Clyde E. Bailey Jr. and Rapheal M. Prevot Jr.; event supports the National Bar Institute scholarship fund and programs.

East/West Golf Classic
Phoenix, Arizona area
Also known as Bill Dickey East/West Golf Classic
www.nmjgsa.org
Traditionally held in the month of January, East/West Golf Classic is a major fundraiser for The Bill Dickey Scholarship Association. The 31st East/West Golf Classic was held in 2013. A Classic Reunion is scheduled for January 2016.

Grid Iron Golf Tournament
Hosted by Franco Harris and Lydell Mitchell
Luana Harris-Scott, Tournament Director
Held in the city of each Super Bowl during Super Bowl week, Harris and Mitchell hosted the first Grid Iron Golf Tournament in 1998. Event supported various charities including Soldiers' Angels, an organization that provides aid and comfort to men and women United States soldiers.

Harlem YMCA Charity Golf Classic
Hosted by Harlem YMCA (New York, New York)
www.ymcanyc.org
The year 2014 marked the 15th anniversary of the Harlem YMCA Charity Golf Classic; proceeds benefited Harlem YMCA Strong Kids Campaign and scholarship program.

Hollywood Women's Open
Presented by Selina Johnson, Hollywood Women's Open was held at Palmer Park Golf Course (Detroit, Michigan). Participants were women amateur golfers from the United States and Canada. The first event was held in 1979 with about 65 golfers. The second year, participation increased to 123. The last Hollywood Women's Open was held in 1982.

James Hughes Memorial Scholarship Fund Golf Classic
Hosted by Pennsylvania State Senator Vincent Hughes and named in honor of James Hughes, the deceased father of Senator Vincent Hughes; four-day event held in the tri-state Pennsylvania area
Proceeds benefited a college scholarship fund for Philadelphia public high school graduates who continued their education in a Pennsylvania state university. In 2006, Walter Morgan was presented the African American Legend of Golf Award. Legends Bill Bishop, Pete Brown, James Clark, Lee Elder, Walter Morgan, Charlie Owens, Calvin Peete, and Charlie Sifford were honored at the 10th anniversary celebration in 2007.

Jethro Pugh / Two Podners Scholarship Invitational
Jethro Pugh (former NFL player)–Host
The Paradies Shops–Host company / Primary underwriters
Benefits United Negro College Fund in the state of Texas
www.theparadiesshops.com
Scholarship awarded to a UNCF Texas college student who has a 3.0 or better GPA and is active in civic affairs. The 20th Jethro Pugh/Two Podners Scholarship Invitational was held in 2012.

Joe Louis Open
Founded and hosted by heavyweight boxing champion Joe Louis, the Joe Louis Open was held at Rackham Golf Course (Huntington Woods, Michigan). A prestigious annual event, the Joe Louis Open was popular for its "big money purse", usually $1000 to $2000—an exceptionally high dollar amount for a black golf event. Most golfing events that offered "big money purses" were all-white tournaments. In August 1941 the first Joe Louis Open was held; Clyde Martin won. No events were held from 1942 to 1944 (during World War II). The second Joe Louis Open was held in 1945. The following year (1946), a women's amateur division was added; Lucy Mitchum placed first. The last Joe Louis Open was held in 1951. *(Read about Joe Louis–page 101)*

Julius L. Chambers Invitational Golf Tournament
Norma Lewis, Tournament Administrator
www.naacpldf.org
Proceeds benefited the NAACP Legal Defense and Educational Fund; the 33rd Julius Chambers Invitational Golf Tournament was held in 2011.

Mid-Winter Golf Classic
Organizers: Jimmie Taylor, Herman Dubois, Eldorado Long
Mid-Winter Golf Classic, part of the United Golfers Association circuit, was held from 1963 until the late 1970s or early 1980s. National Black Golf Hall of Fame resurfaced the Mid-Winter Golf Classic in 2010.

Morgan State University Invitational Tournament
www.events.morgan.edu
Supports athletic fund; 26th invitational held in 2015.

National Colored Golf Championship
(Renamed, in 1926, Negro National Open)
Held in 1925 at Shady Rest Golf and Country Club
National Colored Golf Championship was hosted by United
States Colored Golfers Association. Between 1928 and 1929,
USCGA was renamed United Golfers Association.

National Minority College Golf Championship
(Renamed PGA Minority Collegiate Golf Championship)
Founders: Cleveland Chapter of the National Negro Golf
Association (NNGA), William "Bill" Dickey, Rose Harper,
Eddie Payton, and Dr. Herschel Cochrane (then NNGA
founder/president).
Established in 1986, the first event was sponsored by
National Negro Golf Association and held in May 1987 at
Highland Park Golf Course (Cleveland, Ohio). The following
year, a women's division was added. In 1998, The PGA of
America became a cosponsor. In 2006, National Minority
College Golf Scholarship Fund granted The PGA of America
sole management and operations of the National Minority
College Golf Championship; hence, the event was renamed.

Neckbone Golf Tour–Pete Ball Memorial
Miami, Florida
Supports the fight against sickle cell anemia. The 36th Pete
Ball Memorial was held in 2015.

Negro National Open
(Formerly named National Colored Golf Championship)
In 1926, the event was renamed Negro National Open. First
place received $100, which was the only cash prize; the other
awards were trophies. Sponsored by United Golfers
Association, this was a major golf event for African
Americans. The last Negro National Open was held in 1976.

100 Golf Classic
www.100blackmen-atlanta.org
Hosted by 100 Black Men of Atlanta. 100 Golf Classic benefits Project Success, the organization's youth program.

Original Tee Golf Classic
Hosted by Original Tee Inc.
Wendell Haskins, Founder of Original Tee Inc.
www.originaltee.com
The 15th Original Tee Golf Classic was held in 2015.

P&B Golf Club Mystery Golf Outing
Washington, D.C. metropolitan area
P&B Golf Club was established in the 1960s. P&B Golf Club hosted its first mystery trip in the late 1970s, and for more than 35 years held annual mystery trips for members and guests. Golfers met early in the morning to travel by bus to an undisclosed location.

Pioneer Golf Tournament
Clearview Golf Club
East Canton, Ohio
www.clearview-gc.com
In honor of pioneer golf legend William Powell, this event supports the Clearview Legacy Foundation. The 13th annual Pioneer Golf Tournament was held in June 2015.

Ray Mitchell North-South Tournament
Ray Mitchell, Founder and Event Manager
Noted as one of the major black-sponsored tournaments for amateur and professional golfers, the inaugural Ray Mitchell North-South Tournament was held between 1953 and 1954 in Jacksonville, Florida. In 1955, the host site changed to Miami Springs Golf Course. Theodore "Shorty" Jones served as tournament director from 1954 to 1961. The last Ray Mitchell North-South Tournament was held in 1989. Ray Mitchell was also founder of the Golf School of Harlem.

Sacramento River City Golf Classic

Host: Northern California Minority Junior Golf Scholarship Association

For more than two decades, Sacramento River City Golf Classic has supported collegiate academic scholarships, golf training programs, and financial assistance for deserving youth residents of northern California. Sacramento River City Golf Classic celebrated its 20th anniversary in 2009.

Sisters Across America Golf Invitational

Hosted by Sisters Across America Inc.

www.sistersacrossamerica.com

The inaugural Sisters Across America Golf Invitational was held in May 2007.

Skyview Golf Pro-Am Tournament

The oldest known African American three-day golf tournament, Skyview Golf Pro-Am Tournament inaugural event was held in 1960 and hosted by Skyview Golf Association, which was also founded in 1960.

Southeastern Golf Tournament

In 1964, the year that all state-operating facilities were desegregated on Jekyll Island, Georgia, the first Southeastern Golf Tournament was held on Jekyll Island. Tournament hosts were Earl Hill and the Frontier Club, a social organization formed by Hill. Also known as "The Classic", this event was attended by many notable professional golfers and entertainers including Jim Dent, Jim Thorpe, and soul singer Jerry Butler. The last Southeastern Golf Tournament was held in the early 1980s.

Swing Hope Into Action

Hosted by Great Golfers of Color (GGC)

www.SwingHopeIntoAction.com

Inaugural event was held in 2014 in Augusta, Georgia at Augusta Municipal Golf Course, "The Patch". Honorees in attendance were Pete Brown, Jim Dent, and Charlie Sifford.

Ted Rhodes "The Legends" Tour
"Spreading the Word"
Peggy Rhodes-White, Director
www.tedrhodesthelegendtour.com
Proceeds supported junior golf programs and the Ted
Rhodes Foundation HBCU golf program scholarship fund.

The Herc Golf Tournament
The Herc Golf Tournament: Named after the late Mr.
Hercules L. Joyner, Tom Joyner's father and an avid golfer,
and hosted by The Tom Joyner Foundation. The Herc Golf
Tournament is held every year as a part of the Tom Joyner
Fantastic Voyage™, a week long cruise that raises money to
help keep students enrolled in Historically Black Colleges
and Universities. The Tom Joyner Foundation has raised
more than sixty-five million dollars since it was founded in
1998.

The Unity Golf Classic
www.urbanleaguephila.org
Hosted by The Urban League of Philadelphia and the
Barristers' Association of Philadelphia

University of Maryland Eastern Shore (UMES) Art
Shell Celebrity Golf Classic and Junior Tournament
Hosts: University of Maryland Eastern Shore and Pro
Football Hall of Famer Art Shell
Golf classic benefits University of Maryland Eastern Shore
PGA/PGM™ Program and UMES Athletic Department.

Valley View Golf Club Invitational Golf Tournament
Based in Southern Nevada
www.valleyviewgolfclub.net
Valley View Golf Club was organized in 1958 and the first
Invitational Golf Tournament was held in that same year on
Thanksgiving Day. The 56th Valley View Golf Club
Invitational Golf Tournament was held in 2014.

William "Bill" Dickey Invitational Junior Golf Championship

www.billdickeyscholarship.org

Named in honor of William "Bill" Dickey, founder of The Bill Dickey Scholarship Association; junior golf invitational is a 36-hole event for minority junior golfers with low handicaps and good academic standing. The 16th invitational was held in June 2015.

William Powell Celebrity Tournament

Clearview Golf Course

East Canton, Ohio

www.clearview-gc.com

The 31st William Powell Celebrity Tournament was held in August 2015. Event is named in honor of William Powell. (*Read about William Powell–page 50*)

Women's Collegiate Golf Classic (*also known as National Women's Collegiate Golf Classic*)

LaJean Gould, Founder

Hosted by Women In Golf Foundation

Atlanta, Georgia metropolitan area

www.womeningolffoundation.org

Women's Collegiate Golf Classic features competitive golf among black colleges and universities women's golf teams. In 1994, the inaugural Women's Collegiate Golf Classic was held; five schools were represented—Texas Southern University, Alabama State University, Jackson State University, Southern University, and Talladega College. Women In Golf Foundation hosted the 21st Women's Collegiate Golf Classic in April 2015. Alabama State University took first place, followed by Texas Southern University and Prairie View A&M University respectively.

Billy Gardenhight Sr., Program Director Skyview Golf Pro-Am and Junior Tournament. Gardenhight has served as tournament/program director for more than 40 years. The 56th Skyview Golf Pro-Am and Junior Tournament was held in July 2015.

Vernon L. Echols, Tournament Director L.O.V.E. GolfTech
Connections Invitational Golf Tournament. Event is held in
November at LPGA International (Daytona Beach, Florida).
The 17th L.O.V.E. GolfTech Connections Invitational was
held in 2015. For more information, contact Vernon Echols
at lovegolftech@gmail.com or at 201-658-3935.

Letter, dated December 31, 1986, requesting listings for the first
Black Golf Information Center Calendar.
Courtesy Charles Dorton

BLACK GOLF INFORMATION
CENTER
3090 BIRMINGHAM DR.
RICHMOND, CA 94806
415-223-7414

December 31, 1986

BROOKS, JOHN
19TH HOLE DUFFERS
1014 W. 108TH. PLACE
CHICAGO, IL 60043

Dear JOHN

We are bringing into reality an idea given to us by Mr. Bill
Dickey of Phoenix, Arizona. The idea is to establish a
centralized location and contact person for collecting and
desiminating information related to black golfers. To be more
specific, to put together, a schedule of annual golf tournaments
representing black golf clubs throughout the United States and
other countries where black golfers may reside.

Can you imagine the wealth of information that may be stored at
this center. The camaraderie this could assist in fostering
throughout this and other countries.

Please assist us in this effort by immediately completing the
enclosed form and returning it immediately. There will be no
charge of any kind for the schedules or other information
returned to your club. We would want you to make copies for
your club members.

Thank you and have a good golfing year.

Sincerely,

Charles Dorton

Black Golf Information Center Calendar–1987

Month	Date	Club	Course(s)	Location
Jan.	17-18	Fun-Lovers	Brookside	Pasadena, CA
	21-22	East/West Classic	Over Three Courses	Scottsdale, AZ
Feb.	18-22	N.N.G.A.	Saddlebrook Resort	Tampa, FL
	22	Bay Cities	Greentree	Leisure Town, CA
Mar.	7	Whispering George	Western Avenue	Los Angeles, CA
	8	Bay Area	Alameda	Aladema, CA
	9-16	Golf Adventures	El Cid	Mazatlan, Mexico
	14	SABGC	Green Tree	Leisure Town, CA
	15	Metro	Sharp Park	Pacifica, CA
	28	Jr. Golf Benefit	Lew Galbraith	Oakland, CA
Apr.	4-5	Spear Annual	DeLaveaga/ Pasatiempo	Santa Cruz, CA
	5-11	Tampa (Roots of Golf)	Rogers Park	Tampa, FL
	11-12	Carvon	Mangrove Bay	St. Petersburg, FL
	12	Golden Gators	San Ramon	San Ramon, CA
	19	SABGC	TBA	TBA
	25	Nor-Cal Ladies	Dry Creek	Galt, CA
	25-26	Arroyo	Brookside	Pasadena, CA
	25-26	Unique	Willow Springs	San Antonio, TX
	26	Top-Flight	Mt. Shadows	Rohnert Park, CA
May	1-3	Peoples' Pro-Am	Alameda/Galbraith	Oakland, CA
	9-10	Par 5 Golf Assoc	Indian Pines	Ft. Pierce, FL
	16-17	Nor-Cal Annual	Haggin Oaks	Sacramento, CA

May	16-17	Desert Mashie	Superstition Mts	Mesa, AZ
	16-17	Sickle Cell Anemia	Burns Park	Little Rock, AR
	16-17	Foreball	Langston	Washington, D.C.
	16-17	Rivercity	Helfrich	Evansville, IN
	20-24	N.N.G.A. Atlanta	TBA	Atlanta, GA
	23-24	Louisville-Kentuckiana	Shawnee	Louisville, KY
	23-24	Home City	Veteran's Memorial	Springfield, MA
	23-24	Detroit Golf League	Dun Rovin	Plymouth, MI
	23-24	Winston-Salem	Winston Lake	Winston-Salem, NC
	29-31	West Side (Penn)	Glade Springs	Daniels, WV
	30-31	Golden Tee	Z. Boaz	Ft. Worth, TX
	31	Bay Area	Mt. Shadows	Rohnert Park, CA
June	7	Golferettes	I.M.A. Brookwood	Flint, MI
	7	Top-Flight	Peacock Gap	San Rafael, CA
	6-7	Cosmopolitan	TBA	TBA
	6-7	Douglas	Coffin	Indianapolis, IN
	6-7	North Shore Duffers	Foss Park	Chicago, IL
	13-14	Metro Atlanta Women	Alfred "Tup" Holmes	Atlanta, GA
	14	Herman Marshall	Tyrone Hills	Flint, MI
	14	Golden Gators	Mt. Shadows	Rohnert Park, CA
	14	Pitch & Putt	Pine Ridge	Baltimore, MD
	18-21	Midwestern (Tulsa)	Dainer Hill CC	Siloam Springs, AR
	20	Bay Cities	Mt. Shadows	Rhonert Park, CA
	20	Kappa Alpha Psi	Torry Pines	Flint, MI

June	20-21	Midwest District UGA	Indian Lakes	Bloomington, IL
	26-27	Chicago Women	Cherry Hill	Chicago, IL
	26-27	Friendship	Pontiac Muni	Pontiac, MI
	26-28	W.S.G.A. Annual	Rancho Canada	Carmel, CA
	27-28	V.P.G.A.	I.M.A. Brookwood	Flint, MI
July	4-5	Milwaukee Frontiers	South Hills	Milwaukee, WI
	4-5	Tampa-All American Classic	Rogers Park	Tampa, FL
	4-5	New England-Seniors	Bel Compos	Avon, CT
	5	Inner City Lions	Tyrone Hills	Flint, MI
	5	19th Hole Duffers	Tuckaway	Crete, IL
	8-12	N.N.G.A. New York	TBA	New York, NY
	11	Tee Set	Salt River	Detroit, MI
	11-12	Par Busters	Ted Rhodes	Nashville, TN
	11-12	Metro Annual	Sonoma National	Sonoma, CA
	14-16	Skyview	City	Asheville, NC
	17-19	West Side (Penn)	Kiamesha Lake	Concord, NY
	18	Nor-Cal Ladies	Bethel Island	Bethel Island, CA
	18-19	Vehicle City	Swartz Creek	Flint, MI
	18-19	Chicago Executive	Vernon Woods	Chicago, IL
	18-19	Tire Town	Good Park	Akron, OH
	18-19	Tee Masters	TBA	TBA
	19	S.A.B.G.C.	Kennedy	Napa, CA
	25-26	Midwestern	Detwiller	Toledo, OH
	25-26	Fir State	Bear Creek	Redmond, WA
	26	Gulf Coast	Oso Beach Muni	Corpus Christi, TX

July	26	Ark-Chi	Indian Lakes	Bloomington, IL
Aug.	TBA	Minnesota Metro	TBA	Minneapolis, MN
	1-2	Fairway	Madden	Dayton, OH
	1-2	Leisure Hour	Bowman's Resort	Portland, OR
	1-2	Golden Hawks	Urban Hills	Richton Park, IL
	2	S.A.B.G.C.	Ancil Hoffman	Arbuckle, CA
	6-8	W.S.G.A. Jr. Championship	TBA	Los Angeles, CA
	8	Par-Links Picnic	Sky West	Hayward, CA
	8-9	Linksman	Vernon Woods	Chicago, IL
	8-9	Swinging Duffers	Country Lakes	Naperville, IL
	8-9	Swingers	Gates	Waterloo, IA
	16	West Side	TBA	Elkins Park, PA
	22-23	Mile High Sandbaggers	TBA	Denver, CO
	22-23	S.A.B.G.C.	Wild Creek	Reno, NV
	22-23	Forewood	Warren Valley	Dearborn Heights,MI
	23	Metro	Sharp Park	Pacifica, CA
	28-29	Flint I.C.G.A.	Kearsly Lake	Flint, MI
Sept.	2-7	N.N.G.A. Cleveland	TBA	Cleveland, OH
	5-6	Tee & Turf	TBA	Tacoma, WA
	5-6	Gate City	Bryan Park	Greensboro, NC
	5-6	New England-Seniors	Iyanough Hills	Hyannis, MA
	8-15	Bay Area Excursion	TBA	Bermuda
	12	S.A.B.G.C.	TBA	Manteca, CA

Sept.	12-13	Oil Capital	Page Belcher	Tulsa, OK
	13	Par-Links	Lew Galbraith	Oakland, CA
	19-20	Pro Duffers S.W.	TBA	Dallas, TX
	19-20	Peoria Progressive	Neuman	Peoria, IL
	19-20	Paramount	Torry Pines	San Diego, CA
	20	Top Flight	Mt. Shadows	Rohnert Park, CA
	27	S.A.B.G.C.	Haggin Oaks	Sacramento, CA
Oct.	3-4	Greater Cincinnati	TBA	Cincinnati, OH
	3-4	Pro Duffers West	TBA	TBA
	4	Bay Cities	Greentree	Leisure Town, CA
	10	S.A.B.G.C.	Ancil Hoffman	Arbuckle, CA
	10	Nor-Cal Ladies	Lincoln	San Francisco, CA
	14-18	N.N.G.A. National Championship	Half Moon Bay	Montego Bay, JM
	17-18	20th Century	Riverside	Fresno, CA
	24-25	Desert Trails	TBA	Tucson, AZ
Nov.	2-7	Bermuda Triangle	Over Three Courses	St. George's, BMU
	7-8	Golden Tees	TBA	TBA
	14	S.A.B.G.C.	Van Buskirk	Stockton, CA
	15	Bay Area	Sharp Park	Pacifica, CA
	22	Top Flight	Alameda So.	Alameda, CA
	28-29	Valley View	TBA	Las Vegas, NV

Courtesy Charles Dorton

Charles Dorton, Director Sports
Opportunity and Information
Center

Sports Opportunity and Information Center Calendar–2010

Month	Date	Club	Course(s)	Location
Jan.	16–17	Valdosta	Francis Lakes	Lake Park, FL
	18	M.L. King Memorial	Silverado	Napa, CA
	21–24	East/West Classic	Over Three Courses	Scottsdale, AZ
	TBA	Tiger Sharks	Emerald Hills	Miami, FL
	19	Tampa Bay Black Heritage	Rogers Park	Tampa, FL
Feb.	13	Vernoncrest	TBA	Los Angeles, CA
	13–14	Neckbone Tour	C.C. of Miami	Miami, FL
Mar.	6–13	Hackers Invitation	Over Six Courses	Orlando, FL
	13	Fore Youth Inc.	Mill Cove	Jacksonville, FL
	20	Masters City	Applewood	Augusta, GA
	26–28	MidWinter Classic	Rogers Park	Tampa, FL
Apr.	7	Woody Kinchen Memorial	Silverado	Napa, CA
	9–10	Pacific Desert Classic	TBA	Fontana, CA
	17–18	Capitol City	Hillcrest	Orangeburg, SC
	17–18	Spear	Ridgemark	Hollister, CA
	17–18	Tampa Roots of Golf	Rogers Park	Tampa, FL
	17–18	Unique	Willow Park	San Antonio, TX
	24–25	Old Dominion	Newport News	Newport News, VA
	24–25	Port City	The Cove	Wilmington, NC
	24–25	Sandwedge	Lake View	Meridian, MS
	30	Cosmopolitan	TBA	Palm Springs, CA
	TBA	F.C.A.A.	Grand Palms Resort	Pembroke Pines, FL
May	1	Cosmopolitan	TBA	Palm Springs, CA

Month	Dates	Event	Course	Location
May	1-2	Peoples Celebrity Pro-Am	Metropolitan	Oakland, CA
	5-8	Winston Lakes (Seniors)	Winston Lakes	Winston Salem, NC
	TBA	PGA Intercollegiate Championship	PGA Village	Port St. Lucie, FL
	8-9	Desert Mashie	Wild Horse Pass	Chandler, AZ
	15	MidOcean	Brentwood	Brentwood, NJ
	15-16	Fayetteville Metro	TBA	Fayetteville, SC
	15-16	Home City Pro-Am	TBA	Springfield, MA
	15-16	Par-Five	Fairwinds	Ft. Pierce, FL
	15-16	Port City	City Course	Charleston, SC
	15-16	Pro-Duffers	Hindman	Little Rock, AR
	22-23	Chicago Champs	Meadow	Riverdale, IL
	22-23	Nine Iron	Sonny Guy	Jackson, MS
	22-23	North American	Browns Mill	Atlanta, GA
	29-30	Golden Tee	TBA	Ft. Worth, TX
	29-30	Louisville-Kentuckiana	Shawnee	Louisville, KY
	TBA	Toussaint Golf Association	Les Vieux Chenes	Lafayette, LA
June	5-6	Central Texas Players	Stonetree	Kileen, TX
	5-6	Corn Huskers	Benson Park	Omaha, NB
	5-6	Douglas	Coffin	Indianapolis, IN
	5-6	J.L. Chambers Invitational	PGA Village	Port St. Lucie, FL
	6	Birdcage	TBA	Oakland, CA
	6	Flint Golferettes	TBA	Flint, MI
	12-13	Black Archives	Swope Park	Kansas City, MO
	12-13	Capitol City	Santa Marie	Baton Rouge, LA

June	12–13	Ebony Ladies	Pine Lakes	Hubbard, OH
	12–13	Mid-West Golf Association	Hawthorne Hills	Lima, OH
	12–13	Pine States	Indian Valley	Spokane, WA
	12–13	Trail Blazers	Wind Hollow	Longview, TX
	13	Pitch & Putt	Diamond Run	Baltimore, MD
	14	Rileys Senior Shoot Out	Sharp Park	Pacifica, CA
	12–20	Heart of America	Swope Park	Kansas City, MO
	19–20	Lone Star	Memorial	Houston, TX
	19–20	Pioneer	Clearview CC	E. Canton, OH
	19–20	Ridgewood	Linrick	Columbia, SC
	21	Greater Cleveland Jr. Golf	Little Mountain G & CC	Concord, OH
	24–26	W.S.G.A. Annual	Over three courses	Denver, CO
	26	Kappa Alpha Psi-Madison	TBA	Madison, WI
	26–27	Par-Four	Osceola	Pensacola, FL
	26–27	Purple and Gold (Omega Psi Phi)	Bradley/Patton	Ft. Benning, GA
	26–27	Upstate Elite	River Falls	Duncan, SC
	26–27	Wego Charity	Southlawn	Pine Mountain, GA
July	3–4	Bronze Open	Hiawatha	Minneapolis, MN
	3–4	Eastern	Lincoln	Oklahoma City, OK
	3–4	Jim Thorpe Pro–Am	TBA	Winston-Salem, NC
	3–4	Milwaukee Frontiers	South Hills	Milwaukee, WI
	9	Sacramento River City Classic	Wild Horse	Davis, CA
	9–10	Texas State Amateur Golf Association	The Republic/ Pelican Valley	San Antonio, TX

July	10–11	Caddo Ebony	Huntington Park	Shreveport, LA
	10–11	Central States	Eagle Springs	St. Louis, MO
	10–11	Chicago Executives	Joe Louis	Riverdale, IL
	10–11	Deep Drivers	TBAS	Lake Tahoe, NV
	10–11	Greater Dayton Youth Acad.	Kitty Hawk	Dayton, OH
	10–11	Gulf City	Azalea	Mobile, AL
	10–11	Winston-Lakes Pro–Am	Winston Lakes	Winston-Salem, NC
	13–15	Skyview Pro–Am	Asheville Muni	Asheville, NC
	17–18	Boot Walker	Shadow Ridge	Hattisburg, MS
	17–18	Greater Battlecreek	Bender	Battle Creek, MI
	17–18	High Point Swingers	Blair/Oak Hollow	High Point, NC
	17–18	Linksmen (PC Open)	TBA	Spartanburg, SC
	17–18	Winston-Lakes	Winston Lakes	Winston-Salem, NC
	24	Capitol City	MSU-Forest Akers	Lansing, MI
	24–25	Cosmo Knights	Douglas	Indianapolis, IN
	24–25	Detroit Golf League	TBA	Detroit, MI
	24–25	Fir State	TBA	Seattle, WA
	24–25	Golden Tee	TBA	Buffalo, NY
	24–25	Golden Tee	Heritage Hills	Stuart, FL
	24–25	Knickerbocker	Ailing Memorial	New Haven, CT
	24–25	Mile High Sandbaggers	Thorncreek/Buffalo Run	Denver, CO
	24–25	Twin City	Hiawatha	Minneapolis, MN
	TBA	MGA-National Junior Golf Championship	Hawthorne Hills	Lima, OH
Aug.	2	John Christian Classic	TBA	Pittsburg, PA

Aug.	2	Men of Essex	Maplewood	Maplewood, NJ
	7	R.L. Winn Invitational	TBA	Madison, WI
	7-8	Autocrat	Stone Ridge	New Orleans, LA
	7-8	Bill Bishop Pro-Am	Freeway	Sicklerville, NJ
	7-8	Bull City	Hillandale	Durham, NC
	7-8	Fairway Pro-Am	TBA	Dayton, OH
	7-8	Galesburg Linksters	TBA	Galesburg, IL
	7-8	Golfin With The Guys	Krueger/Haskell	Beloit, WI
	7-8	Jack An Jill	TBA	Ft. Worth, TX
	7-8	Leisure Hour	Resort at the Mountain	Welches, Or
	7-8	Par-Makers	Crosswinds	Bowling Green, KY
	7-8	Pro-Duffers	Tour 18 Dallas	Dallas, TX
	7-8	Swingers	Gates	Waterloo, IO
	8	Capitol City	TBA	Austin, TX
	14-15	Augusta Shot Makers	TBA	Augusta, GA
	14-15	McAdams	Pawnee Prairie	Wichita, KS
	14-15	New Era Pro-Am	Bowden/Heron Lakes	Macon, GA
	14-15	Tee Masters	TBA	Los Angeles, CA
	14-15	Twin City Golf Clubs	Channault	Monroe, LA
	20	Madison Golfers	TBA	Madison, WI
	21-22	Forewood	Warren Valley	Dearborn Heights, MI
	21-22	Grandstrands	Chippendale	Kokomo, IN
	21-22	Metro Columbus Pro-Am	TBA	Columbus, GA
	21-22	Mid-Ohio Valley	New Woodridge	Mineral Wells, WV
	21-22	Par Busters	TBA	Charleston, NC

Aug.	21–22	Sacramento Area Black Golfers	Red Hawk	Reno, NV
	28–29	Michigan Amateur	TBA	Lansing, MI
Sept.	3–4	Little Giant	Lincoln	Oklahoma City, OK
	3–5	Black Enterprise	TBA	TBA
	4–5	Bay Area	Ranch Canada	Carmel, CA
	4–5	Milwaukee Connection	Dretzka	Milwaukee, WI
	4–5	Tri County	TBA	Rock Hills, SC
	4–5	Valley Views	TBA	Las Vegas, NV
	6	Holiday Golf Group	Blue Rock GC	Vallejo, CA
	10	Ed "Too Tall" Jones	Cottonwood	Tunica, MS
	11–12	Desert Trails	TBA	Tucson, AZ
	11–12	Lexington Swingers	Lakeside/Tate Creek	Lexington, KY
	11–12	Paramount	TBA	San Diego, CA
	11–12	Ted Rhodes Foundation Inc	St. Andrews G & CC	St. Charles, TN
	11–12	Tri-Parish	Sugarland	Houma, LA
	18–19	Greater Cincinnati	Clearview	E. Canton, OH
	18–19	Masters City	Forest Hills	Augusta, GA
Oct.	2–3	Florida Sportsman	Harper Hills	Sebring, FL
	7–9	NBT Golfers	TBA	Myrtle Beach, SC
	8–9	W.S.G.A. Women in Golf	TBA	TBA
	9	Delta Sigma Theta	Sunol Valley	Sunol, CA
	16–17	Peoria Progressive	TBA	Peoria, IL
	16–17	Pro Duffers West	TBA	Oxnard, CA
	22	East Orange	TBA	East Orange, NJ
Nov.	6–7	L.O.V.E. GolfTech	LPGA	Daytona Beach, FL

Nov.	26	West Coast Rattlers	Rogers	Tampa, FL
	27–28	Twin City	Lake Marion	Santee, SC
Dec.	11–12	Tri Club Classic	Desert Princess	Palm Springs, CA
	30–31	Holiday Classic	Francisco Grande	Casa Grande, AZ

Courtesy Charles Dorton

We do as much.
We eat as much.
We want as much.

Sojourner Truth

Chapter VI
Before and After

BILL BISHOP
PRO GOLF CLASSIC
WINNERS

HUBERT GREEN 1971	FRED GIBSON 1972	NICK GARDNER 1973	BOBBY MAYES 1974
JIM THORPE 1975	NATE STARKS 1976	WAYNE McGOWAN 1977	CHUCK THORPE 1978
MIKE WILLIAMS 1979	ERNEST BLUE 1980	GEORGE BUTLER 1981	WILEY WILLIAMS 1982
MANNING MULLINS 1983	RICARDO STEVENS 1984	AL GREEN 1985	FRANK EATON 1986
CRAIG DEAR 1987	MIKE WILLIAMS 1988	JAMES BROWNLEE 1989	AL MORTON 1990
DAVE QUINN 1991	FRANK EATON 1992	BILL KENNEDY 1993	EARNEST ANDREW 1994

Time line

Listings under each year—may not be in chronological order.

1800s ♦ ♦ ♦

1879

John Shippen Jr. is born December 5th in Washington, D.C. In later years, Shippen is recognized as the first golf professional born in the United States.

1896

John Shippen Jr., age 16, becomes the first African American professional golfer; Shippen competes in the USGA U.S. Open; ties for fifth and wins ten dollars.

1899

Dr. George Franklin Grant receives the first United States registered patent for a wooden golf tee.

John Shippen Jr. plays in the U.S. Open for the second time.

1900s ♦ ♦ ♦

1900

John Shippen Jr. plays in the U.S. Open; this is Shippen's third U.S. Open appearance.

1902

John Shippen Jr. ties for fifth at the U.S. Open and wins seventy-five dollars. This is Shippen's fourth U.S. Open appearance.

1913
John Shippen Jr. plays in the U.S. Open for the fifth time.

1915
Alpha Golf Club (Chicago, Illinois) sponsors what is credited to be the first black golf tournament. This event is held at Marquette Park Golf Course. Walter Speedy wins the event.

1921
Shady Rest Golf and Country Club (Scotch Plains, New Jersey) is established. It is the first documented African American owned golf and country club. Formerly named Westfield Club, this property is mortgaged to Progressive Realty Company, a group of African American investors.

1923
Tuskegee Institute (Tuskegee, Alabama) develops a five-hole golf course.

Joseph Bartholomew, golf course architect, begins construction of an 18-hole golf course for Metairie Golf Club, an exclusive all-white members golf club in Metairie, Louisiana.

St. Louis, Missouri Commissioner of Parks grants African Americans access to public golf courses on Mondays only— 6:00 AM to 12:00 noon.

1924
Ceremonial dedication is held for Lincoln Memorial Golf Course, a blacks-only golf course in Washington, D.C.

John W. Lewis establishes Booker T. Washington Country Club (Buckingham, Pennsylvania).

1925
United States Colored Golfers Association is established.

Shady Rest Golf and Country Club (Scotch Plains, New Jersey) hosts the National Colored Golf Championship, the first black major golf tournament held in the United States.

Joseph Bartholomew becomes the first golf professional at Metairie Golf Club (Louisiana), an all-white facility.

Citizens Golf Club is established in Washington, D.C.

1926
Robert Hawkins purchases Mapledale Country Club (Stow, Massachusetts).

Tuskegee Institute (Tuskegee, Alabama) opens a nine-hole golf course on Franklin Road.

United Golfers Association sponsors its first official Negro National Open; host site is Mapledale Country Club. First place prize of 25 dollars is awarded to Harry Jackson.

George Roddy Sr. becomes the first African American member of the University of Iowa golf team.

Abraham Lincoln Lewis establishes Lincoln Golf and Country Club (Jacksonville, Florida).

1927
Robert "Pat" Ball captures his first of four UGA Negro National Open Championship victories; Ball later wins the same event in 1929, 1934, and 1941.

Nimrod Allen and Rocky Fork Outing Club establish Big Walnut Country Club (Gahanna, Ohio).

1928
Dewey Brown Sr. becomes the first African American PGA Member.

UGA Negro National Open includes, for the first time, an amateur men's division; Frank Gaskin wins.

United Golfers Association is formally established.

Parkridge Country Club (Corona, California) is purchased by a group of African American businessmen.

1929
Robert Hawkins sells Mapledale Country Club.

Mr. and Mrs. Osmond Barringer deed and convey Bonnie Brae property to the City of Charlotte, North Carolina; the Barringers' gift has specific usage guidelines—*for white people's…only…and requiring that the lands revert to the grantors if such restrictions are not carried out.*

1930
A.D.V. Crosby and R.G. Robinson become the first African Americans to enter a University of Michigan All-Campus Golf Tournament; Crosby wins.

UGA Negro National Open Championship includes, for the first time, a women's division; Marie Thompson is the winner.

Hampton Institute (Hampton, Virginia) begins development of Shellbanks Golf Course.

1931
Howard "Butch" Wheeler wins the Atlanta Open.

1932
The Common Pleas Court awards, to Robert "Pat" Ball, an injunction to play in the USGA Philadelphia Public Links.

Lincoln Country Club (Atlanta, Georgia) is established; nine-hole golf course is on unused cemetery property.

1933
Capital City Golf Club is renamed Royal Golf Club.

Howard Wheeler wins his first of six UGA Negro National Open Championships (1933, 1938, 1946, 1947, 1948, 1958).

1934
Section 1 of Article III (also known as Caucasian-only clause) becomes a formal part of The PGA of America Bylaws. *Section 1 of Article III* limits membership to professional golfers of the Caucasian race.

The PGA of America retracts Dewey Brown Sr.'s PGA Member status.

1935
Solomon Hughes Sr. wins Negro National Open Championship.

1936
The United Golfer is first published.

1937
The first intercollegiate golf match is held between a historically black university (Wilberforce University) and a white university (Ohio Northern University).

1937 (continues)
Wake-Robin Golf Club, founded in Washington, D.C., becomes the first African American women's golf club documented in the United States.

The Chicago Women's Golf Club is organized.

Yorkshire Golf Club is established.

1938
Caddie Willie Stokes has his first of five Masters Tournament wins; other Masters Tournament wins are in 1948, 1951, 1953, and 1956.

Wake-Robin Golf Club and Royal Golf Club petition for African Americans to have access to public golf courses in Washington, D.C.

The first Historically Black Colleges and Universities Southern Intercollegiate Association of Colleges tournament is held at Tuskegee Institute's nine-hole course.

Robert "Pat" Ball joins the staff at Palos Park Golf Course (Chicago, Illinois); thus, Ball becomes one of the first African American golf professionals hired at a desegregated public golf facility.

Shady Rest Golf and Country Club's African American ownership is terminated due to a tax lien foreclosure. The Township of Scotch Plains becomes owner; however, African Americans are allowed to continue to operate the facility.

1939
Langston Golf Course (Washington, D.C.), a segregated blacks-only nine-hole golf course built by the federal government, opens.

1939 (continues)

The Chicago Women's Golf Club becomes the first women's organization to obtain UGA affiliation.

Cosmopolitan Golf Club (Los Angeles, California) hosts the first UGA Negro National Open that is held on the west coast.

1940

The Chicago Women's Golf Club hosts a United Golfers Association tournament.

1941

The first Joe Louis Open is held.

Paris Brown becomes the first woman to hold an executive office in the United Golfers Association.

United States Secretary of the Interior Harold Ickes issues a desegregation order to Washington, D.C. public golf courses.

1942

Beginning this year, the Joe Louis Open is not held from 1942–1944 (during World War II); and United Golfers Association Negro National Open is not held from 1942–1945 (also World War II years).

1945

The second Joe Louis Open is held.

1946

The first Joe Louis Open Women's Amateur event is held; Lucy Mitchum wins.

1947
Hermann Park Golf Course (Houston, Texas) desegregates.

Vernoncrest Ladies Golf Club is established and is recognized as the first African American women's golf club on the west coast.

Dewey Brown Sr. purchases Cedar River House and Golf Club (Indian Lake, New York).

Dr. Pruitt Sweeney Sr. files a lawsuit against the City of Louisville, Kentucky for desegregation of city golf courses.

1948
Solomon Hughes Sr.'s and Ted Rhodes's applications to compete in the PGA Tour 1948 St. Paul Open are denied.

Clearview Golf Club (East Canton, Ohio) opens with nine holes.

William "Bill" Spiller and Theodore "Ted" Rhodes place in the top 25 at the Los Angeles Open.

Bill Spiller's, Ted Rhodes's, and Madison Gunter's entry fees are refunded after they play a practice round at the Richmond Open. Because of their race, The PGA of America rejects their entry to compete at the Richmond Open. Spiller, Rhodes, and Gunter file a lawsuit against The PGA of America and Richmond Open tournament committee.

Theodore "Ted" Rhodes becomes the second African American to play in a USGA U.S. Open Championship.

The PGA of America allows blacks to enter PGA events through an *invitation-only* policy.

Charlie Sifford turns professional.

1949

Rice v. H.H. Arnold is filed in Dade County Circuit Court; lawsuit challenges a restrictive play policy at Miami Country Club, a municipal golf course in Miami, Florida. The restrictive play policy—blacks are allowed to play the course on "Mondays only".

Theodore "Ted" Rhodes claims his first UGA professional championship win.

City Council of Norfolk, Virginia gives Negroes exclusive use of Memorial Park Golf Course on—the second weekend (Friday, Saturday, and Sunday) of each month; during the other weeks Negroes have exclusive use on Wednesdays and Fridays.

1950

Federal court grants African Americans the right to play on municipal golf courses in Baltimore, Maryland.

Theodore "Ted" Rhodes receives a sponsor's invitation to play in the Phoenix Open; Rhodes makes the cut.

Desert Mashie Golf Club becomes a USGA member club; thus, Desert Mashie Golf Club is recognized as one of the first African American golf clubs to join the USGA.

1951

Lions Municipal Golf Course (Austin, Texas) desegregates.

Holmes v. Atlanta (Atlanta, Georgia) is filed; lawsuit seeks desegregation of public golf courses and city parks.

A federal judge orders the City of Louisville, Kentucky to open all city golf course services to African Americans or provide separate golf facilities for African Americans.

1951 (continues)
James Green, Hugo Owens, Harvey Johnson Jr., and Floyd Cooper file a lawsuit against the City of Portsmouth, Virginia; lawsuit seeks, for Negroes, access to City Park Golf Course and Glensheallah Golf Course. Federal District Court orders the City of Portsmouth, Virginia to provide golfing facilities for Negroes; the City of Portsmouth allows Negroes to play—on Fridays only—at City Park Golf Course.

1952
Louisville, Kentucky public golf courses open all services to African Americans.

Eural Clark and Bill Spiller, through sponsors' exemptions, enter the San Diego Open. Spiller makes the cut; Spiller is denied the right to continue to compete in the San Diego Open because he is African American.

Amateur golfer Joe Louis (world heavyweight boxing champion) receives a sponsor's exemption to the San Diego Open; Louis's entry is denied because he is African American. The PGA of America later changes its decision and allows Louis to compete; thus, Louis becomes the first African American to play in a PGA sponsored event.

Charlie Sifford wins his first of six UGA Negro National Open Championships. He also wins from 1953 to 1956 and in 1960.

United States Supreme Court upholds Florida Supreme Court ruling to not remove the "Monday's only" rule at municipal golf courses in Miami, Florida.

Miami Country Club informs the USGA that Negroes will not be permitted to compete in the USGA Amateur Public Links Championship held at Miami Country Club.

1952 (continues)
The PGA of America allows African Americans to enter tournaments through a sponsor's exemption.

Rogers Park Golf Club (Tampa, Florida) opens as a segregated golf course for African Americans.

1953
Joe "Roach" Delancey wins UGA Negro National Open Amateur Championship. This is Delancey's first of three consecutive UGA Amateur Championship wins.

Fir State Golf Club (Seattle, Washington) becomes a USGA member club.

1954
The City of Fort Worth, Texas opens Harmon Field Golf Course, a segregated golf course for blacks only.

Paris Brown becomes the first woman tournament director of United Golfers Association.

Pete Brown turns professional.

Western States Golf Association is founded.

City of Nashville, Tennessee opens Cumberland Golf Course, a nine-hole golf course exclusively for African Americans.

City of Nashville, Tennessee grants African Americans two designated days of the week to play Shelby Park Golf Course, one of three city golf courses.

City of Houston, Texas grants African Americans unrestricted access to municipal golf courses.

1955

African Americans are granted unrestricted access to Tyrrell Park Municipal Golf Course (Beaumont, Texas).

Holmes v. Atlanta U.S. Supreme Court ruling desegregates public golf courses and city parks in Atlanta, Georgia.

Six African American men, later known as "The Greensboro Six", are arrested for "simple trespassing"—playing nine holes at Gillespie Park Golf Course, a Greensboro, North Carolina public golf course operated by a private club for "whites only".

United States Supreme Court bans segregation of public golf courses in Little Rock, Arkansas.

Washington, D.C. golf courses desegregate.

United States District Court grants Negroes unrestricted access to all Fort Worth, Texas city-owned golf courses.

Langston Golf Course expands to 18 holes.

1956

Linwood Bailey, James Gray, and James Holley III file a lawsuit in Federal District Court seeking, for Negroes, unrestricted access to City Park Golf Course (Portsmouth, Virginia); temporary injunction granted.

In Huntsville, Alabama a municipal ordinance that set aside one day a week for Negroes to play the municipal golf course is passed.

Nashville, Tennessee public golf courses are desegregated.

Chicago Women's Golf Association becomes a USGA member.

1956 (continues)

William Powell buys out his partners and becomes sole owner of the 130-acre property—Clearview Golf Club in East Canton, Ohio.

Ann Gregory enters the USGA U.S. Women's Amateur Open at Meridian Hills Country Club (Indianapolis, Indiana); thus, Gregory becomes the first African American female amateur to play in a USGA national championship.

1957

Charlie Sifford wins Long Beach Open, a non-sanctioned PGA event.

Dallas, Texas city golf courses desegregate.

Bonnie Brae Municipal Golf Course (Charlotte, North Carolina) desegregates.

The Greensboro Six is indicted on initial trespassing charges. Guilty verdict; appeal is filed.

Circuit Court of Appeals orders the City of Greensboro, North Carolina to cease operating Gillespie Park Golf Course as a segregated golf facility.

"Monday's only" rule is removed from Miami, Florida municipal golf course policy.

1958

A permanent injunction is granted giving Negroes unrestricted access to City Park Golf Course in Portsmouth, Virginia.

Dewey Brown Sr. becomes Golf Course Superintendents Association of America's first African American member.

1958 (continues)
Wichita, Kansas City Park Board prohibits city golf courses from hosting tournaments that exclude blacks; Chester Lewis, local NAACP president, spearheads this action.

1959
Meadowbrook Country Club and Golf Course (Garner, North Carolina) is established.

Charlie Sifford receives his first golf ball endorsement from United States Rubber Company; and Charlie Sifford receives his first golf club endorsement from Kroydon Company.

Robert Moss is the only African American to compete in the San Diego County Amateur Golf Tournament; Moss wins the sixth flight.

William "Bill" Wright wins the 34th USGA U.S. Amateur Public Links Championship; thus, Wright becomes the first African American to capture a national golf title.

Theodore "Ted" Rhodes and Charlie Sifford are appointed to Ballantine Company Athletic Advisory Board. (Ballantine Company was a brewery company.)

1960
Harold Dunovant becomes the first African American graduate of the PGA Business School.

Stanley Mosk, California Attorney General, challenges the "Caucasian-only clause"—*Section 1 of Article III* of The PGA of America Bylaws.

Federal District Court ruling orders Charleston, South Carolina municipal golf course to desegregate.

1960 (continues)
Charlie Sifford earns PGA Approved Tournament Player card; thus, Sifford becomes the first African American PGA Tour member.

Maggie Hathaway petitions Los Angeles County to hire African Americans as starters at the county's golf courses.

Gulf City Association files a lawsuit seeking access to play Mobile Municipal Park Golf Course (Mobile Alabama).

United States Supreme Court dismisses The Greensboro Six's conviction appeal.

Skyview Golf Association hosts the first Skyview Tournament.

1961
The PGA of America passes a resolution to remove the Caucasian-only clause from its bylaws.

Charlie Sifford becomes the first African American to play on the PGA Tour.

United States District Court rules in favor of Gulf City Golfers Association; African Americans are granted access to play Mobile Municipal Park Golf Course.

Charleston, South Carolina's municipal golf course desegregates.

Richard I. Thomas receives PGA Approved Tournament Player card; thus, Thomas becomes the second African American to receive PGA Tour Member status.

Carl Jackson is caddying in the Masters Tournament for the first time.

1961 (continues)
Charlie Sifford plays in the Greater Greensboro Open and becomes the first African American to play in a PGA event held in the south.

Pete Brown wins the Michigan Open.

Charles L. Bowden Golf Course (Macon, Georgia) integrates; this is the first integrated public facility in Macon, Georgia.

1962
Tuskegee Institute (Tuskegee, Alabama) develops a nine-hole golf course at Moton Air Field.

Jimmie DeVoe becomes a PGA Member.

The PGA of America removes from its bylaws—*Section 1 of Article III*, also known as the Caucasian-only clause.

Gillespie Park Golf Course desegregates (Greensboro, North Carolina).

1963
Althea Gibson becomes the first African American LPGA Tour member; Gibson makes her first professional golf appearance at the USGA U.S. Women's Open.

Pete Brown receives PGA Approved Tournament Player status.

Willie "Pete" Peterson has his first of five Masters Tournament wins as Jack Nicklaus's caddie.

George Roddy Sr. wins the Indiana City Championship; this is Roddy's first of two wins for this event; he also wins in 1967.

1964
William "Bill" Wright joins the PGA Tour.

The state of Georgia's state-operated golf course, located on Jekyll Island, desegregates.

African Americans no longer operate Shady Rest Golf and Country Club; the Township of Scotch Plains, owner of Shady Rest Golf and Country Club, takes over the operation. The facility is renamed Scotch Hills Country Club, and the facility opens to the public.

Charlie Sifford receives full PGA member status.

Pete Brown wins Waco Turner Open; thus, Pete Brown becomes the first African American to win a PGA Tour sanctioned event.

1965
National Negro Golf Association is established.

James Black, age 22, becomes the youngest African American to join the PGA Tour.

The PGA of America reinstates Dewey Brown Sr. as a PGA Member.

1966
Bob Salsbury, James Blocker, Al Letson, and Maxwell Sanford initiate a plan to purchase Freeway Golf Course.

Ben Davis, PGA Member, becomes the first African American admitted to the Michigan PGA Section.

National Negro Golf Association hosts its first tournament in Pittsburgh, Pennsylvania

1967

Renee Powell becomes the second African American to join the LPGA Tour.

Lee Elder receives PGA Tour card.

Charlie Sifford wins the PGA Tour's Greater Hartford Open.

1968

Murphy Street becomes the first African American to win the Gate City Open Tournament.

George Johnson earns his PGA Tour card.

Freeway Golf Course, an 18-hole golf course located in Sicklerville, New Jersey, opens for play. Freeway Golf Course is the first 18-hole golf course owned by African Americans in the United States.

1969

Charlie Sifford wins the Los Angles Open.

Cumberland Golf Course (Nashville, Tennessee) is renamed Ted Rhodes Golf Course.

1970

Jim Dent joins the PGA Tour.

Charlie Owens joins the PGA Tour.

Althea Gibson ties for second in a three-way playoff at the Lem Immke Buick Open—LPGA Tour.

Pete Brown wins Andy Williams-San Diego Open Invitational.

1971

Jackson, Mississippi public golf courses desegregate.

Tuskegee Institute closes its nine-hole golf course at Moton Air Field.

George Johnson wins Azalea Open; thus, Johnson becomes the fourth African American to win a PGA Tour event.

1972

Carrie Russell becomes the first golf coach at Delaware State University; Russell coaches the men's golf team.

Joseph Bartholomew, golf course architect, becomes the first African American inductee to the Greater New Orleans Sports Hall of Fame.

1973

Entertainer Sammy Davis Jr. becomes title host and a major sponsor of the PGA Tour's Greater Hartford Open; this event is renamed Sammy Davis Jr. Greater Hartford Open.

Al Green and Nathaniel Starks join the PGA Tour.

1974

Carrie Russell becomes the first African American LPGA T&CP Member.

Bill Bishop represents Gulf Oil Company at the Nigerian Open.

Lee Elder wins Monsanto Open; this win qualifies Elder to receive the first Masters Tournament player invitation given to an African American.

1975

Charlie Sifford joins the Senior PGA Tour.

Lee Elder becomes the first African American to play in a Masters Tournament.

Maggie Hathaway is the only African American granted a media pass to the Masters Tournament.

Charlie Sifford wins the Senior PGA Championship.

Bide-A-Wee Golf Course board members grant Charlie Sifford a one-time playing privilege; thus, Sifford becomes the first African American to play Bide-A-Wee Golf Course (Portsmouth, Virginia).

Calvin Peete qualifies to play on the PGA Tour.

1976

Justice Department files a lawsuit seeking integration of Bide-A-Wee Golf Club (Portsmouth, Virginia).

Jim Thorpe, Bobby Stroble, and Ron Terry join the PGA Tour.

Jim Dent wins the Florida PGA Championship; this is Dent's first of three consecutive wins for this event.

Carrie Russell becomes the first president of the LPGA T&CP Northeast Section.

Lee Elder wins Houston Open.

1977

Pearl Carey becomes the first female president of Western States Golf Association.

1977 (continues)
Lee Elder plays in the Masters Tournament.

1978
Clearview Golf Club expands to 18 holes.

Lee Elder wins Greater Milwaukee Open in a playoff; Elder defeats Lee Trevino on the eighth playoff hole. Elder shoots a 13 under (275).

Thomas Kenney purchases Spring Lake Golf Course, a nine-hole golf course in Glen Allen, Virginia.

Lee Elder plays in the Masters Tournament.

1979
Calvin Peete wins Greater Milwaukee Open.

Lee Elder plays in the Masters Tournament; he ties for 17th, which later becomes his best finish out of six Masters Tournament appearances.

Pontchartrain Park Golf Course (New Orleans, Louisiana) is renamed Joseph M. Bartholomew Senior Golf Course.

Lee Elder becomes the first African American to play on a U.S. Ryder Cup Team.

1980
Calvin Peete becomes the second African American to receive an invitation to play in a Masters Tournament.

Charlie Sifford wins Suntree Senior PGA Tour Classic.

Lee Carter joins the PGA Tour.

1980 (continues)
Lee Elder plays in the Masters Tournament.

1981
Phyllis Meekins becomes a LPGA T&CP Member.

Lee Elder makes his last appearance playing in the Masters Tournament.

Calvin Peete makes the cut at the Masters Tournament; and from 1981 to 1987, Peete continued to make the cut at the Masters Tournament.

Charlie Owens joins the Senior PGA Tour.

Al Morton and Tom Woodard join the PGA Tour.

1982
Alton Duhon wins USGA Senior Amateur Championship; thus, Duhon becomes the first African American to win a USGA Senior Championship, and second African American to win a USGA championship.

Western Avenue Golf Club is renamed Chester Washington Golf Course in honor of Chester Washington, former publisher of *Los Angeles Sentinel* newspaper.

Jim Thorpe wins Canadian PGA Championship.

Calvin Peete wins Greater Milwaukee Open.

Jim Thorpe plays in the Masters Tournament.

1983
Calvin Peete is a member of the U.S. Ryder Cup team.

1983 (continues)
Adams Park Golf Course (Atlanta, Georgia) is renamed Alfred Tup Holmes Memorial Golf Course.

Calvin Peete wins Georgia-Pacific Atlanta Golf Classic and Anheuser-Busch Golf Classic.

This is the first year, since the first Masters Tournament was held in 1934, that there is not an all-black caddie field at a Masters Tournament.

Calvin Peete receives Ben Hogan Award.

1984
Lee Elder joins the Senior PGA Tour.

Jim Thorpe plays in the Masters Tournament.

Calvin Peete ties for 15th at the Masters Tournament.

1985
Jim Thorpe wins Greater Milwaukee Open.

Calvin Peete is a member of the U.S. Ryder Cup team.

Jim Thorpe ties for 18th at the Masters Tournament.

Calvin Peete receives the Vardon Trophy.

Adrian Stills successfully completes PGA Tour Qualifying School and earns PGA Tour Member status for 1986.

1986
Pipe O Peace Golf Course in Riverdale, Illinois (outskirts of Chicago) is renamed Joe Louis The Champ Golf Course.

1986 (continues)
Calvin Peete wins MONY Tournament of Champions, and Calvin Peete ties for 11th at the Masters Tournament.

Jim Thorpe makes the cut at the Masters Tournament.

Charlie Sifford, at age 64, becomes the oldest player to receive a Champions Tour exemption.

Harold Dunovant establishes National Black Golf Hall of Fame.

Catana Starks becomes the first men's golf coach at Tennessee State University, and the first African American female to coach a men's NCAA Division I golf team.

1987
First National Minority College Golf Championship is held.

Russell Taylor becomes the first African American hired at Pebble Beach Company as assistant golf professional and assistant buyer.

Charlie Owens receives Ben Hogan Award.

Jim Thorpe makes the cut at the Masters Tournament.

Charles Dorton distributes the first calendar issue for Black Golf Information Center.

1988
Bide-A-Wee Golf Course, in Portsmouth, Virginia, desegregates and opens to the public.

First publication of *TEE-CUP Magazine,* the official publication of Western States Golf Association, is launched.

1989

Jim Dent joins the Senior PGA Tour; at the end of the season he ranks 12th on the Senior PGA Tour's money list.

Donald F. Littlejohn becomes the first African American to win the Charlotte City Amateur Golf Championship; Littlejohn also wins the same event in 1991.

Ann Gregory wins gold medal at the U.S. Senior Olympics.

Selina Johnson receives the PGA Tour Card Walker Award for contributions to junior golf.

1990

Tiger Woods is Southern California Player of the Year.

Hal Thompson, president of Shoal Creek Golf and Country Club (Birmingham, Alabama), announces that Shoal Creek Golf and Country Club will not be forced into accepting African Americans as members.

Ron Townsend becomes the first African American member of Augusta National Golf Club.

Louis Willie Jr. becomes the first African American member of Shoal Creek Golf and Country Club (Birmingham, Alabama). Willie's honorary membership becomes effective nine days before the opening of the PGA Championship at Shoal Creek Golf and Country Club.

1991

Tiger Woods is named *Golf Digest* Player of the Year and AJGA Player of the Year.

USGA acknowledges George Grant's United States patented wooden golf tee invention.

1991 (continues)
Walter Morgan joins the Senior PGA Tour.

Tiger Woods, age 15, becomes the youngest to win a U.S. Junior Amateur Championship.

1992
William "Bill" Dickey receives the PGA Tour Card Walker Award.

John F. Merchant becomes the first African American to serve on the USGA Executive Committee.

1993
Pete McDaniel becomes the first African American hired at *Golf World*.

Calvin Peete joins the Senior PGA Tour.

Barbara Douglas becomes the first African American to serve on the USGA Women's Committee.

Jeff Dunovant receives PGA Class A Member status; thus, Jeff and his father Harold Dunovant become the first African American father and son PGA Class A Members. Harold received PGA Class A Member status in 1974.

Tiger Woods is *Golf World* Player of the Year.

Jim Dent posts nine top-10 finishes on Champions Tour.

1994
Tiger Woods claims his first collegiate win (William Tucker Invitational), and first of three U.S. Amateur wins (1994–1996).

1994 (continues)
Joseph Louis Barrow Jr. becomes the first African American member of Denver Country Club.

The first Women's Collegiate Golf Classic is held.

Jim Dent is inducted into the Georgia Golf Hall of Fame.

1995
Craig Bowen is hired as sales representative at Titleist.

Robert Clark Sr. receives PGA Class A Member status and becomes the first African American PGA Member in the state of Oregon.

Leroy Richie becomes the first African American to serve as general counsel of the USGA.

LaRee Sugg becomes the third African American member of the LPGA Tour.

George Lewis becomes the first African American elected to serve on The PGA of America Board of Directors.

National Minority Golf Foundation is established.

Walter Morgan wins Senior PGA Tour GTW NW Classic.

Tiger Woods competes for the first time at the Masters Tournament. Woods enters as an amateur player and is the only amateur to make the cut; Woods ties for 41st.

Bobby Stroble joins the Senior PGA Tour.

Dedric Holmes becomes the first African American to serve in an administrative position at the USGA; Holmes is hired as Coordinator of Junior Golf and Minority Affairs.

1996
Bull Creek Golf and Country Club (North Carolina) opens with nine-holes.

Renee Powell becomes the first African American female to earn PGA Member status.

Walter Morgan wins the FHP Health Care Classic and the Ameritech Senior Open.

Ron Edwards becomes the second African American member of Shoal Creek Golf and Country Club; and first African American equity member of Shoal Creek Golf and Country Club.

Jackson State University men's golf team becomes the first HBCU men's golf team to advance to a NCAA regional championship.

Tiger Woods, age 20, joins the PGA Tour; Woods also records his first PGA Tour victory at the Las Vegas Invitational.

Earl Parham wins the St. Louis PubLinx Open Championship.

1997
Ted Rhodes is posthumously inducted into the Tennessee Golf Hall of Fame.

Andy Walker, member of Pepperdine University men's golf team, becomes the first African American male to play on a Division 1 NCAA championship men's team.

George Johnson joins the staff at Bobby Nichols Golf Course in Louisville, Kentucky; thus, Johnson becomes the first African American hired as head golf professional in the state of Kentucky.

1997 (continues)

Tiger Woods receives Associated Press Male Athlete of the Year Award, and ESPY Best Male Athlete Award.

Earnie Ellison is hired as Director of Finance for Tournament Operations at The PGA of America; thus, Ellison becomes the first African American in a senior management position at The PGA of America.

Tiger Woods becomes the first person of African American descent to win a Masters Tournament; and at age 21, he becomes the youngest Masters Tournament winner and the youngest No.1 golfer.

Tiger Woods has four PGA Tour wins, and is named Player of the Year by the PGA Tour, The PGA of America, and Golf Writers Association of America.

William Powell receives honorary PGA Member status by The PGA of America Northern Ohio Section.

Jack Thompson Golf Course (Los Angeles, California) is renamed Maggie Hathaway Golf Course.

1998

Tiger Woods receives Mark H. McCormack Award.

William Powell is inducted into Ohio Veterans Hall of Fame.

Bull Creek Golf and Country Club (Louisburg, North Carolina) expands to 18 holes.

Eastern Golf Course (Oklahoma City, Oklahoma) is renamed James E. Stewart Golf Course—in honor of civil rights activist James Edward Stewart.

Tiger Woods is year-end world number one ranked golfer.

1999

Renee Powell receives LPGA Teaching & Club Professional honorary member status.

Tiger Woods wins eight PGA Tour events and one major event.

William "Bill" Dickey becomes the first African American recipient of The PGA Distinguished Service Award.

Tiger Woods is named Player of the Year by the PGA Tour, The PGA of America, and Golf Writers Association of America.

Deer Brook Golf Course (Shelby, North Carolina) opens; former NFL player Willie Green is a co-owner.

William Powell receives Life Member status from The PGA of America.

Tiger Woods receives Associated Press Male Athlete of the Year Award.

George Roddy Sr. becomes the first African American inducted into the Indiana Golf Hall of Fame.

Jim Thorpe joins the Senior PGA Tour.

Tiger Woods claims his 13th PGA Tour career win; with this win, Woods breaks Calvin Peete's record of the most PGA Tour wins by an African American.

Tiger Woods is the year-end world number one ranked golfer; Woods receives Mark H. McCormack Award.

William Powell receives the first Unsung Hero Award presented by Congressional Black Caucus Spouses.

2000s ◆ ◆ ◆

2000
Dr. Obie Bender becomes the second African American PGA
Board of Directors member.

Kevin Hall becomes the first African American to attend
Ohio State University through a golf scholarship, and the
first African American member of Ohio State University
men's golf team.

Lee Elder receives the Golf Writers of America Association
Annual Award.

Julius Richardson becomes the first African American to be
listed among the top 100 instructors in *Golf Magazine*.

Tiger Woods receives Associated Press Male Athlete of the
Year Award and ESPY Best Male Athlete Award.

Stephen Reed becomes the first African American to win an
American Junior Golf Association award since Tiger Woods
won in 1992.

Tiger Woods ends the season with nine PGA Tour wins and
three major wins.

Robert Clark Sr. receives Oregon Chapter PGA Junior Golf
Leader award; Clark also receives this award for the next
two years.

Tiger Woods is named Player of the Year by the PGA Tour,
The PGA of America, and Golf Writers Association of
America.

Tiger Woods is the year-end world number one ranked
golfer, and Woods receives Mark H. McCormack Award.

2001

Jameisha Levister, a female member of North Carolina Central University men's golf team, is honored as CIAA Men's Golf Rookie of the Year.

Clifford Sommerville opens Wedgewood Golf Center (Halifax, Virginia).

Tiger Woods receives ESPY Best Male Athlete Award; Woods is named Player of the Year by the PGA Tour, The PGA of America, and Golf Writers Association of America.

Jeff Dunovant is Southwest Section PGA Junior Golf Leader of the Year.

William "Bill" Dickey is the first African American to receive the USGA Joe Dey Award.

Clearview Golf Club (East Canton, Ohio) is listed among the National Register of Historic Places.

Mill Cove Golf Course (Jacksonville, Florida) opens for play under ownership and operation of T. C. Newman and Ruby Newman.

Tiger Woods becomes the first player to hold all four professional major titles at once—U.S. Open, British Open, PGA Championship, and the Masters Tournament.

Tiger Woods has five PGA Tour wins, and Woods wins the Masters Tournament for the second time.

Jackson State University women's golf team becomes the first HBCU women's golf team to advance to a NCAA regional championship.

Tiger Woods is the year-end world number one ranked golfer, and Woods receives Mark H. McCormack Award.

2002
SydMar Golf Management takes over management of Sugar Creek Golf Club, a municipal property in Dekalb County, Georgia; thus, SydMar Golf Management is recognized as the first African American-owned golf management company to win a county golf course management contract.

LaRee Sugg becomes the first African American to coach a women's golf team at a predominantly white university, the University of Richmond.

Tiger Woods captures his third Masters Tournament win, his second U.S. Open victory, and five PGA Tour wins.

The PGA of America, PGA Tour, and Golf Writers Association of America name Tiger Woods Player of the Year.

Tiger Woods is the year-end world number one ranked golfer, and Woods receives Mark H. McCormack Award.

Pearl Carey receives California Golf Writers Association Golden State Award.

Lauren Braswell becomes the first African American to join Rutgers University women's golf team.

2003
The first editon of *African American Golfer's Digest* magazine is released.

Steve Poole becomes the first African American member of Seattle Golf Club (Seattle, Washington).

Tiger Woods is named Player of the Year by the PGA Tour, The PGA of America, and Golf Writers Association of America.

2003 (continues)
Steve Hogan receives PGA Junior Teacher of the Year Award.

Renee Powell receives PGA First Lady of Golf Award.

Fayetteville State University men's team is the only HBCU team to qualify for the NCAA Division II playoffs.

Tiger Woods has five PGA Tour wins.

Oneida Castillo earns LPGA T&CP Class A Member status.

Jim Thorpe wins Charles Schwab Cup Championship.

Susan Lee-Hargrave is recognized as the first African American female to build and own a golf facility in the United States—Jeremy's Golf Center and Academy (South Waxahachie, Texas).

Tiger Woods is the year-end world number one ranked golfer; and Tiger Woods receives Mark H. McCormack Award.

2004
Kenneth Sims becomes the first African American president of a PGA Chapter Section.

Pete Hayes, at North Carolina Central University, is CIAA Men's Head Golf Coach of the Year.

Tiger Woods has one PGA Tour win.

Friends Golf Club takes over management of Pickett-Thomas Golf Course (Camden, South Carolina).

Tiger Woods receives Mark H. McCormack Award.

2004 (continues)
Milton Irvin becomes the first African American member of Baltusrol Golf Club (Springfield, New Jersey).

Eve Wright becomes the first African American hired as Director of Legal Affairs at LPGA national headquarters.

Charlie Sifford becomes the first African American inductee into the World Golf Hall of Fame (St. Augustine, Florida).

2005
Hercules Pitts purchases Lake Arbor Golf Course.

Weldon and Shirley Coleman open Pro Golf at Camp Creek in East Point, Georgia; during years of operation (2005–2008) the Coleman's are the only African American owners of a Pro Golf franchise.

Tiger Woods has six PGA Tour victories, wins the Masters Tournament for the fourth time, and British Open for the second time.

Pearl Carey is the first African American to receive the Northern California Golf Association Grand Master Award; and the second female and second African American to receive the USGA Joe Dey Award.

Barbara Douglas is named second-vice chairman of the USGA Women's Committee.

Tiger Woods is named Player of the Year by the PGA Tour, The PGA of America, and Golf Writers Association of America.

Kevin Hall makes his PGA Tour debut through a sponsor's exemption; this appearance makes Kevin Hall the first profoundly deaf person to play in a PGA Tour event.

2005 (continues)
Jerry Bruner, European Senior Tour member, wins Algarve Seniors Open of Portugal; Bruner also has two previous wins—the 2003 De Vere Northumberland Seniors Classic and 2001 European Seniors Tour Championship.

Tiger Woods is the year-end world number one ranked golfer, and Woods receives Mark H. McCormack Award.

2006
Wendy Boyd becomes a LPGA T&CP Class A Member.

The Tiger Woods Learning Center opens (Anaheim, California).

Hercules Pitts purchases Marlborough Country Club (Upper Marlboro, Maryland).

Lewis Horne Jr. becomes board chairman of The LPGA Foundation.

Sam Puryear becomes full-time assistant coach of men's golf at Stanford University.

Tiger Woods receives Associated Press Male Athlete of the Year Award.

Andy Walker ranks 10th on Gateway Pro Tour season ending official money list.

Charlie Sifford becomes the first African American golfer to receive an honorary Doctor of Laws degree from the University of St. Andrews (Scotland, England).

Albert Crews is PetroSun Independence Bowl Sportsman of the Year. Crews also wins Sunbelt Senior Tour Championship.

2006 (continues)
Andrea Winslow becomes the fourth African American female to enter a LPGA Tour event.

The PGA of America takes over full management and operation of National Minority College Golf Championship; event is renamed PGA Minority Collegiate Golf Championship.

Tim O'Neal has five top-10 finishes on Nationwide Tour.

Tiger Woods posts eight PGA Tour wins and two majors—British Open and PGA Championship; Woods also ties for third at the Masters Tournament.

Julius Erving (former NBA player also known as Dr. J) becomes co-owner of Heritage Golf Club.

Jim Thorpe wins Charles Schwab Cup Championship; Thorpe ranks seventh on the Champions Tour season ending official money list.

Tiger Woods is Player of the Year by the PGA Tour, The PGA of America, and Golf Writers Association of America.

Tiger Woods is the year-end world number one ranked golfer; and Tiger Woods receives Mark H. McCormack Award.

2007
Renee Powell receives the inaugural Rolex For the Love of the Game Award.

Jackie and Percy Hall (parents of professional golfer Kevin Hall, first profoundly deaf person to play in a PGA Tour event) are inducted into the Caddie Hall of Fame under the category Caddie/Coach.

2007 (continues)

William Powell is inducted into the Ohio Golf Hall of Fame.

Charlie Sifford receives an honorary Doctor of Laws degree from Lincoln University (Jefferson City, Missouri).

Barbara Douglas is named USGA Women's Committee vice-chairman.

Charlie Sifford receives Old Tom Morris Award from Golf Course Superintendents Association of America.

Greater Grace Temple purchases The New Rogell Golf Course (Detroit, Michigan).

Sam Puryear becomes head coach of Michigan State University men's golf program.

Tiger Woods is named Player of the Year by the PGA Tour, The PGA of America, and Golf Writers Association of America.

Chris Arceneaux is named Golf Channel Amateur Tour Player of the Year.

Tiger Woods has seven PGA Tour wins and one major win.

Jim Thorpe wins Charles Schwab Cup Championship.

Tiger Woods wins FedExCup, receives Mark H. McCormack Award, and is the year-end world number one ranked golfer.

Sheila Johnson becomes the first African American sole-owner of a golf resort and PGA Tour championship course—Innisbrook© Resort and Copperhead Golf Course.

Saint Augustine's University purchases Meadowbrook Country Club and Golf Course (Garner, North Carolina).

2007 (continues)
Raymond McDougal, Fayetteville State University head golf coach, receives CIAA Golf Coach of the Year Award for the 11th time; McDougal also received this award from 1993 to 2003.

Tiger Woods ties for second at the Masters Tournament.

William "Bill" Dickey receives an honorary Doctor of Public Service degree from University of Maryland Eastern Shore.

2008
Former NFL player Willie Richardson becomes co-owner of Brookwood Byram Country Club (Byram, Mississippi).

Carl Jackson is inducted to the Arkansas Golf Hall of Fame.

Bob Bonner purchases Grand Marais Golf Club (Centreville, Illinois).

Renee Powell becomes the first African American female golfer to receive an honorary Doctor of Laws degree from the University of St. Andrews (Scotland, England).

Tiger Woods is the year-end world number one ranked golfer; Tiger Woods receives Mark H. McCormack Award and ESPY Best Male Athlete Award.

Ulysses "Junior" Bridgeman becomes the third African American sworn in to serve on The PGA of America Board of Directors.

Sam Puryear is named Big Ten Coach of the Year.

University of Maryland Eastern Shore becomes the first HBCU, accredited by The PGA of America, to offer the PGA/PGM™ Program.

2008 (continues)
Tiger Woods posts four PGA Tour wins and one major victory; Tiger Woods places second at the Masters Tournament.

Barbara Douglas serves a second term as vice-chairman of the USGA Women's Committee.

Saint Augustine's University Golf Course and Recreational Complex at Meadowbrook opens to the public.

Tiger Woods is named number one on *Business Week*'s list of "The Power 100 Most Influential People In Sports".

Julius Erving (former NBA player also known as Dr. J) becomes sole owner of Heritage Golf Club.

2009
Nevin Phillips becomes the first African American to receive national PGA Merchandiser of the Year honors.

Vincent Johnson becomes the first recipient of the Northern Trust Open Exemption.

Donna Richardson Joyner becomes the first African American to serve on *Women's Golf Month* Spokeswomen Team.

The PGA of America grants posthumous honorary membership to Joseph Louis Barrow Sr., better known as Joe Louis, world heavyweight boxing champion.

Condoleezza Rice, former United States Secretary of State, becomes a member of Shoal Creek Golf and Country Club.

Barbara Douglas becomes the first African American woman to chair a USGA committee.

2009 (continues)
Shasta Averyhardt claims her first professional win; she wins on the SunCoast Ladies Series Tour.

William Powell receives PGA Distinguished Service Award.

Jamila Johnson becomes the first woman to coach a University of Maryland Eastern Shore men's golf team.

Tiger Woods wins the PGA Tour FedExCup and the Australian Masters.

Miller Park Golf Course is renamed Steve Hogan Golf Course in honor of the late Steve Hogan, PGA Member.

Cheyenne Woods enters Wegmans LPGA Championship through a sponsor's exemption.

Lynn Swann, Pro Football Hall of Famer, becomes a member of Augusta National Golf Club.

Tiger Woods has six PGA Tour wins; Golf Writers Association of America, the PGA Tour, and The PGA of America name Tiger Woods Player of the Year.

2010
Joshua Wooding becomes second recipient of the Northern Trust Open Exemption.

Maulana Dotch becomes the second African American female PGA Class A Member.

John Jacob, former CEO of the National Urban League, is sworn in to The PGA of America Board of Directors.

Renee Powell ties 24th on *Golf Digest*'s list of America's 50 Best Women Teachers.

2010 (continues)
Joseph Bramlett becomes the first African American, since 1985, to earn a PGA Tour card through PGA Tour Qualifying School.

Tiger Woods receives Mark H. McCormack Award for having the number one ranking for the most weeks in this calendar year.

Ginger Howard becomes the first African American female selected to a United States Junior Ryder Cup Team.

Tiger Woods ties fourth at the Masters Tournament and places fourth at the U.S. Open Championship.

Vincent Johnson wins Long Beach Open.

2011
Joseph Bramlett joins the PGA Tour.

Shasta Averyhardt joins the LPGA Tour and becomes the fourth African American LPGA Tour Member.

Dr. Angela Stewart becomes the first African American to win a Carolinas Golf Association event; Stewart wins North Carolina Women's Senior Amateur Championship.

Willie Mack III becomes the first African American to win a Michigan Amateur Championship; he wins the 100th Michigan Amateur Championship.

Ginger Howard receives a special age exemption to enter LPGA Qualifying School.

Ginger Howard wins five SunCoast Ladies Series Tour events, and places first on SunCoast Ladies Series Tour season-ending official money list.

2011 (continues)
Barbara Douglas receives the Ben Hogan Award.

Cheyenne Woods wins the Atlantic Coast Conference women's individual title.

Harold Varner III becomes the first African American male to win the North Carolina Amateur Championship.

Joseph Bramlett receives Northern Trust Open Exemption.

Donna Richardson Joyner is appointed to The LPGA Foundation Board of Directors.

Tiger Woods ties fourth at the Masters Tournament and third at Emirates Australian Open.

Revolution Park Golf Course is renamed Dr. Charles L. Sifford Golf Course at Revolution Park.

E. Lee Coble becomes the 34th president of Virginia State Golf Association; Coble is elected to a two-year term.

2012
Jonathan DePina becomes the first African American president of The Country Club of New Bedford, a private golf facility in North Dartmouth, Massachusetts.

Wake Robin Golf Club celebrates its 75th anniversary.

Jeff Dunovant is PGA Georgia Section Junior Golf Leader.

Gladys M. Lee earns LPGA T&CP Class A status.

Maurice Allen sets a new Guinness World Record for golf ball speed; Allen's 211 miles per hour (mph) speed breaks the previous record of 204 mph that was set in 2007.

2012 (continues)

Andy Walker becomes the fourth recipient of the Northern Trust Open Exemption.

Shasta Averyhardt earns 2013 LPGA Tour member conditional status.

Imani Scott becomes the first female member of Johnson C. Smith University men's golf team.

Don Wright, for the fifth time, is career money winner on the Invitational Golf Tour of America.

Shasta Averyhardt receives the first LPGA Symetra Rising Star Award.

Condoleezza Rice, former U.S. Secretary of State, becomes one of the first two female members of Augusta National Golf Club; and Condoleezza Rice is appointed to the USGA Nominating Committee.

Cheyenne Woods captures her first professional win; Woods wins on the SunCoast Ladies Series Tour.

Oneda Castillo is LPGA Southeast Section Teacher of the Year.

Donald Wright earns top money winner on the Invitational Golf Tour of America. Wright captured the same title in 2005, 2007, 2009, and 2010.

Renee Powell ranks 10th on *Golf Digest* "America's 50 Best Women Teachers" list.

Tiger Woods places third at the FedExCup Championship and closes the year with 74 PGA Tour career wins.

East/West Golf Classic celebrates its 30th anniversary.

2012 (continues)
Paine College wins Southern Intercollegiate Athletic Conference (SIAC) Golf Classic; this is the first of two consecutive SIAC Golf Classic wins.

2013
Jeremiah Wooding becomes fifth recipient of the Northern Trust Open Exemption; and Wooding becomes the first Northern Trust Open Exemption recipient to make the cut.

Jimmy DeVoe and William Powell are posthumously inducted into The PGA of America Hall of Fame.

Jamie Taylor earns LPGA T&CP Class A Member status.

Bill Neal purchases Woodridge Golf Club (Mineral Wells, West Virginia).

Sheila Johnson becomes the first African American female member of the USGA Executive Committee.

Tiger Woods receives ESPY Best Male Golfer Award; Tiger Woods, for the ninth time, receives the Vardon Trophy.

Andrew Walker, age 14, becomes the youngest African American to qualify for the USGA U.S. Amateur.

Timothy O'Neal earns Web.com Tour status for 2014.

Lynn Swann, Pro Football Hall of Famer, is named Independent Director on the PGA Board of Directors; Swann's three-year term begins in 2014.

Tiger Woods is number one in official world golf ranking.

Harold Varner III earns full status for the 2014 Web.com Tour season.

2013 (continues)

The PGA of America and PGA Tour name Tiger Woods Player of the Year for the 11th time.

At the end of the season, Tiger Woods has a total of 79 PGA Tour career victories.

2014

Harold Varner III receives the Northern Trust Open Exemption. Varner makes the cut; thus, Varner becomes the second Northern Trust Open Exemption recipient to make the cut.

Women's Collegiate Golf Classic celebrates its 20th anniversary.

Sadena Parks becomes the fifth African American to earn a LPGA Tour card.

From the Rough, a film based on the true story of Catana Starks, opens in theaters throughout the United States.

Cheyenne Woods becomes the sixth African American to earn a LPGA Tour card.

Dr. Charles Sifford receives the Presidential Medal of Freedom award from President Barack Obama.

Dr. Kneeland Youngblood becomes the first African American member of Dallas Country Club (Dallas, Texas).

Carl Jackson caddies in the Masters Tournament for the 53rd time.

Cheyenne Woods wins Volvik RACV Ladies European Masters; hence, Cheyenne Woods receives a two-year exemption for the Ladies European Tour.

2015

Renee Powell is one of seven women to be the first women granted membership to The Royal and Ancient Golf Club of St. Andrews (United Kingdom).

In honor of Dr. Charles Sifford, the County of Los Angeles, California renames West 120th Street (between Western Avenue and Van Ness Avenue)—Charlie Sifford Drive.

Harold Varner III earns PGA Tour card for the 2016 season; this is Varner's first time securing a PGA Tour card.

Charlie Sifford is posthumously inducted into The PGA of America Hall of Fame.

Harold Varner III captures his first top-10 finish as a PGA Tour member; Varner ties for fifth at the PGA Tour's OHL Classic at Mayakoba (2016 PGA Tour season).

William "Bill" Spiller is inducted into the Oklahoma Golf Hall of Fame.

Carolyn Suttles becomes the first woman elected president in the 70-year history of Desert Mashie Golf Club.

Tiger Woods is named a vice captain for the 2016 United States Ryder Cup team.

Ginger Howard becomes the seventh African American LPGA Tour Member; Howard earns 2016 LPGA Tour Member conditional status through LPGA Q School.

Sadena Parks ranks 100th on the LPGA Tour money list; thus, Parks retains her LPGA Tour member status for 2016.

Cheyenne Woods earns 2016 LPGA Tour card through LPGA Q School; 2016 will be Woods's second consecutive year on the LPGA Tour.

remove your blinders!

Clubhouse Thoughts

Let not these bittersweet turn of events give you a false sense of the symbolic transformations of American racism. The longevity of the African American involvement in the game of golf does not mean that—all is well.

Some may have blinders and take the "missing link of African Americans in golf" as an isolated problem. Others, who still honor the "good old boys cultural traditions", may view the problem as just another incident of common occurrences.

Whatever you conclude, the fact remains that for African Americans in golf, the color line of separation still exist. For more than a century, this racial line—camouflaged, fragmented, and entangled—has yet to be extinguished.

United States Golf Association was founded in 1894; The PGA of America was founded in 1916; LPGA was founded in 1950; LPGA Teaching & Club Professional division was founded in 1959; PGA Tour became independent of The PGA of America in 1968; and the World Golf Hall of Fame, originally under the name Pinehurst Hall of Fame, was founded in 1974. As we entered the last quarter of the year 2015, African American representation within these organizations continued to be at a remarkably low percentage rate.

Will African Americans ever receive fair and equal opportunities in golf?

Take an unbiased view and remove your blinders!

Knowledge is the prime need of the hour.
Dr. Mary McLeod Bethune

Chapter VII
Missing Link IQ

Test your knowledge of African American Golf History.

(Left to right) The professional golfer on the left was the second African American to receive an invitation to play in the Masters Tournament. The professional golfer on the right was the recipient of the first Northern Trust Open Charlie Sifford Exemption Award. What are their names? Answers on page 335.

Missing Link IQ

There are *four levels of difficulty*: Par, Birdie, Eagle, and Hole-In-One. Par is the easiest and Hole-In-One is the most difficult. Answers on pages 331 to 335.

Par
True or False

1. In 1964, the UGA became an affiliate of the PGA.

2. The PGA of America Caucasian-only clause allowed African Americans to only play in PGA Tour events that were held in New York, Maryland, and Pennsylvania.

3. All UGA tournaments were closed to Caucasians.

4. The caddie field for the 1981 Masters Tournament included one Caucasian caddie.

5. Pete Brown played in the 1965 Masters Tournament.

6. In 2006, two African Americans qualified to play on the PGA Tour.

7. Theodore "Ted" Rhodes joined the PGA Tour in the same year that Calvin Peete joined.

8. In 2009, former U.S. Secretary of State Condoleezza Rice became a member of Shoal Creek Golf and Country Club.

9. Women were not allowed to play in the inaugural Joe Louis Open.

10. Following the U.S. Supreme Court's 1954 *Brown v. Board of Education* decision—declaring the *Separate But Equal* doctrine unconstitutional, African Americans immediately received unrestricted access to all municipal and public golf courses in the United States.

11. After Charlie Sifford broke the barriers on the PGA Tour, John Shippen Jr. joined the PGA Tour.

12. In 1979, Pontchartrain Park Golf Course (New Orleans, Louisiana) was renamed in honor of Pete Brown.

13. Before the 1940s, there were no golf teams at any Historically Black Colleges and Universities—there were only football and basketball teams.

14. For more than 40 years, Langston Golf Course in Seattle, Washington has been the host site for the Capital City Open.

15. Golf course architects Joseph Bartholomew and William Powell designed and built Langston Golf Course.

16. When he was 18 years old, James Black qualified to play on the PGA Tour.

17. Tiger Woods was born in the same year that the Masters Tournament had its first African American player.

18. In 2004, Jim Thorpe joined the Web.com Tour.

19. From 2000 to 2001, there were two African Americans listed on the LPGA Tour active players roster.

20. Fifty percent of the caddie field at the 1999 Masters Tournament was African American.

21. In 2004, Charlie Sifford became the first African American inductee to the World Golf Hall of Fame.

22. In 1999, Renee Powell became the first African American female to play in a LPGA Championship.

23. In 1982, the UGA and USGA held joint championships.

More Par Trivia

24. Who received the first United States Patent for a wooden golf tee invention?

25. Who was the first African American to play in a Masters Tournament?

26. Who is the author of *Training A Tiger*?

27. Name the world heavyweight boxing champion who advocated fair and equal opportunities for African Americans to compete in PGA events.

28. Which major championships did Tiger Woods win in the year 2000?

29. In which state is Western States Golf Association located?

30. Who was the third African American LPGA Tour member?

31. In 1941, what major African American inaugural event was held at Rackham Golf Course, and after World War II continued annually from 1945 to 1951?

32. Who won the Masters Tournament in 1997?

33. Who was the second African American to play in a USGA U.S. Open Championship?

34. After joining the PGA Tour, what was Tiger Woods's first PGA Tour victory?

35. Name the educational institution that owned and operated Shellbanks Golf Course.

36. What was Tiger Woods's given birth name (first name)?

37. Who was the LPGA Tour's second African American member?

38. Who broke the color barrier on the PGA Tour?

39. In which year did Tiger Woods join the PGA Tour?

40. In 2006, who was the only African American member of the Nationwide Tour?

41. Name the first documented African American women's golf club in the United States.

42. Who was the LPGA Tour's first African American member?

43. What does the acronym USCGA stand for?

44. Who was the first African American to play in a USGA U.S. Open Championship?

45. Who is the book—*How I Play Golf*—about?

46. What does the acronym NNGA stand for?

47. Prior to Tiger Woods's 13th PGA Tour win, who held the record for the most PGA Tour wins by an African American or person of African American ancestry?

48. What is Lee Elder's first name?

49. Who is the publisher of *African American Golfer's Digest*?

◆ ◆ ◆

Birdie
50. The Midnight Golf Program originated in which city and state?

51. Name the community that is located on the outskirts of Pinehurst, North Carolina, and was known as the "colored settlement" where many black caddies lived.

52. Name the first 18-hole African American-owned golf course. In which city and state is it located?

53. In 2001, which African American-owned golf course was listed in the National Register of Historic Places?

54. Name the university that Tiger Woods attended before he joined the PGA Tour.

55. In 1955 six African American men, who paid green fees and played golf at Gillespie Park Golf Course in Greensboro, North Carolina, were arrested at their respective homes for doing "what" earlier that day on Gillespie Park Golf Course?

56. In 1983, what was Adams Park Golf Course in Atlanta, Georgia renamed?

57. Who was the first African American to become a member of Augusta National Golf Club?

58. In which year was The PGA of America's Caucasian-only clause removed from The PGA of America Bylaws?

59. Who was the first African American female PGA Class A Member?

60. Who was the first profoundly deaf person to play in a PGA Tour event?

61. Who was the first African American to be hired as Director of Legal Affairs for the LPGA?

62. Tiger Woods claimed his first Masters Tournament win by how many strokes?

63. From 1923 to 1971, how many golf courses did Tuskegee Institute (Tuskegee, Alabama) own? (Tuskegee Institute is now Tuskegee University).

64. Who was the first African American member of Shoal Creek Golf and Country Club in Birmingham, Alabama?

65. During a qualifying round at the 1952 San Diego Open, what did Joe Louis, Ted Rhodes, Charlie Sifford, and Eural Clark find in the cup on the first green?

66. Who was the first golf professional at Metairie Golf Club located in Metairie, Louisiana?

67. In 2002, who became the first African American female golf coach at a predominantly white university?

68. Who was the first African American to serve as general counsel of the USGA?

69. How old was the first African American professional golfer when he first competed in a major golf event?

70. In which year did Charlie Sifford receive a PGA Approved Tournament Players Card, and in which year did he earn his PGA Tour card?

71. How many professional major golf championships did Tiger Woods win from 1996 to 2006?

72. Who was the first woman to coach a men's golf team at the University of Maryland Eastern Shore?

73. Who was the 1995 Senior PGA Tour Comeback Player of the Year?

74. In 1996, which African American-owned golf course opened in Louisburg, North Carolina?

75. Name the golf course in Glen Allen, Virginia that Thomas Kenney purchased in 1978.

76. Name the three African American professional golfers whose entry fees were refunded after they played a practice round at the 1948 Richmond Open.

77. Who became sole-owner of Lake Arbor Golf Club in 2005, and one year later, sole-owner of Marlborough Country Club? (Both facilities are in the state of Maryland.)

78. In 1989, at age 76, who won gold medal at the National Senior Olympics golf competition (renamed National Senior Games)?

79. In 2004 and 2006, who ranked in the top ten on the Champions Tour official season ending money list?

80. When the USGA U.S. Open Championship had its first African American player, where did he finish on the final leaderboard?

81. Who was the first African American to caddie in all four professional majors?

82. In which year was the first golf competition held between an all-white university and a HBCU? Name the schools that were represented.

83. Who was the first African American to win an AJGA since Tiger Woods's AJGA victory in 1992?

84. Who won the 1975 Senior PGA Championship?

85. Clearview Golf Course was built on what type of farmland?

86. Who is Langston Golf Course named in honor of?

87. Name the golf facility in Centreville, Illinois that Bob Bonner purchased in 2008.

88. In which year did a Masters Tournament, for the first time, not have an all-black caddie field?

89. How many African Americans were selected to the 1983 and 1985 United States Ryder Cup teams? Give the name(s).

90. In 1986, what was Pipe O' Peace Golf Course (Riverdale, Illinois) renamed?

91. The Caucasian-only clause was a part of which section and article of The PGA of America Bylaws?

92. Name the country club in Corona, California that was purchased in 1928 by a group of African American businessmen.

93. Name the inventor of BMR^2-Putters™.

94. Name the first African American female member of the USGA Executive Committee.

95. Who is noted for being the first to use an extended shaft (belly) putter on the PGA Tour?

96. Name the organization that spearheaded the desegregation of Mobile Municipal Park Golf Course in Mobile, Alabama. In which year did the U.S. District Court rule to desegregate Mobile Municipal Park Golf Course?

97. From 1996–2003, how many Masters Tournaments did Tiger Woods win? In which year(s) did this occur?

98. Who is the author of *Forbidden Fairways: African Americans and the Game of Golf*?

99. Formerly named Bonnie Brae Golf Course and Revolution Park Golf Course, what was this golf course renamed in 2011?

100. Who was the first African American PGA Member? In which year did he initially become a PGA Member?

101. Among the African Americans who played the LPGA Tour from 1963 to 2013, who posted the best finish? In her best finish, where did she place on the final leaderboard?

102. Name the organization that was the first women's golf club affiliate of the UGA.

103. Which chapter of the National Negro Golf Association was a major force in establishing the National Minority College Golf Championship?

104. In July 2008, who received an honorary Doctor of Laws degree from the University of St. Andrews in Scotland, England?

105. Who purchased, in the year 2000, Mill Cove Golf Course located in Jacksonville, Florida?

106. Who was the first African American to receive The PGA Distinguished Service Award?

107. What victory qualified Lee Elder to receive an invitation to play in the Masters Tournament? Give the year.

108. The book *Just Let Me Play* is the autobiography of what legendary golfer?

109. Name the African American who was one of seven women, to be the first women, granted membership into The Royal and Ancient Golf Club.

♦ ♦ ♦

Eagle

110. Who was known as "Golfing Granny of the UGA", and in 1975 at age 75, won her last trophy?

111. Which organization is credited for being the oldest African American golf club in western Pennsylvania?

112. Who invented and received a U.S. Patent for "ZipAir Sport Shirt"?

113. Name the university that Althea Gibson attended.

114. In which state was the United Golfers Association incorporated? The UGA was comprised of how many districts?

115. In 2009, Miller Park Golf Course in Omaha, Nebraska was renamed. Give the course's new name.

116. Who was the first African American to receive a USGA handicap?

117. Cyrus Shippen coached golf at a Washington, D.C. school. Give the school's name.

118. In 1997, what was Jack Thompson Golf Course at Jesse Owens Park renamed?

119. Name the country club in Buckingham, Pennsylvania that John Lewis purchased in 1924.

120. Who was the African American selected as one of the inaugural inductees into the Oklahoma Golf Hall of Fame?

121. Who was the first consecutive winner of the United Golfers Association National Men's Amateur Championship?

122. Who founded Wake-Robin Golf Club? In which year was Wake-Robin Golf Club founded?

123. Name the HBCU that hosted the first HBCU Intercollegiate Golf Tournament.

124. Who received the 2011 Ben Hogan Award?

125. Who was the first African American to play in a PGA Tour event in the South? What was the name of that event? In which year did this occur?

126. In 1956, a North Carolina Supreme Court order gave the City of Charlotte two options regarding African Americans having access to Bonnie Brae Golf Course. What were those options?

127. Who was the first African American female selected to the USGA USA Curtis Cup team? Give first and last names. In which year was she a member of the USGA USA Curtis Cup team?

128. Who was the first African American to work for *Golf World* magazine?

129. In which year was the USCGA established?

130. Who was the first African American golf professional hired at Pinehurst Training Academy?

131. In which year did the LPGA Tour have its first African American member?

132. In which month and year was the first U.S. Patent for a wooden golf tee awarded?

133. Who was the founder and first elected president of The Chicago Women's Golf Club?

134. Who was the first African American to become president of a PGA Chapter?

135. Who is credited for establishing Lincoln Golf and Country Club in Jacksonville, Florida?

136. Who received the Ben Hogan Award in 1987?

137. As a result of a Federal District Court lawsuit filed in 1951 by James Green, Hugo Owens, Harvey Johnson Jr., and Floyd Cooper, what day(s) did the City of Portsmouth, Virginia grant Negroes access to play City Park Golf Course?

138. Before Tiger Woods joined the PGA Tour, who held the record of being the youngest African American to qualify for the Tour? What was his age when he qualified?

139. Name the African American who ranked 22nd, as of 2014, on the Champions Tour all-time official wins of 10 or more events.

140. Who was the first African American member of the USGA Women's Committee?

141. In which year did Clearview Golf Club officially open for play?

142. In 1938, United Golfers Association obtained its first official publication. Name UGA's first official publication.

143. Who was the first African American winner of a USGA Senior Amateur Championship? In which year did this occur?

144. Name the first documented African American-owned country club in the United States. Where was it located (city and state); what year was it established?

145. Who won the first Joe Louis Open Women's Amateur Championship?

146. In which year did the United States Supreme Court rule in favor of *Holmes v Atlanta*?

147. Who was the first African American female to own a golf resort and PGA Tour championship course?

148. Who was the first African American golf team captain for the University of Iowa men's golf team?

149. Who was the first woman to hold the position of UGA Tournament Director?

150. Who was the first UGA Women's National Champion?

151. Meadowbrook Country Club and Golf Course (Garner, North Carolina) was purchased in 2007. Name the purchaser.

152. Who are the first African American father and son PGA Class A Members? In which year did the father receive his PGA Class A Member status?

153. Who was the first African American member of the USGA Executive Committee?

154. From 1973 to 1984, who served as title host of the Greater Hartford Open, and title co-host of the same event from 1985 to 1988? What was the name of this PGA Tour event during these time periods?

155. In 2007, who became head coach of men's golf at Michigan State University?

156. Give the name of the African American who, in 1985, successfully completed PGA Tour Q-School.

157. Who (first and last name) won the first Florida State Junior Golf Tournament? In which year did this occur?

158. Who caddied for Arnold Palmer in his four Masters Tournament wins? Give the years.

159. *Rice v Arnold* challenged what rule? In what year was *Rice v Arnold* first filed?

160. From 1996 to 2013, how many times was Tiger Woods named PGA Tour Player of the Year?

161. Who was the first African American to receive a sponsored exemption in a PGA co-sponsored event?

162. In 1960, State Attorney General Stanley Mosk announced—*as long as the PGA discriminates against African American golfers, the PGA will not be allowed to hold any tournaments in this state.* Name the state.

163. In 2008, who became sole owner of Heritage Golf Club in Tucker, Georgia?

164. Who was the first African American equity member of Shoal Creek Golf and Country Club?

165. Who is recognized as leader of the acquisition of Mapledale Country Club in Stow, Massachusetts?

166. Cumberland Park Golf Course in Nashville, Tennessee was renamed in honor of an African American golfer. What is that golfer's name, and in which year was the course renamed?

167. At the 100th Michigan Amateur Championship, who won the event and became the first African American winner of a Michigan Amateur Championship? What year did this occur?

168. Who was the first African American to be listed among the 100 top teachers in *Golf Magazine*?

169. Who served, for more than 30 years, as head golf professional at Madden Golf Course (Dayton, Ohio)?

170. In 1962, what action did the city government of Birmingham, Alabama take to avoid complying with a federal court order to desegregate specified public facilities including golf courses?

171. In which year were women first allowed to play in a Joe Louis Open event?

172. What are their names—Hal Sutton's caddie for more than 20 years; Gary Player's caddie for more than 15 years?

173. Name the professional golfer that received, in 2014, the Presidential Medal of Freedom award.

174. Who was the first African American member of Golf Course Superintendents Association of America?

175. Taylortown, North Carolina is named in whose honor? Give first and last name.

176. *Beal v. Holcombe* was a federal lawsuit seeking access to municipal golf courses in which city and state?

177. As of December 2014, how many total career wins did Jim Thorpe post on the Champions Tour?

178. In which year did Lincoln Memorial Golf Course, a municipal golf course in Washington, D.C., open as a "colored only" golf course?

179. Who was the first African American to receive the Northern California Golf Association Grand Master Award?

♦ ♦ ♦

Hole-In-One

180. In the 1940s, who established Apex Golf Club? In what city and state was Apex Golf Club located?

181. In which year were women first allowed to enter UGA tournaments?

182. Name the first HBCU to offer a PGA/PGM™ Program.

183. Name the first African American admitted to the Michigan PGA Section. In which year did this occur?

184. In which year did a United States Supreme Court ruling ban segregation at Little Rock, Arkansas public golf courses?

185. Through 2014, how many African Americans have earned LPGA Tour member status? Name them in the order that they earned LPGA Tour member status.

186. Who was the second African American female PGA Class A Member? In which year did she become a PGA Member?

187. Name the first African American-owned golf course in the state of Michigan. In which city was it located? Name the owner.

188. In 2014, who won a major Ladies European Tour event? Name the event.

189. Who is the owner of Wedgewood Golf Center in Halifax County, Virginia?

190. Name the African American who competed in the 1902 USGA U.S. Open. Where did he place on the final leaderboard? How much did he earn in prize money?

191. Who was the first African American to earn a PGA Tour card through the Web.com Tour?

192. How many PGA Tour events did Calvin Peete win?

193. Who was the first African American member of Denver Country Club?

194. Who was the first African American to play on a United States Ryder Cup team? In which year did this occur?

195. In which year were African Americans granted access to play Hermann Park Golf Course in Houston, Texas?

196. In 2001, who was honored as the North Carolina Central University men's golf team CIAA Men's Golf Rookie of the Year?

197. Who was the first recipient of the Unsung Hero Award presented by Congressional Black Caucus Spouses?

198. In 1974, who represented Gulf Oil Company at the Nigerian Open?

199. Who was the fourth African American to win a PGA Tour event? Give the year and name of that event.

200. In 1947, who purchased Cedar River House and Golf Club in Indian Lake, New York?

201. Who invented and received a U.S. Patent for the Jiro Putter?

202. Who was the first African American to win a Carolinas Golf Association event?

203. Who was the first African American to play in a USGA Women's Amateur? In which year did this occur?

204. In which year did The PGA of America reinstate the membership of its first African American member?

205. Who caddied for five Masters wins from 1938 to 1956?

206. Almost a decade after Tiger Woods joined the PGA Tour, who was the first African American to earn a PGA Tour card? In which year did he first earn PGA Tour status through PGA Q School?

207. In 1951, a federal judge order gave the City of Louisville, Kentucky two options regarding African Americans having access to city golf courses. What were the two options?

208. As of 2011, how many African Americans received invitations to play in a Masters Tournament? What are their names?

209. How many consecutive years was Julia Siler club champion at Paramount Golf Club in St. Louis, Missouri?

210. In which year was Lincoln Country Club in Atlanta, Georgia established? Lincoln Country Club was built on what type of unused property?

211. Who was the first African American hired as a head golf professional in the state of Kentucky?

212. Who is recognized as the first African American female to build, own, and operate a golf facility?

213. In 1982, who received a U.S. Patent for a golf flag invention?

214. In 2008, Brookwood Byram Country Club in Byram, Mississippi was purchased. Name the African American co-owner.

215. Who were the two African Americans who entered the University of Michigan All-Campus Golf Tournament in 1930? Who won that tournament?

216. Who was the first African American LPGA Class A Member? In which year, did this occur?

217. In which year were public golf courses desegregated in Jackson, Mississippi?

218. In 1928, a golf course to serve the black community opened in Indianapolis, Indiana. Name the golf course and the person it was named in honor of.

219. Who was the first African American female member of a United States Junior Ryder Cup Team? In which year did she play on the U.S. Junior Ryder Cup Team?

220. In 1929, the City of Charlotte, North Carolina was granted the Bonnie Brae property. Who was the grantor? What were the usage guidelines?

221. In June 2006, who became executive director of the Champions Tour Charles Schwab Cup?

222. In 1949, by authorization of Norfolk, Virginia City Council, what day(s) were designated for Negroes to have exclusive use of Memorial Park Golf Course?

223. Name three of the six schools that had golf teams compete in the first SIAC Black Colleges Intercollegiate Tournament.

224. Name the African American who had entry applications denied for the 1948 and 1951 St. Paul Open.

225. Who was the first African American board member of The PGA of America? In which year did he first serve?

226. In 2013, who became the youngest African American to qualify for a USGA U.S. Amateur? At what age did this occur?

227. In 1999, Deer Brook Golf Club in Shelby, North Carolina opened. Name the African American who was a co-owner.

228. In 1989, who became the first African American to win a Charlotte City Amateur Golf Championship?

229. What municipal golf course did *Fayson v. Beard, Mayor of Beaumont* seek access to play? In what year was the ruling made that granted blacks unrestricted access?

230. Who was the first African American member of a men's Division I-A championship team? Name the university that the championship team represented.

231. On October 5, 1940, Hubert Delaney, Edward Morrow, and Roy Wilkins were denied access to play golf. Subsequently, Delaney, Morrow, and Wilkins filed a lawsuit against the golf facility where they were denied access to play golf. In which state was the lawsuit filed? Name the defendant in that lawsuit.

232. In which year did Charleston, South Carolina's municipal golf course open services to African Americans?

233. In which year did Dallas, Texas city golf courses integrate?

234. Name the Pro Football Hall of Famer that became a member of Augusta National Golf Club in 2009.

235. Who was the first African American female member of Augusta National Golf Club (Augusta, Georgia)? In which year did she join Augusta National Golf Club?

236. Who won the first official UGA National Open Championship? In which year did this occur and where did this event take place? Give name of facility, city, and state.

237. In June 1939, a nine-hole segregated golf facility for blacks-only opened in Washington, D.C. Name the facility and the builder of that facility.

238. Recognized as one of the first segregated—for blacks-only—golf course built by a municipality in the United States, this course was located in Gary, Indiana. Name the golf course.

239. Who was the first African American to play in the Long Beach Open? In which year did this occur?

240. In which year did the PGA withdraw the membership of its first African American member?

241. Who was the first African American male to win the North Carolina Amateur Championship? In what year did this occur?

242. What was the former name of the Negro National Open?

243. As of 2014, how many African Americans have received The PGA Distinguished Service Award? What are their names?

244. In which year did the SIAC hold the first HBCU Intercollegiate Golf Tournament?

245. In which year did Georgia's state operated golf course on Jekyll Island desegregate?

246. Who received the USGA Joe Dey Award in 2001? Who received the same award in 2005?

247. In 1923, what days were African Americans allowed to play public golf courses in St. Louis, Missouri? What were the restricted hours for the designated play?

248. In 2001, what Historically Black University women's golf team became the first HBCU women's golf team to advance to a NCAA regional championship?

249. Who was the first African American member of Baltusrol Golf Club (Springfield, New Jersey)?

250. Who is recognized as the first American professional golfer? In which year was he born?

251. Who caddied for Jack Nicklaus for 23 Masters Tournaments? How many Masters wins did this include?

252. In 2005, who were the only African American owners of a Pro Golf franchise in the United States?

253. Name the person who was the first African American to medal twice at a LPGA Tour Qualifying Tournament.

254. Who was the first Northern Trust Open Exemption recipient to make the cut at the Northern Trust Open? In what year did this occur?

255. In 1947, who filed a lawsuit against the City of Louisville, Kentucky—seeking desegregation of city golf courses?

Rafe Botts, former PGA Tour and Senior PGA Tour Member
Botts joined the PGA Tour the year following Charlie
Sifford receiving Approved Tournament Player status.
In what year did Rafe Botts join the PGA Tour?
Answer on page 335.

LaRee Sugg (right) with the winner of the 1974 Monsanto Open.
What is his name? As a result of that win, what two history-making
occurrences happened? What is LaRee Sugg credited for
accomplishing in 1995? Answers on page 335.

Par Answers

1. false
2. false
3. false
4. false
5. false
6. false
7. false
8. true
9. true
10. false
11. false
12. false
13. false
14. false
15. false
16. false
17. true
18. false
19. false
20. false
21. true
22. false
23. false
24. George Franklin Grant
25. Lee Elder
26. Earl Woods
27. Joe Louis (Joseph Louis Barrow Sr.)
28. USGA U.S. Open, British Open, PGA Championship
29. California
30. LaRee Sugg
31. Joe Louis Open
32. Tiger Woods
33. Theodore "Ted" Rhodes
34. Las Vegas Invitational
35. Hampton Institute (now Hampton University)
36. Eldrick
37. Renee Powell
38. Charles "Charlie" Sifford
39. 1996
40. Tim O'Neal

41. Wake-Robin Golf Club
42. Althea Gibson
43. United States Colored Golfers Association
44. John Shippen Jr.
45. Tiger Woods
46. National Negro Golf Association
47. Calvin Peete
48. Robert
49. Debert Cook

Birdie Answers

50. Detroit, Michigan
51. Taylortown
52. Freeway Golf Course; Sicklerville, New Jersey
53. Clearview Golf Club
54. Stanford University
55. simple trespassing
56. Alfred E. "Tup" Holmes Memorial Golf Course
57. Ron Townsend
58. 1962
59. Renee Powell
60. Kevin Hall
61. Eve Wright
62. twelve
63. three
64. Louis Willie Jr.
65. human feces
66. Joseph Bartholomew
67. LaRee Sugg
68. Leroy Richie
69. sixteen
70. 1960 (ATP card); 1964 (PGA Tour card)
71. twelve
72. Jamila Johnson
73. Walter Morgan
74. Bull Creek Golf and Country Club
75. Spring Lake Golf Course

76. Madison Gunter, Ted Rhodes, Bill Spiller
77. Hercules Pitts
78. Ann Gregory
79. Jim Thorpe
80. tied for fifth
81. Alfred "Rabbit" Dyer
82. 1937; Wilberforce University (HBCU); Northern Ohio University (all-white)
83. Stephen Reed
84. Charles "Charlie" Sifford
85. dairy
86. John Mercer Langston
87. Grand Marais Golf Club
88. 1983
89. one; Calvin Peete
90. Joe Louis "The Champ" Golf Course
91. Section 1 of Article III
92. Parkridge Country Club
93. Craig Stingley
94. Sheila Johnson
95. Charles "Charlie" Owens
96. Gulf City Golfers Association; 1961
97. three; 1997, 2001, 2002
98. Calvin Sinnette
99. The Dr. Charles L. Sifford Golf Course at Revolution Park
100. Dewey Brown Sr.; 1928
101. Althea Gibson; tied for second
102. Chicago Women's Golf Club
103. Cleveland, Ohio Chapter
104. Renee Powell
105. T. C. Newman and Ruby Newman
106. William "Bill" Dickey
107. Monsanto Open; 1974
108. Charles "Charlie" Sifford
109. Renee Powell

Eagle Answers

110. Mary Burton
111. Yorkshire Golf Club
112. Jonathan Wilson II
113. Florida A&M University
114. Illinois; five
115. Steve Hogan Golf Course
116. William "Bill" Wright
117. Dunbar High School
118. Maggie Hathaway Golf Course
119. Booker T. Washington Country Club
120. William "Bill" Spiller
121. Frank Gaskin
122. Helen Harris; 1937
123. Tuskegee Institute
124. Barbara Douglas
125. Charlie Sifford; Greater Greensboro Open; 1961
126. close the park or purchase the land
127. Mariah Stackhouse; 2014
128. Pete McDaniel
129. 1925
130. Paul McRae
131. 1963
132. December 1899
133. Anna Mae Robinson
134. Kenneth Sims
135. Abraham Lincoln Lewis
136. Charles "Charlie" Owens
137. Fridays only
138. James Black; twenty-two years
139. Jim Dent
140. Barbara Douglas
141. 1948
142. *The United Golfer*
143. Alton Duhon; 1982
144. Shady Rest Golf and Country Club; Scotch Plains, New Jersey; 1921
145. Lucy Mitchum
146. 1955

147. Sheila Johnson
148. George Roddy Sr.
149. Paris Brown
150. Marie Thompson
151. Saint Augustine's University
152. Harold Dunovant (father)
    Jeff Dunovant (son); 1974
153. John Merchant
154. Sammy Davis Jr.; Sammy
    Davis Jr. Greater Hartford
    Open from 1973 to 1984;
    Canon Sammy Davis Jr.
    Greater Hartford Open
    from 1985 to 1988
155. Sam Puryear
156. Adrian Stills
157. Ralph Dawkins Sr.; 1928
158. Nathaniel "Ironman" Avery;
    1958, 1960, 1962, 1964
159. Miami, Florida municipal golf
    course's Mondays-only access
    for African Americans; 1949
160. eleven
161. Joe Louis (world heavyweight
    boxing champion)
162. California
163. Julius Erving (former NBA
    player known as Dr. J)
164. Ron Edwards
165. Robert Hawkins
166. Theodore "Ted" Rhodes; 1969
167. Willie Mack III; 2011
168. Julius Richardson
169. Pete Brown
170. the city government closed
    those public facilities
171. 1946
172. Freddie Burns was Hal
    Sutton's caddie; Alfred Dyer
    was Gary Player's caddie
173. Charles "Charlie" Sifford
174. Dewey Brown Sr.
175. Demus Taylor
176. Houston, Texas
177. thirteen

178. 1924
179. Pearl Carey

Hole-In-One Answers

180. Sarah Spencer Washington,
    also known as Madam
    Washington; Pomona, New
    Jersey
181. 1930
182. University of Maryland
    Eastern Shore
183. Ben Davis; 1966
184. 1955
185. Six
    Althea Gibson, 1st
    Renee Powell, 2nd
    LaRee Sugg, 3rd
    Shasta Averyhardt, 4th
    Sadena Parks, 5th
    Cheyenne Woods, 6th
186. Maulana Dotch; 2010
187. The New Rogell Golf Course;
    Detroit; Greater Grace
    Temple
188. Cheyenne Woods; Australian
    Ladies Masters
189. Clifford Sommerville
190. John Shippen Jr.; tied for
    fifth; seventy-five dollars
191. Harold Varner III
192. twelve
193. Joseph Louis Barrow Jr.
194. Lee Elder; 1979
195. 1947
196. Jameisha Levister (female
    golfer)
197. William Powell
198. Bill Bishop
199. George Johnson; 1971; Azalea
    Open
200. Dewey Brown Sr.
201. Alexander McKinnon
202. Angela Stewart

203. Ann Gregory; 1956
204. 1965
205. Willie "Pappy" Stokes
206. Joseph Bramlett; 2010
207. open city golf courses to African Americans, or provide separate city golf courses for African Americans
208. four; Lee Elder, Calvin Peete Jim Thorpe, Tiger Woods
209. twenty-seven
210. 1932; cemetery property
211. George Johnson
212. Susan Lee-Hargrave
213. Bobby Brown
214. Willie Richardson (former NFL player)
215. A.D.V. Crosby, R.G. Robinson; A.D.V. Crosby won
216. Carrie Russell; 1974
217. 1971
218. Douglass Golf Course; Frederick Douglass (African American abolitionist)
219. Ginger Howard; 2010
220. Osmond Barringer–grantor; usage guidelines–lands to be used for white people only, lands will revert to the grantor if restrictions are not carried out
221. Leon Gilmore
222. second weekend (Friday through Sunday) of each month; on Wednesdays and Fridays of the other weeks
223. Six schools were: Alabama State College, Florida A&M College, Fort Valley State College, Morehouse College, Morris Brown College, Tuskegee Institute
224. Solomon Hughes Sr.
225. George Lewis; 1996
226. Andrew Walker; age fourteen

227. Willie Green, former NFL player
228. Donald Littlejohn
229. Tyrrell Park Municipal Golf Course; 1955
230. Andy Walker, Pepperdine University
231. New York; Central Valley Golf Club
232. 1961
233. 1957
234. Lynn Swann
235. Condoleezza Rice, former United States Secretary of State; 2012
236. Harry Jackson; 1926; Mapledale Country Club; Stow, Massachusetts
237. Langston Golf Course; United States federal government
238. North Gleason Park Golf Course
239. Jimmie DeVoe, 1944
240. 1934
241. Harold Varner III, 2011
242. National Colored Golf Championship
243. two; William "Bill" Dickey, William Powell
244. 1938
245. 1964
246. William "Bill" Dickey (2001); Pearl Carey (2005)
247. Mondays only; 6 AM to 12 noon
248. Jackson State University women's golf team
249. Milton Irvin
250. John Shippen Jr. 1879
251. Willie "Pete" Peterson; five
252. Weldon Coleman and Shirley Coleman
253. Ginger Howard

254. Jeremiah Wooding; 2013
255. Dr. Pruitt Sweeney Sr.

Answers for Page 306
(left to right) Calvin Peete,
Vincent Johnson
Photo Courtesy Vincent Johnson

Answer for Page 329
1961

Answers for Page 330
Robert Lee Elder;
(1) first African American to
receive an invitation to play in
the Masters Tournament
(2) first African American to play
in the Masters Tournament.

LaRee Sugg in 1995 became the
third African American LPGA
Tour member

It is not light we need, but fire; it is not the gentle shower, but thunder. We need the storm, the whirlwind, and the earthquake.

Frederick Douglass

Concluding Comments
by Jim Dent

Jim Dent
Former PGA Tour
Member and Champions
Tour Member

Concluding Comments

Embraced by cultural ethnicities from around the world, the odyssey of golf has evolved from a Caucasian-only gentlemen's game to a game of diversity. However somewhere along this extraordinary adventure, the growth of African Americans in golf became stunted and shaded by undulating circumstances and obstacles.

Charlie Sifford broke the color barrier on the PGA Tour in 1961. Following Sifford's historical accomplishment, there have been approximately 30 African American PGA Tour Members from 1961 to 2015; myself included. I played the PGA Tour from 1970 to 1988 and the Champions Tour from 1989 to 2009.

As we entered the new millennium, the number of African American PGA Tour members decreased to "one"— Tiger Woods. A decade later in 2010, Joseph Bramlett earned PGA Tour status for the PGA Tour 2011 season. In 2012, Tiger Woods again became the only person of African American ancestry playing on the PGA Tour. Then in August 2015, Harold Varner III earned his PGA Tour card for the 2016 PGA Tour season. On the Champions Tour, Jim Thorpe remained the only African American active player since 2011.

Since the LPGA Tour's inception in 1950, there were six African Americans who played on the LPGA Tour through the 2015 Tour season—Althea Gibson (1963–1971), Renee Powell (1967–1980), LaRee Sugg (1995–1997, 2000–2001),

Shasta Averyhardt (2011, 2013), Sadena Parks (2015), and Cheyenne Woods (2015). There were three African Americans who secured LPGA Tour cards for 2016—Sadena Parks retained her LPGA Tour card; Cheyenne Woods regained her LPGA Tour membership through LPGA Qualifying School; and Ginger Howard, the seventh African American LPGA Tour member, earned her first LPGA Tour card through LPGA Q School.

These statistics confirm that African American representation on the PGA Tour and LPGA Tour is disproportionately low. Our past and present of professional players, golf professionals, and industry professionals illustrate a growing trend of under representation.

The total combine membership of the LPGA T&CP and The PGA of America is approximately 28,600. The combine African American Class A Members for both organizations is approximately 113; hence, African American representation in both organizations is less than one percent. And even though it may appear that we have a stronger presence as industry professionals—that too is under-served.

Fueled by the revolution of such exclusionary policies as the PGA "Caucasian-only clause", the PGA Invitation-Only Policy, and the Masters Invitation-Only Policy, the game of golf's turning point from exclusion to inclusion is an ongoing battle. Therefore—we must continue the journey and preserve the legacy.

We must always aim for all opportunities—new and old. We must always come out swinging, even when we stumble into life's bunkers. And, as we grasp the joys of this remarkable journey, our grip and stance must always remain firm and strong.

I am proud to be a part of this rich heritage, and I hope encouraging pathways will lead many African American men and women into prosperous career adventures.

To the present and future generations—don't lose heart. Believe and hold steadfast to your visions. Embrace the journey!

—*Jim Dent*

continue
the journey!

∾

preserve
the legacy!

AJGA	American Junior Golf Association
ATP	Approved Tournament Player
BDSA	Bill Dickey Scholarship Association
BCS	Bowl Champion Series
BET	Black Entertainment Television
CEO	Chief Executive Officer
CIAA	Central Intercollegiate Athletic Association
EGA	Eastern Golf Association
GCSAA	Golf Course Superintendents Association of America
GPA	grade point average
ING	International Network of Golf
HBCU	Historically Black Colleges and Universities
LPGA	Ladies Professional Golf Association
MGAA	Multicultural Golf Association of America
MVP	Most Valuable Player
NAACP	National Association for the Advancement of Colored People
NASA	National Aeronautics and Space Administration
NBA	National Basketball Association
NBI	National Bar Institute
NCAA	National Collegiate Athletic Association
NCCU	North Carolina Central University
NHL	National Hockey League
NMGF	National Minority Golf Foundation
NNGA	National Negro Golf Association
PAT	playing ability test
PGA	Professional Golfers' Association
PGM	Professional Golf Management
Q-School	Qualifying School
R&A	Royal and Ancient (governing body for the rules of golf worldwide except for Mexico and the United States)
SIAC	Southern Intercollegiate Association of Colleges
SOIC	Sports Opportunity and Information Center
T&CP	Teaching and Club Professional
UGA	United Golfers Association
UNCF	United Negro College Fund
UMES	University of Maryland Eastern Shore
USCGA	United States Colored Golfers Association
USGA	United States Golf Association
USGTF	United States Golf Teachers Federation
WGC	World Golf Championship
WSGA	Western States Golf Association
YMCA	Young Men's Christian Association

Glossary of Golf Terms and Definitions

Approved Tournament Player (ATP)   category established by The PGA of America sometime in the 1940s after World War II; "enabled those who, for any reason…not eligible for PGA membership to compete in tournaments". (In 1960, Charlie Sifford became the first African American to receive Approve Tournament Player status.)

back nine   second half, holes No. 10 to No. 18, of an 18-hole golf course; final nine holes of an 18-hole golf course.

Ben Hogan Award   awarded by Golf Writers Association of America; presented to an individual who has a serious illness or physical limitations, but has continued to be active in golf.

birdie   one stroke under par. *Example*: on a par 5, a score of 4 is a birdie.

bogey   one stroke over par. *Example*: on a par 5, a score of 6 is a bogey.

bunker   hole or depression (on a golf course) filled with sand.

club face   the surface of the clubhead that has impact with the ball.

clubhead   the part of the club that strikes the ball.

cross-handed grip   holding the club with the left hand below the right hand or vice versa for a left handed golfer.

cut   score set for tournament players to avoid elimination of playing in the final round(s). *Example*: 72-hole event; cut is five over par (+5); all players who do not post a score of +5 or better at the end of the first 36 holes will not qualify to play the final 36 holes; those players will be cut from the tournament.

double bogey   two strokes more than par. *Example*: on a par 5, a score of 7 is a double bogey.

eagle   two strokes under par on an individual hole. *Example*: on a par 4, a score of 2 is an eagle.

even par   score that equals to par for a hole or for a round

fairway   closely mowed surface (width and length) between the tee box and the green.

flagstick   stick with a flag on it; marks the hole location on a green.

front nine   first nine holes, holes No. 1–No. 9, of an 18-hole golf course; first half of an 18-hole golf course.

gallery   spectators at a golfing competition.

green   the last target surface (where the flagstick is located) for playing a hole and where the player will putt-out on to complete playing a hole.

green fee   cost to play a round of golf

handicap   calculated prediction of an amateur's playing ability; allows amateurs of different playing abilities to compete somewhat equally. Administered by the USGA; handicap is not a fixed number.

hole   *(1)* one of the playing areas, from teeing ground to the green, on a golf course; regulation golf course has 18 holes.   *(2)* where a player putts a ball into; marked by a flagstick on "the green".

hole-in-one   ball goes in hole on the first stroke from the tee box; usually occurs on a par 3.

hosel   part of a golf club where the shaft is connected to the clubhead.

leaderboard   scoreboard displaying the names, positions, and scores of the leading players; usually displays the top 5 to 10 leaders.

lie   place where the ball rests (after a shot)—usually referred to as a good lie or a bad lie. *Example*: Good lie–ball is in the fairway sitting up on grass. Bad lie–ball is sitting down in deep rough.

making the cut   player scores within a pre-determined number that has been set under the rules of the event host; at the end of the final elimination round, a player must post a total score that will qualify to play in the final rounds.

missed the cut   after the last elimination round, player fails to qualify to play in the final rounds. (See "making the cut" for example of qualification terms.)

mulligan   second chance on a shot (including putts) when a player doesn't like his/her first attempt. Under the Rules of Golf, taking a mulligan is illegal; mulligans are usually played during a round of social/casual play.

over par   more than par for a hole or for a round. *Examples*: on a par 4, a score of six is two over (+2) par for that hole. Playing an 18 hole–par 72 golf course, a score of 75 is 3 over (+3) par for that round.

par   number of strokes it should take a skilled golfer to play a hole or a round of golf. Standard holes on a golf course are par 3, par 4, and par 5. Other holes (rarely on a golf course) are par 6 and par 7. *Examples*: (1) on a par 4, a score of 4 is par for that hole.   (2) Playing an 18 hole–par 72 golf course, a score of 72 is par for that round.

rough   area other than tee box, fairway, hazard, or green; its surface is usually taller than a fairway; sometimes vegetation.

round   completion of play; usually 18 holes.

scratch golfer   player with a zero handicap.

stroke   intentional swing at the ball to put it into play

tee   peg-like object that golfer sets ball on (in the teeing ground only) and then strikes ball.

tee box   located at the beginning of each hole, it is the only area of ground, on a golf course, where golfers are allowed to use a golf tee.

under par   less than par for a hole or a round. *Examples*: on a par 5, a score of 4 is one under (–1) par. Playing an 18 hole–par 72 golf course, a score of 69 is three under (–3) par for that 18-hole round.

Bibliography and References

Books

Clayton, Ward. *Men on the Bag: The Caddies of Augusta National*, Ann Arbor, Michigan: Sports Media Group, 2004.

Dawkins, Marvin and Kinloch, Graham. *African American Golfers During the Jim Crow Era,* Westport, Connecticut: Praeger Publishers, 2000.

Eubanks, Steve. *Augusta*, Nashville, Tennessee: Rutledge Hill Press, 1997.

Gamerman, Kenneth. *Afro-American History Series*, Volume 3, Separate and Unequal 1865–1910, Chicago Encyclopedia Britannica Educational Corporation, 1969, p. 89.

Gates, Henry Louis. *America Behind The Color Lines*, Warner Books, 2004.

Kennedy, John H. *A Course of Their Own: A History of African American Golfers*, Lincoln, Nebraska: University of Nebraska Press, 2005.

Langston, John Mercer. *From the Virginia Plantation to the National Capitol*, 1894.

McDaniel, Pete. *Uneven Lies: The Heroic Story of African-Americans in Golf,* Greenwich, Connecticut: The American Golfer, 2000.

Meffert, John W., Pyatt, Sherman E., and Avery Research Center. *Charleston, South Carolina*, Mount Pleasant, South Carolina. Arcadia Publishing, 2000.

Nösner, Ellen Susanna. *Clearview: America's Course*, Haslett, Michigan: Foxsong Publishing, 2000.

Robertson, Robert J. *Fairways: How six black golfers won civil rights in Beaumont, Texas*, College Station: Texas A&M University Press, 2005.

Sanderson, Jawn. *The Afro-American in United States History*, New York: Globe Book Company, 1969, p. 2Bibliography and References

Shipnuck, Alan. *The Battle for Augusta National: Hootie, Martha, and the Masters of the Universe*, New York: Simon and Schuster, 2004.

Sifford, Charles with Gullo, James. *Just Let Me Play: The Story of Charlie Sifford The First Black PGA Golfer*, Latham, New York: British American Publishing, 1992.

Sinnette, Calvin H. *Forbidden Fairways: African Americans and the Game of Golf,* Chelsea, Michigan: Sleeping Bear Press, 1998.

Sounes, Howard. *The Wicked Game: Arnold Palmer, Jack Nicklaus, Tiger Woods, and the Story of Modern Golf,* New York: Harper Collins, 2004.

Periodicals

African American Golfer's Digest, New York: African American Golfer's Digest Inc., Summer 2006.

——. Volume 1 No. 4, Winter 2004

——. Volume 2 No. 1, Spring 2004

———. Volume 2 No. 2, Summer 2004

———. Volume 1 No. 2, Summer 2003

———. Volume 1 No. 3, Fall 2003

Black Sports, New York: Black Sports, Inc., Volume 3–Number 1, July 1973.

On The Ball, New York: Goodson, Marion, Winter edition, 1962. Rinehart, and Winston, Inc. Holt. *African American Literature,* 1998.

Tee Cup, The Fentress Press: Los Angeles, California. Vol. 4 No. 1, February 1959.

Time Magazine, Time Inc. *Negro Open,* September 12, 1938.

USGA Journal and Turf Management: August 1959. United States Golf Association.

Internet

Advocates USA, <http://advocatesgolf.org/AboutUs_Events_ProTour>

African American Golfer's Digest, <http://www.africanamericangolfers digest.com/>

Botsch, Carol Sears, *Althea Gibson,* <http://www.usca.edu/aasc/AltheaGibson.htm>

CalendarWerks. 1946, 1947, and 1948 calendars, <http://www.calendarwerks.com/calendars/20th-century>

Cannon, Tina, 2009, Cowtown and The Color Line: Desegregating Fort Worth's Public Schools, <http://libnt3.lib.tcu.edu/etdfiles/available/etd-04212009143244/unrestricted/cannon_c5.doc>

Clay, Bobby, 1996, 'Breaking Par Against Racism: Holmes vs. Atlanta', *Black Enterprise,* September, <http://findarticles.com/p/articles/mi_m1365/is_n2_v27/ai_18600934>

Darlene Stowers – A Golf Story, <http://www.darlenestowers.com/?page_id=2>

Davis, Ronald. *Creating Jim Crow: In-Depth Essay.* The History of Jim Crow, <http://www.jimcrowhistory.org/history/creating2.htm>

Decker, Ed, Black Biography: Lee Elder, <http:www.answers.com/topic/lee-elder>

Digital History, *America in Ferment: The Tumultuous 1960s,* <http://www.digitalhistory.uh.edu/database/article_display.cfm?HHID=365>

Douglass Golf Course, <http://golfnow.com/course-directory/indiana-golf-courses/indianapolis-golf-courses/douglass-golf-course>

Duramed FUTURES Tour,<http://www.duramedfuturestour.com/FormerPlayers.asp>

Gahanna Historical Society: Big Walnut Country Club, <http://www.gahannahistory.com/big_walnut_country_club>

Golf Channel: Golf Central, Iain Page, <http:www.thegolfchannel.com/core.aspx?page=23592>

Golf Nation: New Orleans, Metairie Country Club. Course Information, <http://neworleans.golfnation.org/course294/metairie-country-club>

Griffin, Larry and Steve, *Historic Houston: The Black Community Today*, <http://www.houstonhistory.com/erhnichistory3blacks.htm>

Griffin, Stan. 2005, *Kevin Hall: "Quit Being Afraid and Reach for the Sky"*, <http://www.workersforjesus.com/dfi/1011.htm>

Jamieson, Dave. 2000, 'Conquering The Green: Former Cav Golfer Excels, shoots for PGA Tour card', *The Cavalier Daily*, University of Virginia, <http://www.cavalierdaily.com/contact.asp>

Jim Crow Laws: Alabama, <http://www.jimcrowhistory.org/scripts/jimcrow/insidesouth.cgi?state=Alabama>

JSU Tigers.com: Men's Golf, Eddie Payton, <http://www.jsutigers.cstv.com/sports/m-golf/mtt/payton_eddie00html>

Kessler, Kaye. 2004, 'Feature: Tom Woodard', *GOLFViews Magazine*, <http://www.golfviews.com/aug-05-tomw.htm>

Kentucky's Black Heritage: Timetable on Louisville Desegregation, p. 97, <http://www.kyvl.org/kentuckiana/cgi-bin/Ebind3html/371523?seq=103;trans>

Lieber, Jill 2003, 'Golf's host clubs have open-and-shut policies on discrimination', *USA TODAY*, <http://www.usatoday.com/sports/golf/2003-04-09-club-policies_x.htm>

Little Rock Newspapers Inc., 'Time Line: The State Is Set', <http://www.ardemgaz.com/prev/central/CHSmain.html>

LPGA, <http://www.lpga.com/content_1.aspx?pid=143&mid=0>; <http://lpga.com/content_1.aspx?pid=9613&mid=7>

LPGA Urban Youth Golf Program Wilmington, Delaware "Keeping Kids Out of the Rough": Carrie P. Russell LPGA Urban Youth Compassion and Devotion Award, <http://www.lpgakids.org/LPGAUYGPNews3/page1.htm>

Metropolitan Government of Nashville & Davidson County, Tennessee, *Nashville.Gov: Resolution No. RS 2001-729*, <http://www.nashville.gov/mc/resolutions/prevrs2001_720.htm>

Michigan State, Official Website of Spartan Athletics: Men's Golf, Sam Puryear, <http://www.msuspartans.cstv.com/sports/m-golf/mtt/puryear_sam00.html

Mosk, Stanley 2001, My Shot: The Tour's fear of carts is the same form of bigotry that cause the Caucasian-only clause, *Sports Illustrated Golf Plus,* <http://sportsillustrated.cnn.com/golf/news/2001/06/05/my_shot/>

Ogletree, Charles Jr. 2004. 'The 1954 Brown ruling opened America's doors' *The Boston Globe*, <http://www.boston.com/news/globe/editorial_opinion/oped/articles/2004/05/17/the_1954_brown_ruling_opened_americas_doors?mode=PF>

Oswego County Underground Railroad Contents Page, <http://www.oswego.edu/ugrr/contents.html. Tudor E.and Marie Grant,http://www.oswego.edu/ugrr/grant.html>

Rogers Park Golf Course, "The History of Rogers Park Golf Course" <http://www.rogersparkgc.com/content.php?link=history.php>

Sampson, Curt 2003, 'Augusta vs. the world: Ike, Elder, and Shoal Creek', *Golf Magazine*, <http://sportsillustrated.cnn.com/augusta/magazine/2003/augustavsworld/2/>

Shapiro, Leonard. 'Taking Root: The first club for black women worked to desegregate the game', *GOLF MAGAZINE*, <http://www.golfonline.com/golfonline/features/history/article0,17742,467842,00.html>

Shonberger, Yvonne, compiler, *The Miami Springs Golf Course,* pages 14–16, <http://www.miamispringsgolfcourse.com/history.pdf>

The Official Website of Steve Harvey, <http://www.steveharvey.com/2009hoodies/hotelpackages/hotel-packages.html>

The African American Registry, "John Dendy, Ethiopian golf wiz!", <http://www.aaregistry.com/african_american_history/1427/John_Dendy_Ethiopian_golf_wiz>

The PGA TOUR, <http://www.pgatour.com/players>

Tiger Woods official website (About Tiger), <http://www.tigerwoods.com/defaultflash.sps>

TIME Magazine, 'Negro Open'. Time Inc. Monday, Sep. 12, 1938 <www.time.com/time/magazine/article/0,9171,760178,00.html>

United States Golf Teachers Federation, <http://www.usgtf.com/articles/profiles-french.html/>; <http://www.usgtf.com/articles/winter08/page18.html>

United States Black Golfers Association, <http://www.myusbga.com/>, <http://www.myusbga.com/files/SFTP_08_PR_doc.pdf>, <http://www.myusbga.com/event.html>

University of Illinois Press, 'The Wichita NAACP', <http://www.press.uillinois.edu/epub/books/eick/ch3.html>

Vernoncrest Golf Club, <http://www.vernoncrestgolfclub.com/about_us>

Wellman, Grant. 1998. *Tudor and Marie Grant,* <http://www.oswego.edu/ugrr/grant.html>

World Golf.com, Golf Channel welcomes Scott Walker to on-air team, <http://www.worldgolf.com/newswire/browse/56347-GOLF-CHANNEL-welcomes-Scott-Walker-air-team>

World Golf.com, Metairie Country Club-Private. http://www.worldgolf.com/courses/usa/louisiana/metairie/metairie-country-club-private.html (Jack Daray)>

Cases/Legislation Cited

Beal et al. v. Holcombe, 193F. (2d) 384, (5th Cir. 1951).

Brown v. Board of Education of Topeka, Kansas, 347 U.S. 483 (1954)
   Civil Rights Act of 1964, (Pub. L. 88-352, 78 Stat. 241, July 2, 1964)

Delaney et al. v. Central Valley Golf Club Inc., 28 N.Y. Supp. (2d) 932 (1941)

Fayson et al. v. Beard, Mayor of Beaumont, et al., 134 F. Supp. 379

Holley, Bailey, and Gray v The City of Portsmouth, 150 F. Supp. 6 (1957 U.S. Dist. LEXIS 3653).

Holmes v. Atlanta, 350 U.S. 879, (1955)
Leeper et al. v. Charlotte Park and Recreation Commission et al.,
    (U.S.S.C., #648) (88 S.E. 2d 114).
Mayor and City Council of Baltimore v. Dawson, 350 U.S. 877, (1955)
Palmer v. Thompson, 403 U.S. 217, (1971)
Plessy v. Ferguson, 163 U.S. 537 (1896)
Simkins et al.v. Greensboro, 149 F. Supp. 562 (D.C.N.C.) 1956.
Rice v. Arnold, 340 U.S. 848 (1950)
Wolfe v. North Carolina, 364 U.S. 177 (1960)

◆ ◆ ◆

List of Contributors

Persons interviewed and/or sent information to the author

Adger, Levy
Aikens, Robin
Alexander, Ezra
Anderson, Ashleigh
Andraes, Peter
Andy, Delores
Apley, Shirley
Barber, James
Barksdale, Gus
Barnes, Sam
Baron, Betty
Barry, Rory
Beavers, Maureen
Biggers, Robert
Bishop, Bill
Bolden, Carlton
Bolton, Toby
Bourdeaux, Andrea
Bowen, Craig
Bowens, Burl
Bowers, Walt
Bowman, Douglass
Boyd, Wendy
Brawley, Tom
Breckenridge-
    Haywood, Mae

Brown, Bobby
Brown, Margaret
Brown, Pete
Brown, William
Buck, Marian
Burns, Vern
Callahan, Aileen
Castillo, Oneida
Chandler, Dana
Childs, Smitty
Clark, Robert
Clark, Vic
Clement, Michelle
Coleman, John
Coleman, Shirley
Collida, Bart
Cook, Debert
Cooper, Michael
Countee, Ted
Creech, Ruth
Cropper, Marshall
David, John
Davis, Larry
Day, S. E.
Denney, Bob
Dent, Jim

Donaly, Brice
Dorton, Charles
Douglas, Barbara
Douglass, Lisa
Dumpson, Kimberly
Dunovant, Jeff
Dunton, Nancy
Echols, Vernon
Eckert, Jack
Elder, Lee
Elder, Sharon
Erving, Julius
Evans, Todd
Everett, Kimberly
Fleming, Gordon
Flowers, Eddie
Fluker, Renee
Foster, Maurice
Freeman, Ulysses
Fullard, Bill
Gaines, Fletcher
Galloway, Tyrone
Garret, Johnny
Garvey, James
Garvin, Jimmy
Gaskins, Irene

Geilberger, John	McClain, Preston	Simmons, Thurman
Gill, Zollie	McDaniel, Pete	Simmons, Willie
Gould, LaJean	McFadden, Judy	Sims, Kenneth
Gray, James	McNair, Jarem	Sinnette, Calvin
Gregory-Overstreet,	McRae, Willie	Smith, Hanno Shippen
JoAnn	McShane, Stephen G.	Sommerville, Clifford
Griffin, Lanie	Mickey, Lisa	Snye, Angela
Griffin, Rob	Miles, Anthony	Stark, Doug
Gross-Rhode, Dana	Miller, Brian	Staton, Sandra
Haas, Matt	Millender, Dollie	Stroble, Bobby
Hall, Jackie	Molton, Mary Roddy	Stingley, Craig
Hampton, George	Moore, Alphonso	Stulack, Nancy
Hampton, Leo	Moore, Buck	Summers, Ellen
Hamrick, Ken	Moore, Johnny	Sykes, Tiffani-Dawn
Harris, Esaw	Moore, Stanley	Szabo, Margo
Hart, Thomas Jr.	Moran, Patty	Taylor, Russell
Hawkins, Burdette	Newman, T. C.	Terry, Ron
Heard, Quincy	Nyhan, Gail	Thomas, Bennie
Hemphill, Yvette	Oden, Edward	Tiller, Andre´
Hill, Harry Max	Osborn, Jerry	Toohey, Anne
Hogan, Steve	Patterson, Lillian	Trantow, Chris
Holley, James	Peete, Pepper	Troublefield, Mike
Hollingsworth, Ada	Person, Orville	Turner, Jandie
Holmes, Dedric	Peters, Tony	Turner, Roberta
Houston, Arnold	Pique, Joely	Waddell, Roland
Howard, Robert	Pitts, Gloria	Wallace, Tyrone
Hughes, Janet	Pitts, Hercules	Williams, Ken
Hughes, Joyce	Powell, Larry	Williams, Patricia E.
Hughes, Shirley	Powell, Renee	Wilson, Jonathan II
Hurley, Ramona	Powell, William	Wilson, Roy
Jackson, Carl	Prior, Terry	Woodard, Tom
Johnson, Richard	Quarles, Al	Wright, Chuck
Johnson, Selina	Rani, Kelly	Wright, Hampton
Jones, Jessie	Rhodes-White, Peggy	Wright, William
Jones, Lavern	Rice, Joseph	Youman, Robert
Jovanovic, John	Rich, Carter	
Kelly, Charles	Richardson, Willie	
King, Andrew	Roker, Renny	
Lee, Gladys M.	Russ, Michael	
Lee-Hargrave, Susan	Sammons, Jeffrey	
Lewis, Alana	Savoy, Ray	
Lightfoot, Charles	Schuster, Marilyn	
Lindsay, Mason	Scott, Sheila	
Loehr, Bennie	Sheffield, Wanda	
Lowe, Lonnie	Sifford, Charles	

Acknowledgments

My experience in writing, *A Missing Link In History*, gave me opportunities to hear people express their gratitude to those who helped break barriers, and who paved the way so others would have the privilege of enjoying the game of golf. I met people who yearned to give patronage to pioneers like Pete Brown, Ann Gregory, Joseph Rice, Carrie Russell, John Shippen Jr., and Charlie Sifford—all whom you read about in this book.

I thank all who took the time to answer and ask questions, send materials, and share personal stories. To all who are listed and to the many nameless who helped, thank you for your interest in this project and please know that if your name is not listed, it is not intentional.

I extend appreciation to: Rory Barry, Bill Bishop, Geoff Bryant, Bart Collida, Robert Clark Sr., Lee Elder, Sharon Elder, Earnie Ellison, Susan P. Garrett, Joanne Gregory-Overstreet, Dana Gross-Rhode, Carl Jackson, Nelson Jorden, Caity Kivitt, Gladys Lee, Judy McFadden, Pete McDaniel, Orville Person, Dr. Renee Powell, Dr. Richard Selcer, Dr. Charles Sifford, and Dr. Calvin Sinnette.

To the following, I extend a special thanks for telling me to persevere and don't give up: Margaret Brown, Charles French, Gladys Lee, Michael Moore, Alma Reece, Dr. Elinor Sinnette, Dana Torrence, and Robert Youman. Also special thanks to Dr. Maxine Mimms, my most memorable college professor, who inspired me to research and write.

Appreciation is also extended to: Ken Anderson (index consultant), Julia Bachrach (Chicago Park District), Bob Denney (The PGA of America), Harry Max Hill (researcher, Fort Worth, Texas), Arnold Houston (Tuskegee University), and Eric Soderstrom (Titleist).

For permission to use quotes and reprint material, I acknowledge: Charles Dorton (Sports Opportunity and Information Center); Landmark Corporation–*Virginian Pilot;* Ellen Nösner, author of *Clearview;* JaZette Marshburn (*AFRO-American Newspaper*); Debert Cooke (*African American Golfer's Digest*), and *Star-Telegram* (Fort Worth, Texas).

Grateful acknowledgment is made to the staff at various libraries and museums: Doug Stark and Patty Moran (USGA Library and Archives), Shirley Apley (Fort Worth, Texas Public Library), Jim Baggett (Archives Birmingham Public Library), John Jovanovic (James Branch Cabell Library, Virginia Commonwealth University), Lillian Patterson (Alexandria Black History Resource Center), Gloria Pitts (North Carolina A&T University Bluford Library Archives), Terry Prior (Richardson-Bates House Museum Oswego, New York), and Angela Snye (The Adirondack Museum). Also Norfolk, Virginia Public Library Main Branch (for cataloging assistance), Mercer Museum (Doylestown, Pennsylvania), Bucks County Historical Society, Churchland Public Library (Portsmouth, Virginia), Library of Congress Humanities and Social Sciences Division, and Tufts Archives/Givens Memorial Library.

For various forms of never-ending encouragement and support, I am deeply thankful to my family Barbara Wright, Robert McDonald, and Wanda Valk; and my dear friends Casey Allen, Gwendolyn Hardy, Reverend Sydney Moore and Edith Moore, Marvin and Barbara Seidman, Dr. Ella Townsend, Reverend Charles White, Barbara Whiting-Wright, and Patricia E. Williams.

And finally to my parents, grandparents, and aunt—in love, peace, and grace, your spirits have guided me through this chapter of my life. For this, I am grateful.

Index to Chapters One–Five

General Index

About the Author

Ramona Harriet is a research historian of African American golf history. Ramona is founder and executive producer of the traveling exhibition—*Epochs of Courage: African Americans in Golf,* and she is founder of Swing Hope Into Action—a program to preserve and teach African American Golf History. In addition to writing *A Missing Link In History*, Ramona is the author of *African American Golf History Brain-Aerobics*, a book of brain teasers.

In 2010, Ramona was selected to be a member of the PGA/USGA African American golf history task force. In 2012, she was selected to serve on the World Golf Hall of Fame and Museum advisory committee for the permanent exhibition "Honoring the Legacy: A Tribute to African Americans in Golf".

Ramona is also a book publishing consultant, and has served as lead consultant for the publication of two self improvement adult books, a religious studies book, and a children's book. A former educator, Ramona is a former governor's appointee to a state education committee; and she has held administrative and teaching positions in the United States and London, England. She has logged in more than 30 years on the links in the United States and abroad.

Ramona enjoys playing golf and chess; however, her passion is spending time with her daughter. Together they enjoy Broadway musicals, church events, and horse shows.

Supplement
A Missing Link In History:
The Journey of African Americans in Golf
with
African American Golf History Brain Aerobics
Fun challenging enrichment activities
and word puzzles
by Ramona Harriet

African American Golf History
traveling exhibition and projects
are available for events.

For more information visit:
www.AfricanAmericanGolfHistory.com

Barbara Whiting-Wright, exhibition coordinator
at the *Epochs of Courage: African Americans in Golf*
traveling exhibition showing at North Carolina
A&T University H.C. Taylor Art Gallery. Circa 2001

Made in the USA
Charleston, SC
18 December 2015